Tanglewood

By Herbert Kupferberg

McGraw-Hill Book Company
New York • St. Louis • San Francisco • Düsseldorf • Mexico • Toronto

Book design by Judith Michael.

1 2 3 4 5 6 7 8 9 RABP 7 9 8 7 6

Library of Congress Cataloging in Publication Data

Kupferberg, Herbert.
    Tanglewood.

    Includes index.
    1. Berkshire Symphonic Festival. I. Title.
ML200.8.B5K86   780′.79′7441   76-11772
ISBN 0-07-035643-2
        0-07-035644-0 (pkb.)

To the Memory of My Father

Contents

Introduction

The official name of the musical manifestation that takes place every summer between the towns of Lenox and Stockbridge in Massachusetts is the Berkshire Festival. But hardly anyone aside from its sponsor, the Boston Symphony Orchestra, ever calls it the Berkshire Festival; it is known universally as Tanglewood, and that is how I have alluded to it, more often than not, in the following pages.

Although Tanglewood has been in existence for more than forty years, no previous attempt has been made to write a book recounting in depth its past, surveying its present, and perhaps offering a glimpse of its future. The earlier works, which are listed in the Bibliography, have either been specialized brochures or picture booklets.

But Tanglewood has been since its inception one of the most widely reported cultural developments in American history, the subject of countless magazine and newspaper articles, reviews and critiques. I do not claim to have read every one, but in retrospect I find I have gone through an amazing (to me, at any rate) number of them. Similarly, I have interviewed dozens of Tanglewood alumni, some of them now famous, others working in less prominent but no less essential musical jobs. An awesome array of American and foreign musicians has passed through Tanglewood; I truly regret my inability to consult them all and can plead only the exigencies of space and the brevity of life itself.

The names of those who have helped me in my researches are listed elsewhere in this book. However, I must acknowledge special indebtedness to Mrs. Olga Koussevitzky, widow of the greatest figure associated with Tanglewood, for sharing her memories with me; to Leonard Bernstein for what to me, at least, are some remarkably candid and vivid recollections; to the late Jay C. Rosenfeld, who, though stricken with a mortal illness, courteously and generously provided me with difficult-to-obtain material; and to the officials and administrators of the Boston Symphony Orchestra who, while they neither instigated nor authorized this book, helpfully answered my questions, supplied me with information, and extended to me every courtesy during my long stay at Tanglewood in the summer of 1975.

Finally, I wish to express to the members of my own family, three generations of them, my gratitude for having shared this journey with me, as they have so many others.

Herbert Kupferberg

Capacity of the Shed has varied through the years with various seating arrangements tried and the original benches giving way to individual chairs. Current capacity is around 5,000, and the edifice is usually filled to overflowing. (Courtesy Whitestone Photographers)

1. The Tanglewood Experience

The visitor to Tanglewood, that beautiful estate in the Berkshires devoted to summer music, is likely to follow a certain customary, almost ritualistic procedure. Especially if he is a first-time visitor, he will arrive on a weekend rather than in midweek, with the intention of attending one or more concerts by the Boston Symphony Orchestra. Upon purchasing his ticket and entering the gate, he will automatically turn to the left, crossing a spacious, impeccably manicured lawn toward a low, seemingly circular structure called the Shed. The lawn itself is already occupied by a sizeable throng of people, some dressed casually, some elegantly, who have brought along picnic dinners to enjoy before the concert in the last rays of the afternoon sun. Some of them will remain on the grass throughout the concert, listening beneath the stars as the music wafts out through the open sides and rear of the Shed. But most will pack up their hampers and take their places inside the gracefully curving, 5,000-seat structure to listen to the concert. When the program is ended, the visitor will again cross the lawn, this time in darkness, find his car in one of the several enormous parking lots, gingerly ease his way out through the inevitable traffic tangle and eventually reach his abode for the night, convinced that he has seen Tanglewood.

In a way, of course, he has, for the Boston Symphony concerts are central to this great summer festival—in fact they established it firmly some four decades ago. But Tanglewood as it exists and flourishes today is far more than a music festival. It also is an educational institution, a touristic attraction, a business enterprise and a state of mind. And only by experiencing it in all these aspects can one fully appreciate the unique and irreplaceable position it holds in American cultural life.

If, for example, our visitor had arrived not on a Friday or Saturday evening but on a Tuesday or Wednesday morning, and if he had walked straight ahead past the gate rather than turning to the left, he would have encountered a far different kind of musical activity. He would have heard, coming from a large neo-Gothic manor house at the highest point of the lawn, and from a dozen other buildings discreetly hidden among the great

An aeriel photo of the Shed as a concert audience gathers.
(Courtesy the Boston Symphony Orchestra)

trees that shade the grounds, the sounds of string quartets and wind quintets, of music being put together in practice sessions by young men and women who will help shape the next generation of American music.

Some of these players, in fact, are not inside the buildings at all. They are out on the lawn in the clear Berkshire air, practicing their instruments either alone or in groups. A barefoot girl, with a music stand before her, goes over a flute passage in the shade of a hemlock tree. A boy plays a bassoon at the edge of the curving, now empty Shed, explaining that he likes the resonance the vacant building adds to his deep-sounding, burnished instrument. Two tuba players under a group of pines perform a duet of their own concoction—where else but in these vast, open spaces can tubas be played with such abandon? Other young men and women walk by carrying violin or cello cases; one youth intrepidly balances a double bass on his shoulder. Even the small talk is of music. On the porch of the manor house one may hear assignations between boys and girls being made in these terms: "Say, would you be interested in playing some chamber music tonight? We're doing the Brahms E-flat. I'll bring down the music and we'll meet at the library."

These are the students enrolled at the Berkshire Music Center, founded by Serge Koussevitzky and the Boston Symphony Orchestra in 1940 for the express purpose of training young people to positions of leadership—not by teaching them the art of playing an instrument, but what is far more demanding, the art of playing music. The Berkshire Music Center is the world's most intense and concentrated school of ensemble performance. From its ranks have come many of today's leading conductors, from Leonard Bernstein and Lukas Foss to Seiji Ozawa and Michael Tilson Thomas.* From it also have come more than 10 percent of all the instrumentalists now playing in America's symphony orchestras, several chamber music ensembles, scores of opera singers, dozens of composers, and a large body of alert, informed and generally superior performers, all trained and taught by members of the Boston Symphony Orchestra.

Throughout the eight-week Festival season the Berkshire Music Center students present their own concerts, a tremendously broad and lively array, all open to the public at a nominal charge. They give chamber music evenings and vocal recitals, perform a remarkable series of contemporary works and present full symphonic performances every week. The Berkshire Music Center

*Three of the present (or incoming) music directors of America's "Big Five" orchestras are Tanglewood-trained—Ozawa in Boston, Lorin Maazel in Cleveland, and Zubin Mehta at the New York Philharmonic.

Concert crowds come early, make themselves comfortable, and find no trouble passing the time pleasantly. (Photo by Marian Gillett)

Orchestra is, after the Boston Symphony, the chief pride and joy of Tanglewood, playing sometimes under its own student conductors and sometimes under the likes of Bernstein and Ozawa. Only by experiencing the combination of the week-long performances by the student groups and the weekend concerts of the Boston Symphony can a visitor share in the full excitement and exhilaration of Tanglewood.

It is curious, even paradoxical, that all this intellectual activity and artistic stimulation should take place in an area of the United States that is rural in location, conservative in outlook, wary of outsiders and barely tolerant of summer residents. In forty years, Tanglewood has developed into one of the Berkshires' major industries, pumping 12 million dollars a year into its economy, sustaining its hotels, motels, restaurants and rooming houses, all of which unfailingly raise their prices to peak levels during the eight-week Festival season. A woman from Pittsfield on the New York bus tells admiringly how her thrifty neighbors send their children off to summer camp so they can rent their empty rooms to concertgoers. A men's lavatory near the main Tanglewood gate was adorned in 1975 with two penciled graffiti, one apparently from a student, the other a visitor. The first read "Liszt piszt here"; the second "Reincarnate me as an innkeeper in Lenox."

Nevertheless, the musical attractions of Tanglewood and the beauty of its surroundings for most visitors far outweigh the all too familiar travails of vacationing in America. "Nobody ever seems to regret that he came to Tanglewood, no matter how much he was charged outside the grounds or how long he was trapped in an immobile line of automobiles," wrote the critic Cecil Smith—in 1952.

Certainly audiences show no sign of falling off at Tanglewood, even in face of the growth of festivals elsewhere. The first Berkshire Festival, one of the few in the country at the time, drew fewer than 10,000 listeners at $1 and $2 a head. In the 1970s, when the top price in the Shed was $10.50 (with $3.50 for a place on the lawn), the annual attendance reached well over 300,000. Surprisingly it is the New York metropolitan area rather than Boston which supplies the largest single concentration of visitors, but Tanglewood's audience, like its student body, actually is national and even international in origins.

It is an audience that seems remarkably at ease and at peace with itself as it awaits the start of the concert. Age differences, distinctions in dress, variety in life-styles all seem less important here than elsewhere. Gazing upon the dashikis and bikinis, the T-shirts and tank-tops, it is hard to remember that not so long ago the Boston Symphony administration was virtuously

Pre-concert picnickers bring their own furniture, tablecloths, hampers, and even their formal attire. (Photo by Marian Gillett)

handing out skirts to swathe the limbs of girls who turned up wearing shorts. However, the old guard has by no means died or even surrendered; for many Tanglewood habitués the accepted dress continues to be summer gowns and jackets and ties.

For those who dine on the lawn, the picnic menus seem to gain yearly in ingenuity and elaborateness. They range from prepackaged hero sandwiches and containers of coffee to gourmet dinners carefully laid out on tablecloths spread on the grass or set up on folding tables. Some concertgoers bring pitchers of martinis and chilled champagne bottles in their portable coolers, and there even are a number of candelabra set upon the ground, their candles glowing in the gathering darkness. Romance has always flourished at Tanglewood, but in recent years it has become increasingly open and visible. Some couples lie beneath their blankets, some atop them; at Tanglewood, as in Illyria, music has been known to be the food of love.

Despite the great crowds which gather in the Shed and on the lawn for the weekend concerts, and the steady trek of visitors throughout the summer, Tanglewood has managed to avoid all symptoms of what Thomas D. Perry, Jr., executive director of the Boston Symphony, calls "festival sprawl." The vista across Lake Mahkeenac to Monument Mountain is as untroubled as it was in Nathaniel Hawthorne's day; no matter how huge the audience the night before, the grounds are immaculate the next day. There isn't a sign in sight; to find even the men's and ladies' rooms one must rely on instinct or seek guidance from a volunteer usher or knowledgeable stranger. The public cafeteria and the book and souvenir shop near the gate are unobtrusively bucolic in appearance. Even the surrounding roads are free of billboards and hot-dog stands; it is not until one passes through Lenox and heads down the Pittsfield highway that one reenters the world of neon lights, fast-food restaurants and shopping centers. The tranquillity of Tanglewood extends to the skies above, for the site is blessedly far from commercial aviation routes, so that the only aerial interference comes from flocks of sparrows which nest amid the girders of the Shed and sometimes provide a cheerful counterpoint to the symphonies of Brahms or Mahler.

In few other places on this earth are the beauties of nature and the beauties created by the human mind in such a state of perfect equilibrium. For once, man seems to be in accord with his world. And yet that harmony was not achieved overnight, nor did it come without striving, struggle and conflict. Even at Tanglewood, it sometimes rains. . . .

Tanglewood has long since given up on the rules of attire which marked an earlier epoch (see page 154). (Courtesy Whitestone Photographers)

The road to Tanglewood in the 1930s. Neither the sign nor the tieup has changed. (Courtesy the Boston Symphony Orchestra)

The only time Gertrude Robinson Smith missed a Tanglewood season was when she was summering in Europe. This shipboard picture was made in 1937, three years after she launched the Festival. (Courtesy the *Berkshire Eagle*)

2. Founding a Festival

"A True Public Festival"

That sturdy Londoner Samuel Pepys, who once said that he could resist everything except music and women, wrote in his *Diary* for May 28, 1667, after a visit to the Vauxhall Gardens, the Tanglewood of his day: "A great deal of company, and the weather and the garden pleasant . . . to hear the nightingale and other birds, and here fiddles, and there a harp . . . and here laughing, and there fine people walking, is mighty divertising."

People undoubtedly have been deriving similar pleasure from outdoor music ever since the first shepherd fashioned the first pipe, or as Rudyard Kipling once expressed it, since "'Omer smote 'is blooming' lyre." The ancient Greeks used to hold musical agones, competitive festivals which encompassed all varieties of song and instrumental playing, and at which old and new compositions were presented. The Romans also had musical contests in which the Emperor Nero, who played the cithara, participated and managed to do reasonably well. Festivals remained a welcome interlude of life in medieval times—Richard Wagner has recreated one of them for us in the opera *Die Meistersinger*.

The music festival as we know it today seems to stem, like so much else in our cultural life, from nineteenth-century European origins. Especially in Germany and England outdoor musical events began to supplement the regular indoor concert seasons about 150 years ago. Often they were built around a theme, or set forth works not customarily heard inside the concert hall. People traveled considerable distances to attend these events. They were packed eight or ten in a room in crowded hostelries or into improvised accommodations; they paid steeply advanced prices for food and drink; and they made their way home along clogged roads and busy waterways—all of which suggests that festivals haven't changed much in some respects over the years.

Felix Mendelssohn's father, a Berlin banker, has left a vivid description of the Lower Rhine Music Festival held in 1833 in Düsseldorf, at which his famous son, then twenty-four years old, conducted Handel's oratorio *Israel in Egypt.* Wrote Abraham Mendelssohn to his family:

> Since Friday steamboats, diligences of every description, station-wagons, private carriages, convey whole families from all parts of the country . . . to this festive town of Düsseldorf. . . . Here they have no court, no meddling influence from higher quarters, no *General-Musik-direktor,* no royal this or that. It is a true public festival. . . .
>
> During the pauses . . . all rush into the garden, where quantities of bread and butter, Maywine, Seltzerwater, curds and whey, etc. are served. . . . Meanwhile the doors and windows of the concert-room are opened, after which, when the air is sufficiently renewed and the time allowed for the pause has passed, a loud flourish is blown from the orchestra, and the hall fills again with speed and spirit. Lazy and thirsty stragglers are called in by a second flourish, and again Israel cries to the Lord. Thus things went on morning and evening. . . .

The German festivals had their counterpart in England; as a matter of fact, as late as 1893, Bernard Shaw, then the music critic of *The World,* called them "our leading musical institution"—and denounced them for turning over their proceeds to hospitals and similar local charities rather than using them for the benefit of music and musicians.

The city of Birmingham launched a festival in 1768, and over the next fifty years developed it into one of Europe's most celebrated musical institutions. Felix Mendelssohn, who was an inveterate festival man, composed his oratorio *Elijah* for the Birmingham Festival of 1846. Later composers whose works were performed there included Gounod, Dvořák and Elgar. Festivals were held at other English cities like Leeds, Norwich and Sheffield; inevitably they became social occasions as well as musical events. In 1913 Rutland Boughton, the British composer, commented:

> At best these festivals have been gatherings of such wealthy folk as are too kind, or too lazy, to pot grouse. These, the aristocrats of their class, have done what they could for musical art by producing such works as Mendelssohn's *Elijah,* Gounod's *Redemption,* Costa's *Naaman,* Macfarren's *Jerusalem,* Sullivan's *Golden Legend,* Prout's *Hereward,* and other such polite stuff; and if nobody wants to hear the majority of these works again, at least the composers have had their chance. . . .

These nineteenth-century British festivals have mostly passed out of existence, along with their massive *Naamans* and *Jerusalems.* In the 1930s the Glyndebourne Festival came into being, concentrating on exquisite productions of Mozart's operas, and catering largely to an elite audience. It was not until the launching of the Edinburgh Festival in 1947 – more than a decade after Tanglewood came into being—that the British for the first time achieved "a true public festival."

German festivals also tended toward specialization. Bayreuth always was a specifically Wagnerian enterprise, producing the complete *Ring des Nibelungen* in 1876 when no other theater was prepared to take it on, and re-producing it ever since. Salzburg in Austria was almost as purposefully devoted to its native son, Mozart, especially during the Festival's early years, between 1877 and 1910. However, Salzburg broadened out in the era between the two world wars, encompassing operatic and instrumental works by other composers, and enlisting the talents of the world's leading conductors, performers and stage designers. Although Salzburg has continued to flourish, its most brilliant epoch remains the 1930s, when musical travelers came from all over the world to attend performances led by Arturo Toscanini, Wilhelm Furtwängler and Bruno Walter. No other festival was in a class with Salzburg in those days; so it was no wonder that when Tanglewood's founders wished to measure their dreams for their own budding enterprise, they spoke of it hopefully as "an American Salzburg."

American festivals, like those in Europe, began their real development in the nineteenth century. The earliest tended to gigantism in size and were not always impeccable in their musical tastes. One of the most spectacular was a "World Peace Jubilee" that ran in Boston from June 17 to July 4, 1872, in a specially constructed "Coliseum" alleged to seat 100,000. Among the musical highlights was the Anvil Chorus from *Il Trovatore* played on a hundred anvils imported from Birmingham, England; the Sextet from *Lucia* sung by 150 vocalists; and "The Beautiful Blue Danube" played by an orchestra of 1,087 led in person by the Waltz King, Johann Strauss.

The first festival to establish itself in the United States on a continuing basis seems to have been the Worcester Music Festival in Massachusetts, which became an annual event in 1858, specializing in choral music. Chautauqua, New York, and Ann Arbor, Michigan, inaugurated festivals in 1874 and 1894 respectively, and Bethlehem, Pennsylvania, began its annual Bach performances in 1898. In the following year Norfolk, Connecticut, became the site of annual performances on the estate of Carl Stoeckel; in 1914 Jan Sibelius, then forty-nine years old and with his greatest popularity yet to come, was invited there to conduct his own music—the only appearance he ever made in the United States.

Subsequent festivals tended to develop either in or near large urban areas. Opera was performed in Ravinia Park near Chicago as early as 1911, developing eventually into the symphonic festival of the 1930s. The Hollywood Bowl began its "Symphonies Under the Stars" in 1922, and in 1930 the players of the Philadelphia Orchestra organized the first Robin Hood Dell concerts in Fairmount Park.

Perhaps the most important of America's pre-Tanglewood music festivals were the concerts inaugurated in 1918 at Lewisohn Stadium, a curved concrete amphitheater on the campus of the College of the City of New York in Manhattan. The Stadium Concerts, as they were called, were given nightly for eight weeks during the summer, and, from 1922 on, the orchestra that performed there was the New York Philharmonic-Symphony, at first under its own name and later officially redesignated as the Stadium Symphony Orchestra.

Few of the thousands who traveled to 137th Street and Convent Avenue to listen to Beethoven and Brahms vying for attention with passing fire engines and neighborhood street cries (airplanes added their own obbligato in later years) thought of themselves as attending a "festival." They were there simply to hear the Philharmonic play great music at low prices (50 cents for a place on the stone benches; cushions a quarter extra). Yet especially in the Depression years of the 1930s a festive spirit was often in evidence nonetheless, particularly among the young men and women who made up a large proportion of the Stadium's regular audience. And although history has largely overlooked its contribution, it was the Lewisohn Stadium concerts in New York City that played a crucial role in the establishment of the Berkshire Festival in Massachusetts by providing it with its first orchestra.

Dr. Hadley Meets Miss Robinson Smith

The first conductor associated with the Berkshire Festival spent much of his early career in Europe, had a Bostonian background and became one of America's most persistent advocates of contemporary music. But his name wasn't Serge Alexandrovich Koussevitzky; it was Henry Kimball Hadley.

The years that have passed since his death in 1937 have not been very kind to Henry Hadley. His music, once regarded as among the most substantial produced by an American composer, is unplayed, and his contributions to the artistic life of his time are forgotten. Yet in his own day, Hadley was one of the most prolific, active and adventurous musicians in the land— associate conductor of the New York Philharmonic-Symphony Orchestra, illustrious composer of seven operas, five symphonies, two string quartets and a large assortment of tone poems, suites, concert overtures and songs. In 1920 he became the first American ever to conduct his own opera at the Metropolitan Opera House—*Cleopatra's Night,* an exotically staged, conservatively scored work which received a fair amount of praise from Richard Aldrich in *The New York Times* but disappeared permanently after seven performances.

Hadley was born in 1871 in Somerville, Massachusetts, just outside Boston, and studied at Tufts, which gave him an honorary Doctor of Music degree in 1925, and the New England Conservatory of Music. He was one of the most widely traveled conductors of the time, leading orchestras in Europe, South America and the Far East. As associate conductor of the New York Philharmonic under Willem Mengelberg, he was in charge of evaluating scores by American composers and selecting the best of these for performance. Several programs he conducted were transmitted on the radio in 1922—the first broadcasts ever made by the Philharmonic. Conservative as he was in his own musical tastes, Hadley was both imaginative and energetic in his efforts to find as wide an audience as possible for new American symphonic works. When he left the Philharmonic in 1927, he went to work with a short-lived group called the Manhattan Symphony Orchestra, which had a policy of playing at least one American composition on every program and which also managed to get itself broadcast regularly on the radio.

Although Hadley underwent cancer surgery in 1933, he never lost his zest for seeking out new audiences for music. Among his other activities, he began to conduct at summer festivals. He appeared at Worcester as far back as 1924, and he became a familiar figure at festivals on the West Coast, where he served for a time as conductor of both the Seattle and San Francisco orchestras.

In the spring of 1934 Hadley was casting about for a likely site in which to stage summer concerts, and friends suggested the Berkshire region of Massachusetts as a possibility. Hadley was well acquainted with the area and came up to make an exploratory tour with a friend, Roy Chandler. As they were driving around, they passed a farm near the little town of Interlaken, between Lenox and Stockbridge. The property was owned by Dan Hanna, the son of politician Mark Hanna, and among its installations was a large horse-show ring. "Look!" Hadley said to Chandler. "There's a perfect amphitheater! And a good sounding board, too. This farm would be a wonderful place to have a summer festival. It would be as good as the Hollywood Bowl."*

Another Berkshire friend suggested to Hadley that he go to Pittsfield to seek the advice of Carey Hayward, the regional correspondent of *The Springfield Republican,* who was well acquainted with the social and business leaders of the area, especially the well-to-do summer residents. Hayward, with scarcely a moment's hesitation, told Hadley that if he wanted to organize a music festival in the Berkshires, the person to see was a summer resident from New York City named Gertrude Robinson Smith. It was, as it turned out, an inspired suggestion.

Historians of the flowering of feminism have unjustly ignored Gertrude Robinson Smith, as determined, dynamic and purposeful a champion of female independence as ever asserted herself. All who met her remembered her vividly—though some without much affection—and the prim, modest plaque that commemorates her at the entrance of the Tanglewood Shed hardly seems to measure the force of her achievements or her personality.

Like most of the Berkshire Festival's early supporters, Gertrude Robinson Smith wasn't a New Englander but a New Yorker. She was the daughter of Charles Robinson Smith, a Wall Street lawyer and Allied Chemical director whose family always used the "Robinson Smith" designation, presumably to distinguish themselves from the ordinary tribe of Smiths. Gertrude, who was born in 1881, lived all her life in the luxurious surroundings of 1 Sutton Place, Manhattan. On her mother's side she traced her ancestry back to one of the original settlers of Massachusetts, Richard Mather, father of Increase Mather and grandfather of Cotton Mather. As befit a distinguished New York family of pre–World War I vintage, the Robinson Smiths maintained a salon at their Sutton Place dwelling, traveled frequently to Paris and summered in the Berkshires.

Miss Robinson Smith's mother was one of the society beauties of her time, but Gertrude herself was a rather plain girl, built along stocky, four-square lines. She had one sister, Hilda, who married Lyman Beecher Stowe, author, lecturer and grandson of Harriet Beecher Stowe. Gertrude herself never evinced any interest in marriage; for some forty years her constant companion was Miss Miriam Oliver, the sister of a New York architect. In the artistic world Gertrude knew everybody from Edith Wharton and Ger-

*The Hanna Farm in later years became the site of the Stockbridge School, a private preparatory institution.

18 • Tanglewood

trude Stein to Emma Calvé and Sarah Bernhardt. For years she corresponded regularly with Nadia Boulanger, the great French musician and teacher.

The Robinson Smiths maintained something of a tradition of noblesse oblige. Gertrude's first great moment of service came in World War I when with her friend Edith Wharton she launched a campaign to raise $70,000 for medical equipment to send to France, including ambulances and surgical motor units. When she heard that refrigeration facilities were needed badly in Allied field hospitals, she promptly organized an Ice Flotilla Committee which raised $100,000 for ice-making machines. In the course of her activities she crossed the ocean on a blacked-out ship and had herself flown over the front lines in the rickety planes of the day, to see where her machines were being installed. For her services she was made a Chevalier of the French Legion of Honor.

Home from the war, Gertrude turned her full attention to the Vacation Association, a woman's organization dedicated to helping city working girls spend a few weeks in the country during the summer by setting aside small weekly sums in the form of "Vacation Savings Stamps." In 1922, with Anne Morgan, daughter of financier J. P. Morgan and a Sutton Place neighbor, she helped organize the American Women's Association, with the intention of building a great clubhouse and residence hall on West Fifty-seventh Street in New York. The luxurious edifice was to cost $8,000,000, stand twenty-six stories high, and have 1,224 rooms with bath, as well as lounges, a gymnasium, a restaurant and a roof garden. Unfortunately the Depression intervened, and although the building was completed, it wound up not as the haven for women that Gertrude envisioned, but as the Henry Hudson Hotel.

The Robinson Smith family took up summer residence in the Berkshires during the war, when their leisurely annual sojourns in France were no longer feasible. Gertrude's father acquired a 115-acre estate in a wooded area called Glendale near Stockbridge. But Gertrude and her friend Miriam wanted their own place. So she persuaded her father to give her a corner of the estate for her own, and there she and Miriam set out to design and build their own vacation retreat.

They had some outside help for such tasks as putting up the chimney and setting the heavy beams in place, and their neighbor, the sculptor Daniel Chester French, whose studio was nearby, sometimes dropped over to offer advice. But the two women, clad in blue-jean trousers (in 1919!) actually did most of the work themselves, constructing a capacious, com-

Gertrude Robinson Smith, who leaped at Henry Hadley's idea for summer concerts in the Berkshires, little dreaming that they would grow into a national institution. (Courtesy the *Berkshire Eagle*)

This unusual picture, taken in 1919, shows a hammer-wielding Gertrude Robinson Smith (right) and her inveterate companion, Miriam Oliver, at work constructing their Berkshire hideaway, The Residence, where they were to live for many years. The man in the middle is sculptor Daniel Chester French, a neighbor, who used to drop over from his nearby estate to see how the work was coming along. (Courtesy the *Berkshire Eagle*)

fortable cabin they dubbed "The Residence." To furnish it they brought up some family antiques from New York, and they added a few personal touches including a set of silver spoons engraved with the intertwined initials M and G, for Miriam and Gertrude. A female reporter from the *Boston Post,* visiting The Residence shortly after its completion, described it enthusiastically as a "manless Eden" built by "two society women chums."*

It was to The Residence that Henry Hadley came in May, 1934, seeking support for his summer concert plan. He found a woman of fifty-three, positive, decisive and imperious, knowledgeable in music, a born organizer temporarily without a project to occupy her time and talents.

"Gertrude pounced on the idea," remembers Mrs. Alice Edman, whose husband George was county editor of the *Berkshire Eagle,* the Pittsfield newspaper. "She thought it would be wonderful to give music to the farmers around here. As it turned out, the farmers didn't go, but the social people did."

After a long afternoon's discussion that first day at The Residence, Hadley and Miss Robinson Smith tentatively agreed to arrange for three outdoor concerts to be held the following August. He returned to New York to engage a suitable symphony orchestra, while she remained in the Berkshires organizing local supporters to finance the enterprise.

Dan Hanna's Horse Ring

The year 1934 was not especially auspicious for launching new projects in the United States. Despite the recovery measures instituted by Franklin D. Roosevelt, who had been President for two years, the nation was still in the grip of the Depression. Berkshire County, with its paper mills, textile plants and General Electric facilities, was hard hit. People lost their jobs; local shopkeepers began closing as their volume of business dwindled. The well-to-do also felt the pinch: some of the palatial estates in the hills either shut down or struggled along with reduced staffs of gardeners, cooks and housemaids. In this atmosphere a summer festival might hardly seem like the dawn of a new economic era, but it at least gave promise of some increase in trade, tourism and job opportunities.

*The Residence, considerably enlarged, is still in existence and in 1975 was owned by New York summer residents who had purchased it some ten years previously. Many of Miss Robinson Smith's papers are still in the attic, including letters written to her by French soldiers whose lives she helped save in World War I.

A horse ring on a farm near Interlaken, Massachusetts, was the site of the first Berkshire Festival ever held, with Henry Hadley conducting sixty-five members of the New York Philharmonic-Symphony Orchestra. Here the audience assembles for the first afternoon concert on August 25, 1934. (Courtesy Stockbridge Library Association; photo by David Milton Jones)

The Junior League of Pittsfield ran the first food concession at the Festival. (Courtesy The Berkshire Symphonic Festival, Inc.)

This modest hut was the ticket booth for the opening concert of the first Berkshire Symphonic Festival. In the foreground are three officials: John C. Lynch, Henry W. Dwight and George W. Edman (back to camera). (Courtesy Stockbridge Library Association; photo by David Milton Jones)

A cultural tradition had flourished fitfully in the Berkshires for several decades. In 1918 Mrs. Elizabeth Sprague Coolidge, who for several years had been sponsoring Sunday musicales at her home in Pittsfield, organized a Berkshire Festival of Chamber Music at nearby South Mountain. She built a concert hall, known as the "Temple of Music," along with cottages for the performers; she created the Berkshire String Quartet, commissioned new works, awarded prizes and invited distinguished guests to help make up the audience. But after seven annual fall festivals, feeling remote and circumscribed in the Berkshire surroundings, Mrs. Coolidge moved her activities to Washington, D.C., where she built a small chamber music hall—the Coolidge Auditorium—in the Library of Congress, which still is the site of the concerts.

Another Berkshire cultural manifestation was the Jacob's Pillow Dance Festival, which had its inception in 1933 when Ted Shawn turned an eighteenth-century farm he had purchased near the town of Lee into a summer dance theater and residence for his company of male dancers. And in Stockbridge the Berkshire Playhouse was one of the East's most successful and prestigious summer theaters. Something about the Berkshire air seemed conducive to artistic enterprises.

But to set up a major symphonic festival in a few weeks' time was a challenge that called for vigorous action, thoroughgoing organization and substantial capital. Miss Robinson Smith set out to provide all three. "She was a steamroller," says Alice Edman, "but smart and dedicated." Very quickly Miss Robinson Smith enlisted the help of two other Berkshire socialite friends, Mrs. Owen Johnson, whose husband was the author of *Stover at Yale* and other books, and Mrs. William Felton Barrett, a summer resident of Great Barrington whose home was New York and who had often heard Hadley conduct at Carnegie Hall.

Early in June, 150 leading residents of Lenox, Stockbridge, Great Barrington and other communities in the area received a letter from Gertrude Robinson Smith inviting them to a late afternoon meeting at The Residence on June 18 at which Henry Hadley, in person, would explain his proposal for a Berkshire Festival that summer. Sixty-four, nearly all of them women, turned up at the session; committees, subscription teams and regional chairmen were promptly appointed. Gertrude Robinson was named president of the enterprise, and subsequently Elizabeth Sprague Coolidge accepted the title of honorary president. Thus the Berkshire Symphonic Festival, Inc., as the new organization was legally designated, came into being, although its formal incorporation did not take place until August 21, 1934.

Working on a budget of around $10,000—which they hoped to cover through subscription sales for the three scheduled concerts—the Festival committee immediately set about turning Dan Hanna's horse ring, which had been contributed for the occasion, into an outdoor concert arena. A New Deal agency, the Civil Works Emergency Relief Administration, agreed to provide labor to install wooden benches to accommodate an audience of 2,000 as well as a stage and a plywood shell for the orchestra. Additional labor was furnished by the towns of Stockbridge, Lee and Lenox, which hired unemployed electricians, carpenters and plumbers to assist in the construction and also to lay out a parking lot in a nearby cow pasture. Although it began as a society event, and indeed remained one through its early years, the Berkshire Festival very quickly also developed into a community project.

But although a subscription covering all three concerts was modestly priced at from $2.75 to $5.50, three weeks before the scheduled opening the Festival found itself short of necessary funds by $4,000. Nobody knew how many single tickets, priced at $1 and $2, would be sold at the gate for the individual concerts. Eight members of the executive committee promptly pledged $500 apiece to meet the expected deficit, and the season was assured.*

The date set for the first concert was Thursday, August 23, 1934, at 8:30 P.M., with two others to follow on Saturday, August 25 at 4:30 P.M. and Sunday the 26th, again at 8:30. The dates were cannily chosen. In the first place, the lunar schedule promised a full moon for both evening concerts. In the second, Hadley had decided to engage for his orchestra the New York Philharmonic-Symphony, which was playing through July and most of August at Lewisohn Stadium. The season at the Stadium would end just in time for the musicians to make the expedition to northeastern Massachusetts.

For its appearance in the Berkshires, the orchestra was listed as "Sixty-five members of the New York Philharmonic-Symphony Orchestra." The cost of engaging the musicians, including rehearsal time in New York, was given in the Festival's budget as $4,875, and Hadley received a conductor's fee of $600. The men traveled from Carnegie Hall to Stockbridge in two long-distance buses chartered from the New England Transportation Company at a cost of $560. Their instruments followed on a seven-and-a-half-ton

*Since there might never have been a Tanglewood without them, their names merit recording: Mrs. C. C. Griswold, Clarke W. Tobin, John R. Hopkins, Mrs. John Bross Lloyd, Norville H. Busey, Jr., Mrs. Halstead Lindsley, Mrs. Arthur F. Schermerhorn, Mrs. Bruce Crane.

truck. They were put up gratis at various hotels and private homes in the area, with no fewer than fifteen housed free at the Red Lion Inn, Stockbridge's most fashionable hostelry. Miss Robinson Smith, sensing that the concerts were of more than local interest, set up a $1,000 advertising budget that included display ads in *The New York Times* and *Herald Tribune* suggesting: "Why not run up for the Berkshire Symphonic Festival in Stockbridge August 23, 25 and 26—New York Philharmonic Orchestra?"

Engelbert Brenner, then an oboist with the Philharmonic, still remembers the trip with pleasure four decades later. "It was an adventure for most of us," he says. "Some even took their wives along. Hadley was a quiet-spoken person; quite a contrast from Toscanini, our regular conductor. We wore the same clothes we did in the Stadium: dark jacket and light trousers. To the players it was an extra job in nice surroundings. Jobs were at a premium then. Certainly nobody had the feeling that he was participating in anything historic. Even today, I find that people don't believe me when I tell them that it was the New York Philharmonic, not the Boston Symphony, that really started Tanglewood."

As the dates of the concerts neared, excitement grew among the summer residents of the area, most of whom were New Yorkers—well-to-do Bostonians tended to take their vacations either on Cape Cod or in Maine. Berkshire society activities, quiescent since the 1929 stock market crash, suddenly underwent a revival. There were garden, cocktail and dinner parties, all preliminary to the concerts; girls from the Junior League of Pittsfield operated a refreshment stand, vending ice cream and soft drinks; other young women in evening gowns handed out programs, and young male volunteers, clad in dark jackets and white trousers, served as ushers. It became known that Massachusetts Governor Joseph B. Ely and Norman Davis, United States Ambassador at Large, would attend the first concert, and that Mrs. James Roosevelt, mother of the President, would motor over from Hyde Park for the Saturday and Sunday performances. All these notables were to occupy box seats—metal folding chairs placed in a special section, which has persisted at Tanglewood to this day.

An unexpected problem arose concerning the wooden benches upon which the ordinary members of the audience were to sit. These had been painted on the day before the concert, and when the skies turned cloudy the next morning it became painfully obvious that they would not be dry in time. A desperate order was sent to Pittsfield for heavy coated paper, which was cut in strips and placed over the benches, thus saving the concert, not to mention dozens of new frocks. By starting time the skies had cleared, and the first symphony concert ever given in the Berkshires was held—as promised—under a full moon.

For that first concert Hadley played a program consisting of Berlioz' *Roman Carnival* Overture, the Nocturne and Scherzo from Mendelssohn's *A Midsummer Night's Dream,* the Largo movement from Dvořák's "New World" Symphony, Richard Strauss' *Don Juan,* Chabrier's *España* Rhapsody, Respighi's *The Pines of Rome* and the last two movements of Tchaikovsky's Fourth Symphony.

It was not a program excessively complimentary to its audience's sophistication; obviously Hadley had no intention of going much beyond a pleasant summer evening of fairly light music. For the second concert he introduced a vocal soloist, the American contralto Sophie Braslau, who sang in de Falla's *El amor brujo.* Also on this program, again of a popular nature, were Smetana's *Bartered Bride* Overture, Bizet's *L'Arlésienne* Suite No. 1, the Polovetzian Dances from Borodin's *Prince Igor,* Debussy's *Prelude to the Afternoon of a Faun,* and three American pieces—Edward MacDowell's *Clair de lune,* John Powell's *Natchez on the Hill,* a set of three Virginia country dances and Hadley's own *Streets of Pekin* Suite, one of his more popular works.

The third and final concert was more substantial, containing three Wagner works, the *Meistersinger* Prelude, the *Siegfried Idyll,* the Prelude and Liebestod from *Tristan und Isolde,* and Beethoven's Fifth Symphony. The audience demanded an encore, and Hadley played his own "Scherzo Diabolique," which, he announced to his entranced listeners, was designed to depict a terrifying automobile ride "at an excessive speed from Stockbridge to New Haven to catch a train in the rain and darkness at night."

By most standards, the first Berkshire Festival was a triumph. Total attendance for the three concerts was 5,000. Many wore full evening regalia, with observers commenting upon the "glistening jewels and gowns" in evidence. All the notables turned up as advertised, with a newspaperman solemnly recording Miss Robinson Smith and Mrs. James Roosevelt in a typically vacuous ceremonial exchange:

Miss Robinson Smith: "It is a great honor to have you here, Mrs. Roosevelt."

Mrs. Roosevelt: "It is a great honor to be here."

About the only discordant incident, as noted by Jay C. Rosenfeld, the music critic of the *Berkshire Eagle,* occurred in the parking lot on opening night and was caused by "a luckless chauffeur who fell on his F-sharp horn during a passage in D-flat major."

Financially, too, the first Berkshire Festival was a success. The gross income was $9,820.06, leaving—no one had expected a profit—a total deficit of only $413.30. That meant that the eight guarantors who each had been willing to risk $500 were actually assessed only $51.67 apiece. Departing the grounds after the first concert, Governor Ely predicted, with more accuracy than in most political pronouncements: "The Festival is destined to become a notable Berkshire institution of far-reaching importance in attracting people to this wonderful section of the country."

Exit Hadley

The only real complaint over the first Berkshire Festival had to do with Hadley's programming. Murmurings were heard against the composer's selections of such numbers as isolated movements from symphonies. Hadley must have realized that he underestimated the sophistication of his listeners; in a lengthy statement to the board, although he tried to blame some of the "patrons" for his choices, he also promised to mend his ways:

> My many years of experience in preparing and building programs for audiences of all types, the selection of music suitable for the various tastes of different cities and countries all over the world, has sharpened my intuition and judgment as to what will succeed in a particular place.
>
> One of my first questions among the ladies was "What will you play?"
>
> My first choice was and always would be the type of the last program, the Wagner, Beethoven—a program worthy of the audience and the artists' performance. However, after much discussion it was thought best to ask the patrons for suggestions, which we did.
>
> The programs were formed after these suggestions, and therefore were not altogether an index to my taste and to whatever skill I possess in program building, but was rather a temporary yielding to the popular suggestions. The success of the last program completely vindicated my judgment and convinced me that only the greatest works of the masters should be presented on these programs. . . . I wish to go on record as saying that next season we will include only those masterpieces which we would play on a similar program at Carnegie Hall.

Thus reassured, Miss Robinson Smith and her cohorts decided not only to continue the concerts in 1935, but to augment the orchestra to eighty-five members. All through the winter of 1934–35 she worked aggres-

Clad in their summer-concert garb are three oboists from the New York Philharmonic-Symphony Orchestra, ready to play at the first Festival. From left, Engelbert Brenner, Bruno Labate and Michel Nazzi. (Photo courtesy Engelbert Brenner)

sively to spread the word of the Berkshire Symphonic Festival. It is indicative of the New York rather than the Boston connection of the Festival's originators that so much of her activity took place in Manhattan. On April 7, 1935, a meeting was held in the East Seventieth Street home of Mrs. Carlos de Heredia, wife of a Spanish nobleman and also a Berkshire summer resident, to interest new subscribers. Said Miss Robinson Smith determinedly: "It is high time that America had its own Salzburg, and we are taking a step in that direction. The people of the Berkshires are prepared to receive and serve visitors from all over the United States."

To avoid any possibility of rain interfering with the second season of concerts, the Festival directors decided to invest $550 for the rental of a circus tent 250 feet long, 70 feet wide, and 28 feet high from the Martin–New York Tent and Seat Company. Although the canvas was actually erected on the Hanna Farm, it was intended only as a form of weather insurance; the concerts were to be held in the open, with the tent serving as a refuge in case of need. The price of single tickets was raised 50 cents to $2.50 and $1.50. The concert dates were moved up two weeks from the previous summer, being set for August 8, 10 and 11 (again a Thursday night, Saturday matinee and Sunday night sequence). "The moon will be full and the weather a little warmer," explained Miss Robinson Smith.

But the advanced dates also meant that the Berkshire Festival would run into a conflict with Lewisohn Stadium for the services of the Philharmonic musicians, for the Stadium season was scheduled to last through mid-August. To Miss Robinson Smith the solution was simple: the Stadium would simply have to move up *its* season by two weeks. To make the necessary arrangements she paid a visit to Mrs. Charles "Minnie" Guggenheimer, who ran the Stadium concerts as authoritatively as Miss Robinson Smith ran the Berkshire. But in the redoubtable Minnie, Gertrude ran into a body as immovable as herself. Mrs. Guggenheimer informed her that the Stadium dates could not be changed for *anybody,* and Miss Robinson Smith, frustrated and furious, told Hadley he would have to recruit his players elsewhere. Actually, the task was not of inordinate difficulty; New York was filled with unemployed musicians who would have gone far beyond the Berkshires for a paying engagement. Hadley quickly assembled an orchestra made up of a nucleus of Philharmonic members who were not playing at the Stadium, a considerable number from the Metropolitan Opera Orchestra on furlough for the summer and an assortment of others. To maintain an appearance of continuity, these performers were billed as "Eighty-five members of the New York Philharmonic-Symphony and other Orchestras."

Hadley's remuneration for running the Festival was raised to $1,000 and he also was promised, somewhat optimistically, 25 percent of any profits up to $2,000.

By now enthusiasm for the Festival was spreading through the hills, sparked by Miss Robinson Smith's war cry to her women workers: "We must eat, sleep and drink Berkshire Symphonic Festival, and so we will get the whole country Berkshire-minded!" Stamps inscribed "Berkshire Symphonic Festival—Music Under the Moon" were printed and affixed like Christmas or Easter seals to mail going out of the region. The Berkshire Playhouse timed its stellar attraction of the summer, Ethel Barrymore in *Déclassée,* for the Festival weekend. It was noted in a publicity release that a "two-header baseball game" would be played in Stockbridge that weekend. Ted Shawn promised a special program at his Jacob's Pillow theater.* The South Mountain Quartet in Pittsfield scheduled afternoon recitals before the evening Festival concerts. The Festival itself opened an information bureau in Stockbridge; ticket booths were set up in half a dozen towns in the area, and the main streets of Lenox and Stockbridge were strung with banners advertising the Festival dates.

Despite Hadley's assurances that rigorous programming standards would henceforth be followed, the opening concert of the second Berkshire Festival on August 8, 1935, was a hodgepodge. A local chorus of 300 voices had been invited to appear, as had Richard Hale, a baritone. Hale was primarily an actor; in later years he participated as the narrator in the Boston Symphony's first recording of *Peter and the Wolf.* He currently was appearing at the Berkshire Playhouse opposite Miss Barrymore in *Déclassée.*

Hale's reputation as a singer was modest. Nevertheless, he was engaged to perform as the soloist in the Coronation Scene from Moussorgsky's *Boris Godunov.* His number was so placed on the program that a waiting car could speed him back to the Playhouse in Stockbridge in time for the curtain. The first half of Hadley's program also included a transcription of a Bach fugue, four excerpts from Mendelssohn's *Elijah* and the final chorus from Bach's

*The relations between Shawn at Jacob's Pillow and the Symphonic Festival underwent a curious reversal. At first Shawn took a benign, big-brotherly attitude toward his new neighbor. But in later years, as Tanglewood developed into a national institution, its success irritated him. According to William Judd, the concert manager: "Ted always cussed the whole thing out, although the Tanglewood overflow provided a public for him. He was just getting started when the Boston Symphony overwhelmed him." William Kroll, a violinist who often played in Mrs. Elizabeth Sprague Coolidge's nearby Temple of Music, recalls a similar attitude on her part: "Mrs. Coolidge didn't show that she didn't like Tanglewood, but she didn't. She was worried about it. It overshadowed her activities."

St. Matthew Passion, all sung by the "Berkshire Musical Association," as the amateur choir assembled for the occasion was called. After the intermission Hadley conducted the orchestra in Beethoven's "Eroica" Symphony.

Whatever the musical vagaries of the program, the evening was a roaring success socially and fiscally. With a bright moon shining down, a huge crowd of 3,500 descended on the concert site, clogging the access roads and jamming the parking field. Standing room was put on sale at 50 cents a head, thus providing the first of the Berkshire Festival's many overflow crowds. Two New England governors had promised to put in appearances— Theodore F. Green of Rhode Island and James M. Curley of Massachusetts. Curley, however, didn't arrive until 9 P.M. , and the Festival officials, with much muttering, delayed the start of the performance until he got there.

Curley, however, proved well worth the wait, entering in white tie and full evening dress that quite outdid in elegance Hadley's striped trousers and dark jacket. At intermission James Michael, who never missed a chance to harangue a crowd of whatever size and circumstances, advanced to the microphone, extended his congratulations to "the local committee," told of his own love of great music and announced to the surprised multitude that immediately upon return to the State House he would direct "the proper authorities" to allocate $5,000 to the Festival. A whole year later George W. Edman, the *Berkshire Eagle* editor who had been appointed clerk of the Festival organization, was still trying to collect. After repeated inquiries, Curley finally wrote to Edman, blaming "the Republican majority of Beacon Hill" for his failure to produce the promised money. To this day, Tanglewood has never collected on Curley's pledge, but at the time it seemed like a nice thought.

Hadley's next concert, without vocal assistance from singers or politicians, continued to emphasize popular showpieces, including two movements of Rimsky-Korsakov's *Scheherazade* and all of César Franck's Symphony in D Minor, along with Dvořák's *Carnival* Overture and an American piece, Burnet Corwin Tuthill's *Bethlehem,* a "pastorale for orchestra." At the final Sunday evening concert, the Festival's rented tent, which had stood unused, finally repaid its investment. All day long the skies were overcast, and a few hours before concert time it was decided to move the benches and stage structure into the tent. Naturally, by 9 P.M. the skies had cleared and the moon shone brightly, but the performance was nevertheless given under cover—to the betterment, many thought, of the acoustics. Rudolph Ganz was piano soloist in Tchaikovsky's Concerto No. 1 in B-flat minor, giving a particularly exciting performance; the program also included the Bacchanale from Wagner's *Tannhauser* and Brahms' First Symphony.

Although the three concerts attracted a total audience of 9,000, nearly double that of the first year, and brought a gross income of $11,161.88, many of the sponsors were dissatisfied. With a larger orchestra on the payroll, the budget had risen considerably, and so had the deficit. Discontent continued over Hadley's programming; some people felt that only Ganz's pianism had saved the last concert. George Edman, the clerk of the board, made so bold as to assert that in his opinion "the opening program had not been up to Dr. Hadley's usual standard" and that the gate receipts for the two following programs had suffered accordingly.

Remarkably, this entire second Berkshire Festival had taken place without benefit of the presence of Gertrude Robinson Smith. Her mother's brother, a Polish count, had died in Paris in July, just before the concerts were to start, and she felt obligated to travel to France for the funeral. In her absence Mrs. de Heredia became acting head of the enterprise, and Mr. Edman's role was also expanded.

When Miss Robinson Smith returned, she lost no time reasserting her prerogatives. Purposefully she pored over newspaper clippings, consulted her fellow board members, restudied the programs and checked the financial returns. She arrived at the conclusion that while Hadley was providing pleasant enough summer listening, he had not established the "American Salzburg" she wanted.

For his part, the conductor, who was sixty-three and in failing health (he died two years later) perhaps realized that gathering an ad hoc orchestra every summer was not the answer to the needs of a continuing Festival in the Berkshires. And so, after a meeting with Miss Robinson Smith and other directors of the Berkshire Symphonic Festival, Henry Hadley resigned, saying in a statement he had "made other plans which will preclude my being with you." He received from the board an expression of "deep gratitude and appreciation," and the assurance that "his name will always be associated" with the Berkshire Festival—as indeed it is, on a bronze tablet alongside Miss Robinson Smith's at the entrance of the Tanglewood Shed.

So far as the Festival's future was concerned, the board members made a momentous decision. They determined that instead of again utilizing a band of "pick-up" musicians, they would try to engage the services of one of the country's established orchestras for next summer's season in the Berkshires. And unknown to themselves, they hit upon an orchestra whose conductor had been waiting for such an opportunity all his musical life.

One of the first signs of the Berkshire Symphonic Festival's success was the interest evinced by the New England politicians. While conductor Henry Hadley (left) stands aside, Massachusetts Governor James M. Curley (center) extends a welcome to the 1935 Festival to Rhode Island Governor Theodore F. Green. (Courtesy the Berkshire Symphonic Festival, Inc.)

Ever since the start, the Boston Symphony has had to pay a $3 fee—$2 to the state, $1 to the town—for a license to give each Sunday performance. This copy dates from 1940. Although exempted from other taxes, the Festival pays them voluntarily to Lenox and Stockbridge in acknowledgment of the protective and other services given by the towns. (Courtesy Ted and Larry Gross)

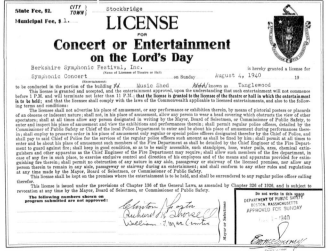

Serge Koussevitzky at his home in the Berkshires, "Seranak." The name is an anagram of "Serge and Natalie Koussevitzky." Mrs. Olga Koussevitzky, his second wife and the niece of his first, still lives there during the summer months. (Courtesy the *Berkshire Eagle*)

3. The Koussevitzky Era

Aristocrat from Russia

Serge Koussevitzky would have been a great man in American musical history even if he had never set a foot in the Berkshires. He was one of the most exciting and creative conductors this country has ever seen; he raised the Boston Symphony to the preeminent position it still holds; he was a friend, counselor and often a discoverer of young musicians; and he championed the cause of contemporary music, especially American contemporary music, with a passion displayed by few of his colleagues.

Oscar Levant once said of Koussevitzky: "He is unparalleled in the performance of Russian music, whether it is by Moussorgsky, Rimsky-Korsakov, Strauss, Wagner or Aaron Copland." Although in later years Koussevitzky became perfectly at home in America, his musical tastes and techniques were developed in Russia and he never lost any of their emotional fervor and luxuriant color, any more than he ever lost his flavorful Russian accent.

Koussevitzky was born July 26, 1874, in Vishny-Volotchok in central Russia. His father, Alexander Koussevitzky, gave violin lessons; his mother, Anna Barabeitchik Koussevitzky, played the piano. Young Serge took piano lessons, but harbored ambitions to be a conductor early in life. According to one family story, he used to set up a score on a music stand and conduct an orchestra of empty chairs. Once he also managed to conduct a band of musicians who accompanied a troupe of strolling actors. But the place for a young musician intent on a serious career was the Moscow Conservatory. So at the age of fourteen Koussevitzky, with a few roubles in his pocket, left behind him the provincial Jewish community of which he was a part and headed for Moscow and the world that lay beyond.

In Moscow he applied for admission to the Conservatory, attempting to get one of the scholarships it offered to worthy but needy students. However, by the time he arrived the only openings left were for the relatively unpopular instruments—the trombone, horn and double bass. Koussevitzky chose the double bass, and worked at it so assiduously that he eventually became one of the greatest virtuosos that that unwieldy instrument has ever known.

In school he was proficient enough to be awarded a job in the double-bass section of the Bolshoi Theater Orchestra. But Koussevitzky wasn't satisfied; all his life he took pleasure in occupying the limelight, and the obscurity of a pit band befitted neither his talents nor his temperament. Solo double-bass recitals were as rare then as they are now, but Koussevitzky began to supplement his orchestral work by lugging his instrument around on a concert tour of European cities. A recital in Berlin attracted particular attention, with critics praising the young virtuoso's mastery. To eke out the meager repertory, Koussevitzky at the age of thirty composed a double-bass concerto, which he performed for the first time in Moscow in 1905. The same year he married Natalie Ushkov, the daughter of a wealthy tea merchant.

Koussevitzky's marriage transformed his life. With his economic security assured, he was able to quit his job at the Bolshoi. But far from seeking a life of ease, he began to widen his musical interests and activities tremendously. First he and Natalie moved for a time to Berlin so he could study conducting with Arthur Nikisch. His first appearance on the podium was with a student orchestra at the Berlin Hochschule für Musik, and in 1908 he conducted the great Berlin Philharmonic itself. Back in Russia Koussevitzky, with his wife's money behind him, established his own orchestra and embarked upon a series of brilliant concerts encompassing music by Russian composers and by the classic masters. He immediately displayed his affinity for new music, becoming an early champion of Alexander Scriabin, and he imported leading European soloists and conductors to Russia. Koussevitzky also established a publishing house called Editions Russes de Musique, signing contracts with Stravinsky, Prokofiev and Rachmaninoff in their early days. By 1914, when he was forty, he was Russia's most brilliant and innovative musical director.

Among his notable contributions was his pioneering work in bringing music to masses of people who had no other opportunity to hear it. All his life Koussevitzky was imbued with a passion to discover not only new music and musicians, but also new audiences. Koussevitzky always refused to believe that there were people who could not love music once they were exposed to it. He was the first conductor in Russia to introduce student tickets, and young men and women lined up to pay fifty kopecks for admission to his concerts.

In 1910 he conceived the idea of chartering a large pleasure steamer

The first of the annual birthday parties for Koussevitzky was given by the Berkshire Music Center students on July 26, 1940. Leonard Bernstein conducted Stravinsky's *L'Histoire du Soldat*—with a specially written text making Koussevitzky the hero—while the conductor and his wife Natalie listened from their balcony at Seranak. (Courtesy the Boston Symphony Orchestra)

for a concert tour of cities and towns along the Volga. Up and down the river he went with his sixty-five-man orchestra on a journey of 2,300 miles, going ashore at night to perform. Accompanying him was Scriabin, who played his own piano concerto. So warmly were he and his musicians received by everybody from municipal officials to school students, few of whom had ever heard a symphony orchestra before, that the Volga voyage was repeated in 1912 and 1914. Claude Debussy, who visited Russia in 1913, described Koussevitzky as "unique" and "burning with a will to serve music," and said his orchestra had more "discipline and devotion" than most European ensembles.

The success of his Volga trips and the huge crowds they drew gave him the idea of doing something to draw people closer to music in the heart of Russia, Moscow itself. He decided to build a great musical center just outside the city for both musical and educational activities, and actually engaged an architect to draw up the plans. The onset of World War I caused the project to be abandoned, but not forgotten.

Koussevitzky remained in Russia after the Bolshevik Revolution, and for a time became conductor of the State Symphony in Leningrad. But in 1921 he decided to get out although he had to leave much of his money behind and his property was expropriated. After some time in Berlin and Rome he settled in Paris. There he organized the Concerts Koussevitzky and soon was playing as brilliant a role in French musical life as he had in Russian. It was Koussevitzky who premiered Arthur Honegger's *Pacific 231,* which created a sensation with its graphic depiction of a railway locomotive. Similarly he played new music by Ravel, Prokofiev and Stravinsky, and gained a reputation as one of the most exciting and innovative conductors in Europe.

In 1924 the Boston Symphony was in the market for a new conductor. The orchestra, established in 1881 by Henry Lee Higginson, a philanthropic but authoritarian music-loving banker, had rapidly become one of the most outstanding in the United States. But in recent years it had undergone a series of vicissitudes, most of them extramusical in nature. Its German conductor, Karl Muck, had been hounded from his post as an "enemy alien" in 1918, and under Pierre Monteux, its music director from 1919 on, it underwent a period of labor difficulties occasioned by Higginson's fervid opposition to unionization. As admired as Monteux was as a musician, it was generally agreed that only a new conductor could restore the orchestra to its former eminence. The offer was made to Koussevitzky. He accepted, stipulating that he would continue to return to Paris each summer to conduct the Concerts Koussevitzky. At his first concert in Symphony Hall, Boston, on October 10, 1924, he made it a point to play the kind of repertory for which he had been noted in Europe, including *Pacific 231* and Scriabin's *Poem of Ecstasy.*

Koussevitzky's early years in Boston have been the subject of some controversy. He never was noted for his impeccable technique, and some players professed difficulty in following his cues. Koussevitzky was an instinctual rather than an intellectual conductor; to him music existed in sound and feeling rather than on paper, and score-reading always was something of an effort for him. But he knew what he wanted and, as it turned out, how to get it. The musicians learned to respect him, even though he worked them hard and rehearsed them at length.

While Koussevitzky spoke both English and French, everything came out sounding Russian, and his accent and his malapropisms sometimes helped lighten, if not shorten, a rehearsal session. "Do not spik. If you spik I go home," was one of his threats. "Gentlemen, you are awfully not togedder," he would tell the musicians. "You play all the time the wrong notes not in time." When a player arriving late for a rehearsal took his seat rather slowly, Koussevitzky called out: "Vy you not come in so fast as you go out?" One of the most famous Koussevitzky tales, perhaps apocryphal, tells of the time he turned on a musician who repeatedly played wrong notes. "Ged out, ged out, you're fired," he shouted. On his way out the musician passed the office where the conductor sat hunched over a score. "Nuts to you, Koussevitzky," he bellowed. Koussevitzky looked up with disdain. "It's too late to abologize," he snapped.

Symphony Hall audiences, although surprised by some of the strange music Koussevitzky was playing, gradually took to the new conductor. They found him a trim, rather patrician figure on the podium, and a leader who knew how to perform music with éclat and excitement. Some even learned to look for a large blood vessel on the side of his head that seemed to pulsate in rhythm with the music. This was before the era of *wunderkind* conductors; Koussevitzky was fifty years old when he came to Boston. In the full maturity of his powers, he was able to bring the orchestra to an eminence even higher than in the past and to take his place, along with Toscanini in New York and Stokowski in Philadelphia, in the ruling triumvirate of American conductors. The Boston began to be called "The Aristocrat of Orchestras" and Koussevitzky's brilliant musical style, his elegant bearing, his penchant for wearing a cape, and his courtly European manner all helped sustain the image.

From his very first season he began to search out American music. "Who are your composers in America?" had been one of the first questions he asked upon accepting the Boston post, and he lost no time in finding out. But he was nothing if not discriminating in his choices. Charles O'Connell, who recorded Koussevitzky for RCA-Victor for years, told of a composer reproaching the conductor when an anticipated performance failed to materialize. "But Maestro, you said you would play my piece this season. You promised. You know you have a terrible weakness for making promises," cried the composer indignantly. "Yes, my dear," replied Koussevitzky smoothly, "but thank God I have the strength not to keep them."

Koussevitzky found plenty of American compositions to his liking, and premiered them as enthusiastically as he had performed new works by French and Russian musicians. Aaron Copland credits him with being the conductor who established him as a composer in the United States. "He was brave enough to introduce me to conservative audiences," says Copland.

The two first met in Paris, where Copland, still in his twenties, was studying with Nadia Boulanger. Copland played some of his music for Koussevitzky shortly before his Boston appointment was announced. About the same time, Boulanger was invited to the United States to appear with Walter Damrosch and his New York Symphony Orchestra, and she commissioned Copland to write an organ concerto for her to play at the concert. Some in the New York audience thought it a daring piece, and when it was finished, Damrosch turned smiling to the audience and said: "If a young composer of twenty-three can write a piece like that, in five years he'll be ready to commit murder." The comment did not exactly fill Copland with joy.

A short time later Koussevitzky also played the piece in Boston. "He didn't say anything to the audience," Copland recalls. "But to me he said: 'What are you going to write next?' From then on, most of my orchestral music was introduced to America by Koussevitzky and the Boston. Koussy was a terrific fellow—an utterly dedicated soul—passionately interested in all aspects of musical experience, whether it was playing the double bass, conducting, or gathering around him the best musicians and getting them to transmit their knowledge to younger musicians. That was his special passion—passing on the wisdom of the old guys to the young kids."

Despite his eagerness to play and promote American music, for many years Koussevitzky was careful to keep one foot in Europe. The end of the Symphony Hall season invariably found him on a liner bound for France, and he plunged into his Paris concerts as avidly as those in Boston. He traveled little in the United States and for years he never bought property here, preferring to live in a rented house in Brookline.

But gradually "Koussy"—as he was universally called, though not to his face—found himself more and more involved in American life. It became borne in on him that musical creativity, education and appreciation were all on the ascent on this side of the Atlantic even as they were being adversely affected in a Europe that was deteriorating politically and moving toward war. In 1935 he applied for United States citizenship and received his first papers. A few months later came the offer to conduct in the uniquely American summer festival that had been organized in the Berkshires.

Enter the Boston Symphony

The Boston Symphony was only one of several organizations considered by the officials seeking a permanent orchestra to play at their summer festival. They gave up the idea of the New York Philharmonic with the utmost regret, and they also explored the possibilities of the Detroit and Cleveland orchestras. Arthur Rodzinski, the conductor of the Cleveland, who later became a Berkshire summer resident, presumably was interested in the idea, but his orchestra's board of directors was not scheduled to meet for a number of weeks, and quick action was imperative.

It seems to have been George W. Edman, rather than the omnipresent Gertrude Robinson Smith, who suggested the Boston Symphony. With Miss Robinson Smith's approval—nothing was done without *that*—Edman contacted the Boston's manager, George E. Judd, to inquire about the availability of the orchestra and its conductor.

Judd told him that the Festival could have the former but not the latter. "Dr. Koussevitzky always goes back to Europe for the summer," he said.

According to the conductor's second wife, Olga Koussevitzky, Miss Robinson Smith thereupon resolved to see the conductor herself. "She was a very determined person," recalls Mrs. Koussevitzky. "She went to talk to him in Boston, and to the great surprise of Mr. Judd, Koussevitzky immediately said 'Splendid—it's a great idea.'"

In subsequent years Koussevitzky and Miss Robinson Smith were to have their differences, even their quarrels, but at that first meeting his charm and her bluntness seemed to make for a perfect formula. They talked for two hours while she dilated on the beauties of her summer concerts and he began to envision possibilities beyond mere performances. When Miss

Robinson Smith returned to the Berkshires, she was filled with enthusiasm, and on October 17, 1935, the board of trustees of the Berkshire Symphonic Festival, over her signature, reported to its members that it had "the great privilege of announcing that Dr. Serge Koussevitzky will conduct the Boston Symphony Orchestra at the 1936 Festival on August 13th, 14th and 16th." The letter continued: "You certainly must be as happy about this rare and unique opportunity as we all are. Dr. Koussevitzky is tremendously interested and sees a great future for the Festival."

The Boston Symphony management may not have had precisely the same vision of the future as Koussevitzky, but it certainly was quick to seize the opportunity of some summer dates in the Berkshires. The contract was drawn up by Judd, a native of Stamford in upstate New York, who had graduated from Harvard and gone to work for Henry Lee Higginson in 1911 in his Boston banking office. Later on Judd had become assistant to Charles A. Ellis, the orchestra's first manager. Now, stepping into the managership himself, he shrewdly saw the possibilities of the Berkshire engagement, as did Bentley W. Warren, president of the orchestra's Board of Trustees and himself a summer resident of nearby Williamstown. Warren issued a statement saying that the orchestra was happy "to add to its schedule of winter symphonies, spring pops and free Esplanade concerts, a summer festival of unrivaled importance, both from a musical and from a public point of view."

Under an agreement signed on February 13, 1936, the Boston Symphony Orchestra was to receive a fee of $9,500 from the Berkshire Symphonic Festival, Inc., for three concerts, $4,750 payable before the first concerts, $4,750 after the last. Koussevitzky's fee was included. It was specified that the orchestra would supply at least eighty players, and that the Festival would pay their round-trip rail fare between Boston and Pittsfield, the rate being put at $4 a man. The Festival also assumed the costs of housing and feeding the musicians, as well as providing ushers, ticket takers and similar help.

One point Koussevitzky insisted upon was that the concerts be held under cover. Accordingly an even larger tent than the previous year was ordered, at a cost of $795. When a Boston woman who had attended the subscription concerts for years in Symphony Hall expressed surprise that the orchestra had consented to play under a tent, Koussevitzky is said to have drawn himself up loftily and replied: "Madame, the tent is where the priests were."

With the largest budget in the Festival's history confronting them, Miss

George E. Judd, the manager who helped bring the Boston Symphony to the Berkshires and ran its business affairs during its early years there. (Courtesy the *Berkshire Eagle*)

Robinson Smith and her cohorts both in the Berkshires and New York worked more determinedly than ever to find supporters. An unexpected problem arose early in 1936 when it developed that the Hanna Farm, site of the Festival in both of Hadley's years, had been sold to new owners, who instead of making the property available without charge were demanding a rental of $700 for the weekend and were prohibiting any parking on their land. For a time the future of the whole project was in jeopardy, but another Berkshire resident, Mrs. Margaret Emerson—the former Mrs. Alfred Gwynne Vanderbilt—offered the use of her 500-acre estate, Holmwood, at the town boundaries of Stockbridge, Lenox and Lee.* There a tent 250 feet by 120 was erected on a lawn in front of a grove of pine trees, and the benches, stage and shell transported from the Hanna property about a mile away, under the direction of Joseph Franz, a Stockbridge engineer. Describing the musicians' facilities, *The New York Times* reported: "A small cottage near Mrs. Emerson's villa will be used by Mr. Koussevitzky as dressing quarters during the festival, and the spacious stables will be placed at the disposal of the musicians for similar purposes." The horses, it may be assumed, had been removed.

The advent of the Boston Symphony seemed to turn the Berkshire Festival into a musical event of national importance. At the opening concert, Francis D. Perkins, critic of the *New York Herald Tribune* and an inveterate statistician, noted that autos were arriving every six seconds in the parking lots and among them were license plates from twenty-five states, including California and Florida, not to mention Canada. With 5,000 tickets sold, so great was the traffic jam that the starting time had to be set back half an hour while a second gate was hastily opened to the parking field, which had room for 3,000 cars. Innkeepers and tourist homes reported every room in the area sold out and began to envision an end to the Depression, at least locally.

Press coverage was extensive with more than twenty newspapers, from Boston to Pittsburgh, sending their music critics. On the local level, the *Berkshire Eagle* of Pittsfield, an outstandingly high-quality paper for a city of 50,000, provided full and competent coverage of the Festival, as it had from the start. George Edman, who eventually became the *Eagle*'s managing editor, was clerk of the Festival association. Jay Rosenfeld, its music critic, was a trained violinist who had studied in Europe and whose family happened to own a leading Pittsfield men's clothing shop. Edman later left newspaper work to go into the diplomatic service, but Rosenfeld continued

*The site was subsequently occupied by the Foxhollow School for Girls.

writing about the Festival with tireless devotion and keen musical judgment until his death at the age of eighty on October 21, 1975.

Journalistically, the Festival's most brilliant coup was in attracting the attention of the New York press, especially *The New York Times.* Olin Downes, a critic in Boston before moving to the *Times,* was an old friend of Koussevitzky, who advised Miss Robinson Smith to invite him to lecture on the works to be performed. Accordingly, Downes was engaged to give talks at the Berkshire Playhouse on the morning of every concert, and naturally he remained on hand to review the performances for his newspaper.

For his first concert on Thursday, August 13, Koussevitzky played a program consisting of Bach's Chorale Prelude "Komm Gott, Schöpfer, heiliger Geist" in Arnold Schoenberg's arrangement; Beethoven's *Egmont* Overture and Seventh Symphony; and Sibelius' Second Symphony. As in Hadley's time, there was no Friday concert. On Saturday afternoon the major work was Brahms' Second Symphony, and on Sunday evening Koussevitzky played Mendelssohn's "Italian" Symphony, the preludes to Wagner's *Lohengrin* and *Die Meistersinger,* and Tchaikovsky's Fifth. All three concerts were jammed, and the delighted Festival authorities were able to report that despite their vastly increased scale of operations they had actually turned a profit—expenditures $18,259, receipts $21,194.

The press notices for each concert were almost universally favorable. Downes was particularly rhapsodic in his important dispatches to the *Times;* never one to temper his enthusiasm or abbreviate his reportage, he filled columns with praise for Koussevitzky's conducting, the orchestra's playing and the general ambiance of the Festival. The programs, he said, had been "fortunately chosen from the most popular but also the most representative masterpieces of the orchestral repertory" and the audiences had displayed "immense enthusiasm" throughout and given a "mighty demonstration" at the close of the final concert. It had been, he wrote in a Sunday article, "a season which promises to have far reaching results," for the performances had been "of a quality to set them wholly apart from any others the writer has ever heard at summer concerts in America."

With notices like these, and a financial profit besides, both the Berkshire Festival board of trustees and the Boston Symphony trustees were eager to extend their partnership into a second summer, and possibly beyond. In fact, the length of the Festival was forthwith doubled, with a tentative decision to have six concerts, rather than three, spread out over two weekends in 1937. But Koussevitzky, who was by now formulating in his mind plans to expand the summer activities into a educational institution, wanted to give his concerts not in a tent, but in a permanent structure. The

Berkshire Festival authorities estimated such a project would cost $100,000, and convoked a meeting of local bankers and businessmen to find, first, whether such a sum could be raised and, second, whether any property owner would donate land for a suitable site.

The replies, to put it mildly, were cautious. The businessmen concluded that it might be possible to obtain the land, but that only about $25,000 could be reasonably expected to be raised in the area for a building. They also sorrowfully reported "that there is a grave question as to the desirability, from the viewpoint of the summer residents of Berkshire County, of having an enlarged Berkshire Symphonic Festival." Thus, not for the last time, a strain of opposition to the Festival was revealed to exist among certain residents who rather resented the intrusion of so many outsiders, particularly from the New York area, upon the private preserves of their hills.

Nevertheless, Miss Robinson Smith and the Berkshire Festival board were determined to go ahead. They even talked about inviting the Cleveland or Philadelphia Orchestras in case the Boston pulled out. But Koussevitzky was equally committed; he had developed an affinity for the region, with its lovely landscape and bracing air. Despite the businessmen's report, Miss Robinson Smith promised she would continue working to find the money to build a "music pavilion." Koussevitzky told her he had just the man in mind to design the structure—Eliel Saarinen of Bloomfield Hills, Michigan, the noted Finnish architect, whom he had met on a transatlantic voyage in 1934, and whose work he admired.

So in the fall of 1936 Koussevitzky and Miss Robinson Smith set out on a tour of the Berkshires to examine possible permanent sites for the Festival. They were still looking when they received word that the Hanna Farm, the scene of Hadley's two years of concerts, had again become available and could be obtained the next year at a nominal rental of $1. On the whole it seemed best to postpone the search for a permanent home for another year and to return to the Hanna property on a temporary basis. But before this decision could be made official, another summer resident of the Berkshires, Mrs. Gorham Brooks by name, unexpectedly called on Koussevitzky and made him an offer that was to give the Festival a new home, a new name and a new permanence.

Hawthorne's Tanglewood

Unlike many Berkshire summer residents, Mrs. Gorham Brooks—later to become Mrs. Andrew H. Hepburn—was a Bostonian rather than a New

Yorker, and she had long been an admirer of the Boston Symphony and its dynamic, debonair conductor. In later years she recalled: "One day I attended a concert of the Boston Symphony in Symphony Hall and the thought came to me of how beautiful it would be if Tanglewood could be the home of music. By intermission I made up my mind to make the offer."

Tanglewood, the Brooks property, had originally borne the name Highwood and was one of the parklike millionaire's estates that came into being in the Berkshires during the nineteenth century. This particular property, with especially magnificent pines and hemlocks, had been bought by William Aspinwall Tappan, a Boston merchant and banker. In 1849 he erected a gabled Victorian mansion with some twenty rooms and, amid beautiful lawns, laid out reflecting pools, a formal garden, a rose bower and all the other accouterments of a luxurious nineteenth-century country establishment.

Among the subsidiary buildings on the estate, at a considerable distance from the main house, was a small red cottage overlooking Lake Mahkeenac, or the Stockbridge Bowl, as it also was known both then and now. In 1850 this house was rented to Nathaniel Hawthorne, author of the recently published *The Scarlet Letter*. Hawthorne, who was forty-six years old, had been removed from his political job as surveyor of customs at the Customs House in Salem. Weary and dispirited, he was in the market for a "cheap, pleasant and healthy residence" for himself and his family, preferably far from Salem. Hawthorne's wife, Sophia, knew Tappan's wife, Caroline, and the offer of the red cottage in the Berkshires was made. Hawthorne lived there for a year and a half, during which he wrote *The House of the Seven Gables;* his third child, a daughter, was born in Lenox.

During his stay in the cottage Hawthorne also wrote two children's books, *A Wonder-Book for Girls and Boys* and *Tanglewood Tales*. Neither, it must be said, is read with much avidity by children today. Both books consist of a retelling, in a rather frigid style, of the tales of classic mythology. The supposed narrator is a college student named Eustace Bright, and the setting is a country house and estate very much like the Tappans', to which the author gives the name "Tanglewood." In later years Hawthorne's son Julian confirmed that his father had indeed referred to the Tappan property as Tanglewood. As for the Tappans themselves, they were so delighted with the literary distinction thus bestowed on their property that they dropped the name Highwood and henceforth called their home Tanglewood.

It seems ironical that Nathaniel Hawthorne should have invented the name eventually given to a great music festival, for music was a subject that interested him little. He once bewailed his inability to dinstinguish between "Hail, Columbia" and "Yankee Doodle." One of the characters in *The House*

In 1936, with the Boston Symphony providing the music, the Festival moved under a huge tent set up on a private estate called Holmwood. (Courtesy Stockbridge Library Association; photograph by David Milton Jones)

of the Seven Gables, inspecting an antique harpsichord, remarks, "I have forgotten all my music, long ago," and so it was with the author of *Tanglewood Tales.*

To compound the irony, Hawthorne didn't much like the Berkshires. At first he admired the beauties of his surroundings, especially the view from his window over the Stockbridge Bowl. He wrote: "Beyond the lake is Monument Mountain looking like a headless sphinx wrapped in a Persian shawl, when clad in the rich and diversified autumnal foliage of its woods; and beyond Monument the dome of Taconic, whose round head is more

distinct than ever in winter, when its snow patches are visible but which generally is a dark blue unvaried mountain top.'' He had plenty of literary company, for among the residents or visitors who came to call upon him were Oliver Wendell Holmes, Henry Wadsworth Longfellow and Fanny Kemble, the English actress and author. Such calls were reflective of his own growing repute, for *The Scarlet Letter* was beginning to find readers and to bring in royalty checks.

Hawthorne's closest friend in the Berkshires was Herman Melville, who was residing in Pittsfield, six miles away, where he was working on

Moby Dick. The two men met, quite by accident, during a summer thunderstorm on Monument Mountain, where both had gone for a climb and a picnic. They both happened to take refuge from the rains in the same crevice. It was one of the more fortuitous encounters in American literary history, for they were confined together for two hours and laid the foundations for a continuing friendship. Afterwards they visited each other frequently. When Melville published *Moby Dick* it bore the dedication: "In token of my admiration for his genius, this book is inscribed to Nathaniel Hawthorne."

Despite such attractions and amenities, Hawthorne wound up bored and unhappy in his country surroundings. He had a disagreement with the Tappan family about the use of some land as a garden, and although he won his point, the dispute irked him. His family found the winter snows and storms severe. "This is a horrible, horrible, most horrible climate," he wrote in 1851. "I detest it! I hate Berkshire with my whole soul, and I would joyfully see its mountains laid flat." To his publisher he confided: "To tell you a secret, I am sick to death of Berkshire and hate to think of spending another winter here." In November of 1851, while a raging snowstorm blew, Hawthorne and his family left Lenox and began an all-day trip to a new residence in West Newton. He never returned to the Berkshires.

In 1890 Hawthorne's little red house was destroyed by fire. A plaque was placed on the site in 1929. In 1947 a replica of the building was put up after a campaign headed by Mrs. Guy Patterson Gannett, president of the National Federation of Music Clubs. The original foundations were used and the fireplace built up from the ruins of the old one. But while the exterior is a replica of the house Hawthorne occupied, the interior is quite different, consisting principally of two airy, soundproof studios used by Tanglewood students. The house is always kept open to visitors, who may take a guided tour and also inspect, through the large windows, the view across the lake that almost reconciled Nathaniel Hawthorne to the Berkshires.

The Tanglewood estate itself continued in the hands of the Tappan family into the twentieth century, when it began to be subjected to the same economic pressures as the other palatial establishments in the area. In 1936, for the first time in eighty-eight years, it was unoccupied by members of the Tappan family and was let instead to summer tenants. However, when it became known that the lessees would not return the following summer, Mrs. Gorham Brooks—the granddaughter of the original owner of the estate—and her aged aunt Miss Mary Aspinwall Tappan reluctantly decided to close it down altogether. To Mrs. Brooks, offering it for the site of the Berkshire

Replica of house where Nathaniel Hawthorne lived and worked in 1850 is used for classroom instruction. Koussevitzky stands near the entrance. (Courtesy the Boston Symphony Orchestra; photograph by Howard S. Babbitt, Jr.)

Festival was a graceful means of bringing new usefulness to a property that had outlived its original purpose.

A Storm and a Shed

As attractive as the prospect of receiving Tanglewood as an outright gift seemed, Koussevitzky knew very little about the place and asked George Judd for information. "Tanglewood?" cried the manager. "Every child knows what Tanglewood is! It would cost a fortune." Koussevitzky replied, according to Olga Koussevitzky, "Then I present you with Tanglewood."

Although Koussevitzky, Judd and the Boston Symphony trustees were all delighted with Mrs. Brooks' present, Gertrude Robinson Smith had strong reservations. The gift had been made not to her, but to Koussevitzky. It was obvious to her that if the Boston Symphony became the outright owner of the property on which the Festivals were held, her own organization's importance and influence in the enterprise would inevitably diminish. Ernest B.

During a 1936 performance under a tent, Koussevitzky found the heat so uncomfortable that he asked for—and received—the audience's permission to doff his jacket. The *Berkshire Eagle* considered this sartorial breach page one news. (Courtesy the Berkshire Symphonic Festival, Inc.)

Dane, speaking on behalf of the orchestra's trustees, sought to reassure her by offering to the Berkshire Symphonic Festival, Inc., the right to hold the Festival on the land "for a period of years, provided suitable structures are erected by you, and that you meet all expenses of the upkeep."

After considerable internal wrangling, the Berkshire directors finally voted to accept the conditions. They signed a five-year contract, running through 1941, with the Boston Symphony for summer concerts on the property, and approved Eliel Saarinen as the architect for the proposed music pavilion. They even voted to add Mrs. Brooks to their own board of trustees. Alice Edman, the wife of George W. Edman, was put in charge of the most intense and widespread fund-raising campaign to date.

Construction of the new building was not envisaged before 1938, which meant that the 1937 season, scheduled to run for two weekends, would once more be held in a tent. This time, of course, the site was Tanglewood, and Koussevitzky chose to open the orchestra's permanent summer home on August 5, 1937, with an all-Beethoven program including the *Leonore* Overture No. 3, the Sixth Symphony and the Fifth Symphony. Once again, great crowds began swarming into the Berkshires; in Pittsfield the *Eagle* reported that "public interest outside the Berkshires never has been so aroused over a Berkshire event." The National Broadcasting Company's Blue Network announced that two of the concerts would be carried nationally on the radio, with Olin Downes among the commentators.

Just at this juncture, for the first time in the four years of the Festival, the Berkshire weather began to manifest its well-known perversity. Rain fell on Tanglewood all afternoon before the first concert, and the trees were dripping wet at starting time; nevertheless, a somewhat moist audience of 5,000 filled the tent to capacity. On Sunday afternoon of the first weekend, with a Schubert–Stravinsky–César Franck program scheduled, it suddenly turned unbearably hot and humid. Tanglewood audiences in those days dressed rather formally, and it occasioned a stir when a number of men were observed slipping out of their jackets, opening their collars and loosening their ties. Finally Koussevitzky himself, whom many believed impervious to such considerations, turned to the packed benches and said: "It is awfully hot. You will escuse if we remove our kowts." A roar of approval went up, and for the first time in its history the Boston Symphony played a concert in shirtsleeves. The incident seemed so newsworthy that the *Eagle* ran its account on page one the next day under the headline: "Serge Koussevitzky Removes Coat."

The torrential storm of August 12, 1937, when rain poured through the tent during a Wagner concert by Koussevitzky, was a turning-point in Tanglewood's history. As the audience sat under open umbrellas and picked its way across sodden parking lots, plans were launched to raise money for a permanent "pavilion." (Both courtesy the *Berkshire Eagle*)

But the major meteorological event of the 1937 Festival, and one that had a profound effect on its future, occurred on Thursday evening August 12, the first concert of the second weekend. Koussevitzky had scheduled an all-Wagner program, and despite the sultriness of the skies all day, the largest crowd of the Festival's brief history, well in excess of 5,000, turned out for it. The first number was the *Rienzi* Overture, and no sooner had its opening A-natural on the solo trumpet swelled out than thunder began to rumble. Soon rain was beating on top of the tent. The overture went on, but so did the thunder and lightning, and the downpour became furious. At times the thunder drowned out the music—no easy matter in the *Rienzi* Overture. Three times Koussevitzky actually stopped conducting momentarily until the thunderclaps subsided. Upon completing the overture he decided to revise and shorten the program, skipping the *Siegfried Idyll*, which seemed too idyllic for such a night, and going on to the *Ride of the Valkyries*. Concertmaster Richard Burgin announced the changes to the audience. Rain was still pouring down, and by now the tent was leaking badly, especially around the tent poles. Many in the audience raised umbrellas where they sat. "Even the French horns were shipping water," Jay Rosenfeld reported.

Finally intermission time arrived. To some the storm was an annoyance, even a peril, but to the doughty Gertrude Robinson Smith it was a godsend. While Koussevitzky sat in his little retiring room, morosely watching the drops splash around his feet, she mounted to the stage and told the drenched audience: "This storm has proved conclusively the need for a shed. We must raise the $100,000 to build it." A soggy cheer went up and within a few minutes some $30,000 had been pledged.

Meanwhile, trouble was reported from the radio booth, where Downes, co-commentator Lisa Sergio and announcer John McNamara sat on raised boxes in an effort to keep their feet dry. The commentators said they were running out of material to talk about while efforts were being made to resume the concert. Finally the rest of the broadcast was canceled. Somehow, the second part of the program finally got under way, and the orchestra played without a break to the end, even when the stage lights temporarily went out during the *Tannhäuser* Overture. At 11 P.M., considerably behind schedule, the audience surged out into the still rainy night. Not surprisingly, the parking lots (unpaved then as they still are now) had turned into a mass of mud, and wrecking trucks had to be summoned from Lenox and Pittsfield to pull out dozens of mired cars. Several ladies were observed walking across the fields in their bare feet, clutching expensive evening slippers in their hands.

It was an evening that nobody could have forgotten, and even if they had wanted to, Miss Robinson Smith had no intention of letting them. When she got home that night she immediately sat down and wrote out the text of a circular appealing to the public to support the building fund and to become patrons and members of the Festival. The leaflets were distributed at the two remaining concerts, held in drier weather, and enough money came in to begin on the active planning of the "music pavilion."

Eliel Saarinen, whom Koussevitzky had selected as designer of the structure, was one of the foremost architects in the country, usually working in partnership with his son Eero, a Yale graduate who had joined his father's company in 1936. After inspecting the property, he advanced the idea of a wedge, or pie-shaped, open-sided structure, with a vast audience area fanning out in an arc from the stage. One faction among the Berkshire Symphonic Festival trustees, led by George Edman, argued for more of a "New England design," possibly an oblong, churchlike building. Miss Robinson Smith sided with Saarinen, however, and the architect's original concept is strikingly similar in shape to the structure eventually erected.

However, it also was far more elaborate. Saarinen's model of the site called for studios, lecture halls, a library and a Greek amphitheater in addition to the pavilion, which by itself would require an outlay of $167,000. The entire complex would have cost $232,000. Staggered by these estimates, the Festival trustees requested him to modify his plans to keep the cost within $100,000. Saarinen drew up a set of new designs but warned that there was no way he could reduce the cost to less than $125,000. "Of course," he wrote, "a solution could have been easily had by erecting just a shed without any consideration as to good proportions, good architectural qualities, and a proper fitting into the landscape. And as any builder could accomplish this, why then, hire an architect?"

After some reflection, Miss Robinson Smith and her associates decided that it would be preferable to have "just a shed" they could afford, rather than a "pavilion" they couldn't. From then on, the structure was always referred to as the "Shed," a designation from which it seems not to have suffered at all.

The Berkshire trustees also took up Saarinen's other "suggestion" by calling in Joseph Franz of Stockbridge to make some cost-saving revisions in the architect's blueprints. Franz, though not a professional architect, was a skilled and imaginative engineer who had been in charge of the physical set-up of the Festival since the Hadley days.* In October, 1937, he journeyed to Saarinen's studio in Michigan to discuss his proposed modifications. The major change was to put three slender steel columns in the middle of the Shed, which in Saarinen's design was unencumbered by pillars of any kind. Although an obstruction in sight lines would thus be introduced into a few areas of the hall, the structure would be simplified, the overall use of steel reduced, and the cost cut substantially. Saarinen told Franz that if pillars were

*In 1942 Franz designed the Ted Shawn Theater at Jacob's Pillow.

introduced into the audience area he no longer wished to be associated with the project—which is the reason that it is Franz's name and not Saarinen's that is commemorated in the lineup of plaques near the Shed entrance. However, Saarinen permitted the Berkshire Symphonic Festival to retain his plans and use them as they saw fit upon payment of a fee of $4,000, which was promptly remitted to him.

Franz was appointed construction engineer at a fee of $1,000, and Prof. Richard D. Fay of Massachusetts Institute of Technology was engaged as acoustical expert for another $500. Franz called for new bids on the project, and the main construction contract went to a local firm, Graves and Hemmes of Great Barrington. Ground was broken on December 31, 1937, and although the ground was hard with winter frosts, supports were sunk for the seventy-eight steel supports (reduced from Saarinen's original ninety) which were to support the weight of the huge wooden roof. It was so cold that workmen had to cover the holes with hay to keep the bottoms from freezing. When the spring thaws set in, trucks bearing the huge Bethlehem steel trusses, ninety feet long and sixteen tons in weight, became mired in mud and had to be pulled out by bulldozers. Firwood for the roof was shipped from the West Coast through the Panama Canal and up the Atlantic coast and Hudson River to Albany and thence transported overland to Tanglewood.

In this day of cost overruns, construction delays and acoustical disasters, it is instructive to note that the Tanglewood Music Shed was erected well within its budget (the total cost was $90,000*), was completed a month ahead of schedule (on June 16, 1938) and was celebrated from the very start for the excellence of its sound. Discussing the Shed in later years, Franz was inclined to ascribe its success to the very necessity of building it on a shoestring. To save money, he retained the weather-beaten plywood shell that had provided resonance for the orchestra since the Hadley days. Re-erected on the new stage at Tanglewood it functioned admirably for many years. Limited funds also dictated that the structure be left unfinished on the inside, meaning that the open maze of steel girders under the roof served to break up and diffuse the sound of the orchestra, effectively preventing echoes or dead spots. Whatever the reason, the Shed at Tanglewood, which accommodates 5,000 visitors beneath its one-and-a-half-acre roof, provides clear, rich and resonant sound not only within the structure but for a considerable distance

*By contrast, the Saratoga Performing Arts Center in New York State, which seats 5,100, was constructed in 1966 at a cost of $3,600,000—a tremendous increase, even allowing for inflation.

beyond. Commented a writer for *The New Yorker* after a visit to the new edifice: "They've arranged the shed so the music comes out and the rain doesn't get in."

A Home in the Berkshires

Completion of the Shed provided the last touch in making the Berkshire Festival the most prestigious summer musical event in America. A journey to "Tanglewood," as both the site and the Festival now became universally known, took on the aura almost of a pilgrimage. Especially as Europe moved toward an inevitable war, threatening the future of festivals far longer established, did Tanglewood assume a significance far beyond the pleasures of its six concerts a year by the Boston Symphony Orchestra. The concept of great music, performed in a structure of simple but bold and graceful design, in a natural setting of the utmost beauty, seemed to symbolize eternal values being challenged and threatened everywhere.

Koussevitzky was as conscious as any of this deeper significance. For his inaugural concert in the Shed on August 5, 1938—a perfect summer evening—he chose to play two works, Bach's chorale "Ein' feste Burg ist unser Gott," in which the overflow audience of 6,000 was asked to raise its voices, and Beethoven's Ninth Symphony with Jeanette Vreeland, soprano, Paul Althouse, tenor, Anna Kaskas, contralto, and Norman Cordon, bass, and the Cecilia Society Chorus, whose conductor was listed as none other than Arthur Fiedler. In his dedicatory remarks, the orchestra's president, Bentley Warren, made the first public allusions to Koussevitzky's plans to launch a summer academy for young conductors and orchestral musicians at Tanglewood. "Who can predict how great may be the contribution of the Berkshires to the musical culture of America?" Warren asked. Miss Robinson Smith also spoke and predictably appealed to the audience for funds, this time to beautify the grounds, illuminate the parking fields and provide roll-up curtains to close against the winter weather. Koussevitzky had not been listed as a speaker, but on the spur of the moment decided to address the audience, telling them that he had chosen to play Beethoven's Ninth "because it is the greatest work in musical literature" and "because Tanglewood could, through Schiller's *Ode to Joy,* call all nations to brotherhood." It was no bad thought a few weeks before Munich.

Perhaps it was symbolic of the new stature and significance of the Festival that, throughout the six concerts, Koussevitzky made up programs which,

The Shed under construction in the spring of 1938. When architect Eliel Saarinen bowed out because he regarded the allocation of funds as insufficient, local experts took over and completed the edifice under budget and ahead of schedule. (Both courtesy Stockbridge Library Association; both photographs by David Milton Jones)

while largely drawn from standard repertory, consisted entirely of music of substance, some of it from the twentieth century. Following Beethoven's Ninth, the first weekend was given over to Haydn's Symphony No. 99 in E-flat, Debussy's *La Mer* and Sibelius' First Symphony on Saturday night, followed by Mozart's *Eine kleine Nachtmusik,* Brahms' Fourth, Aaron Copland's *Music for the Theater,* Ravel's *Ma Mère L'Oye* and Respighi's *Pines of Rome* on Sunday afternoon. The second weekend of concerts started with an all-Wagner program consisting of the final scene of *Die Walküre* and the complete Act III of *Siegfried.* Cordon, Kaskas and Beal Hober were the singers. On August 13 the "Angelus" movement of Henry Hadley's Third Symphony was played as a tribute to the Berkshire Festival's first leader, who had died the previous September in New York. The major works on this program were the Sixth Symphonies of Beethoven and Tchaikovsky. The last concert of the 1937 Festival, on August 14, included Schumann's Symphony No. 1, Prokofiev's *Lieutenant Kije* Suite and Brahms' Symphony No. 2. No one that first summer in the Shed, certainly, could have complained of being musically shortchanged.

The crowds that year were similarly solid and satisfying. Stockbridge merchants from Frank Grande's shoe repair shop to Herman Cohen's clothing store reported the best business since 1929. For innkeepers, hotel owners and restaurateurs, the long Depression was over. Even the churches were packed with Sunday visitors. One clergyman was actually inspired to a sermon in which he concluded that the Festival showed how Recovery could be achieved by other techniques besides "proceeding on a crude material basis alone." But those not yet ready to abandon materialism could note with crass satisfaction that the Festival was in the black by $4,300 for the summer of 1938—a surplus split equally between the Berkshire Symphonic Festival and the Boston Symphony Orchestra.

One of the season's more curious sidelights occurred when a New York newspaper, the *World-Telegram,* suggested editorially that Arturo Toscanini, who had publicly announced that he would not conduct at the 1938 Salzburg Festival because of the Nazi take-over of Austria, go instead to Tanglewood. It was, no doubt, a measure of Tanglewood's growing significance that after five years' existence it be equated with the famous Austrian festival. The New York newspaper's suggestion was promptly echoed by the *Berkshire Eagle,* which also felt Toscanini would lend lustre to Tanglewood. However, it was Koussevitzky and not the editorial writers who was issuing the invitations, and none was tendered to Toscanini. Koussevitzky was no great admirer of the guest-conductor concept in general; he himself seldom directed any American orchestra beside the Boston, and he habitually was present for nearly the entire Symphony Hall season. At Tanglewood he saw no need for outside conductors, and indeed none except himself and his students ever conducted the orchestra there until his very last year.

Koussevitzky kept a close watch on doings in the Shed even after the Festival season ended. Understandably proud of the facility they had created with their own resources, the Berkshire Symphonic Festival, Inc., had ideas of putting it to use after the Boston Symphony had packed up its instruments and departed. Among the events considered were local dog and flower shows, and appearances by the Goldman Band and even a "swing band." A Catholic group in Springfield suggested the possibility of using the Shed for "a sort of Oberammergau performance." But the Boston Symphony authorities were not receptive to such ideas. Discussing the dog-show proposition, Miss Robinson Smith tartly informed her board members at a meeting late in 1938: "Dr. Koussevitzky is apparently upset about the fact that there will be dogs singing in the Shed." The Berkshire trustees finally adopted a resolution "that the use of the Shed be not given to anyone"—a policy that has been modified in recent years for certain civic and educational events.

The pattern established by the 1938 concerts—serious programs, capacity crowds, and a slight but satisfying profit—was carried out again in the 1939 Festival. The opening concert ranged a gamut of musical epochs and styles, starting with Bach's Brandenburg Concerto No. 3 in G, going on to Rimsky-Korsakov's *Scheherazade* and winding up with Brahms' First Symphony. During the fourth movement of *Scheherazade,* depicting the splitting and sinking of Sinbad's ship, a violent Berkshire downpour struck the Shed, reinforcing the thunderings of the orchestra. "The general effect," reported the *New York Herald Tribune* the next day, "was almost cinematic." Unlike the famous Wagner thunderstorm of two years previously, the audience sat snug and dry through the storm; nevertheless, during the intermission the indefatigable Miss Robinson Smith mounted the stage and asked the crowd for contributions of anything from $1 to $1,000 to "put shutters in the Shed, so we need not mind thunderstorms."

During the five concerts that followed, Koussevitzky again played a scattering of twentieth-century works, including two Sibelius symphonies, Stravinsky's *Le Sacre du Printemps,* Ravel's *La Valse,* Walter Piston's Concerto for Orchestra and Prokofiev's *Peter and the Wolf,* which had had its premiere in Moscow only three years before. In *Peter and the Wolf,* which the audience heard with obvious delight, the narrator was Richard Hale, the actor who had sung excerpts from *Boris Godunov* in the second Berkshire

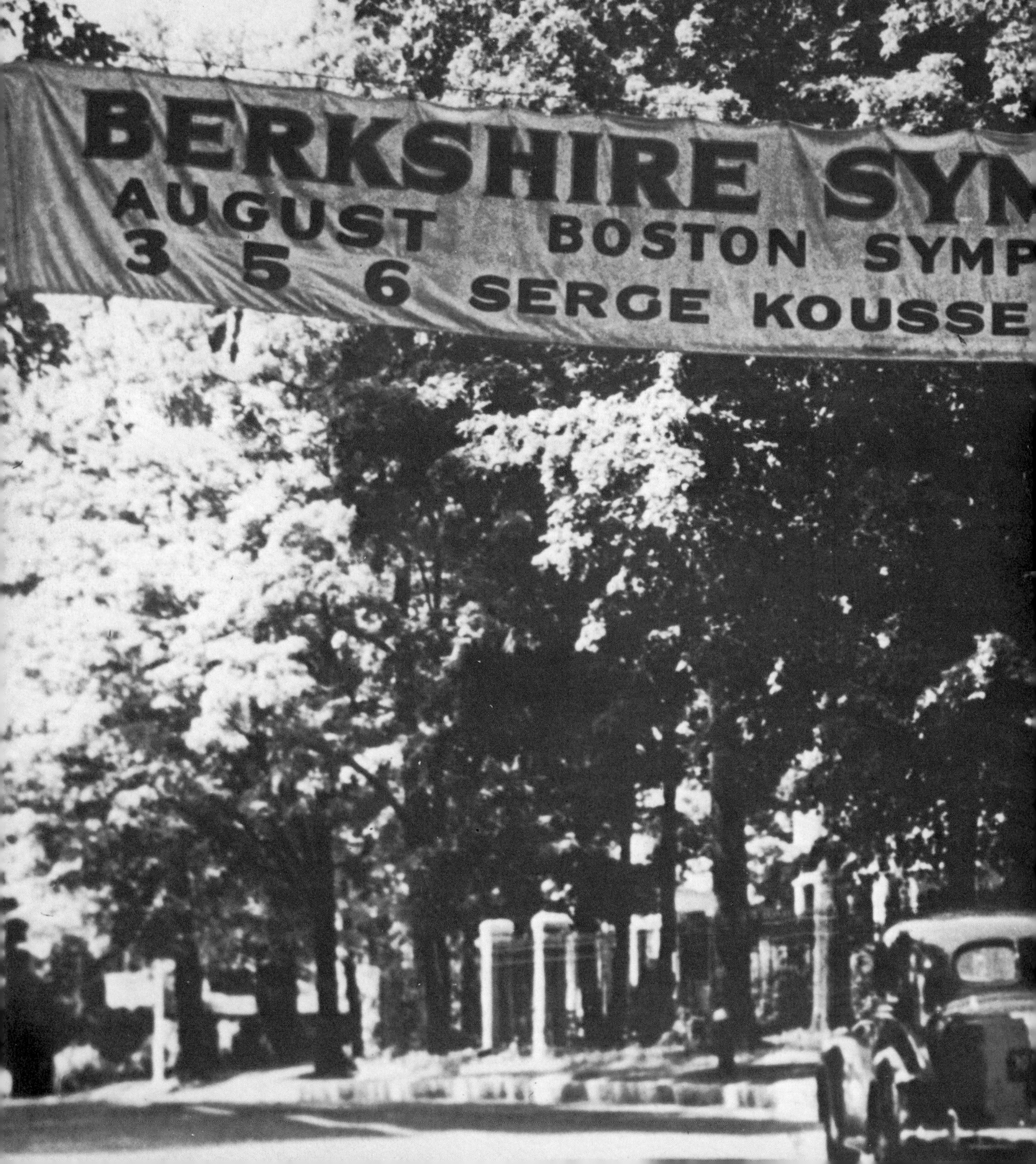
BERKSHIRE SYM
AUGUST
3 5 6
BOSTON SYMP
SERGE KOUSSE

Berkshire towns were quick to recognize the economic benefits accruing from a summer festival in their midst. This 1939 banner was typical of advertising signs that went up in Lenox and Stockbridge. (Courtesy the Boston Symphony Orchestra)

season under Henry Hadley. Aided by a record single-concert crowd of 7,000 on August 13, total attendance for the season reached 38,000, a rise of 2,000 over the previous summer. Not included in this figure was a total of 1,000 schoolchildren who were invited to attend the orchestra's rehearsals as part of a course in musical appreciation in six Berkshire County high schools arranged by the Festival and taught by Harriet Johnson, who later became music critic of the *New York Post*. In her two years at Tanglewood, Miss Johnson extended her lectures to take in the local music-going public.

The 1939 Festival did not quite end with the last concert, for immediately following it Koussevitzky gave a picnic in the Shed for the musicians of the orchestra at which he presented the first of many "finds" he was to make at Tanglewood over the years.

The new and virtually unknown artist he introduced was a twenty-eight-year-old black soprano named Dorothy Maynor. Despite the success of Marian Anderson, Paul Robeson and one or two others, black singers were still a considerable rarity then; it was not until 1955 that they were invited to join the ranks of the Metropolitan Opera. Miss Maynor, who had just signed her first contract with a New York management and had a Town Hall debut scheduled for the fall, went to Tanglewood in August on a vacation trip with friends. Several people who had heard her sing urged Koussevitzky to listen to her. Among them was Mrs. Brooks, the donor of the Tanglewood site. Koussevitzky happened to be in the midst of auditions to select a new first double bass for the orchestra, but with no great graciousness he agreed to an interruption so he could hear her. In the empty Shed, a light coat over his shoulders, he sat and listened to her sing one number after another. Finally he cried out: "A new musical revelation! The world must hear her!"

Koussevitzky was ever prone to glowing pronouncements over talented newcomers, but it was remarkable how frequently his enthusiasms were sustained by subsequent developments. He immediately invited Miss Maynor to sing at his picnic the next day, accompanied by the orchestra's pianist Bernard Zighera. The audience of 200 musicians and their families and friends gave her an ovation as she sang a program that included "Oh, Sleep! Why Dost Thou Leave Me?" from Handel's *Semele,* "Ach, ich fühl's" from Mozart's *The Magic Flute* and "Non mi dir" from his *Don Giovanni,* "Depuis le jour" from Charpentier's *Louise* and a group of spirituals. So memorable was her account of "Depuis le jour" that the aria became a kind of touchstone for nearly every black soprano who followed her. Several critics had been invited to the picnic, and their enthusiastic dispatches assured Miss Maynor's career on the spot.

Seranak, the mansion in the Berkshires, adjacent to Tanglewood, which Koussevitzky purchased at a bargain price and turned into his summer home. (Courtesy the *Berkshire Eagle*)

Koussevitzky with soprano Dorothy Maynor. A hastily arranged, postseason appearance he arranged for her in the Berkshires opened the way to her career. The cape the conductor is wearing is now owned by Leonard Bernstein. (Courtesy the *Berkshire Eagle*)

During the summer of 1939 Koussevitzky had been a houseguest of Artur Rodzinski, the conductor of the Cleveland Orchestra, who owned a goat farm near Stockbridge. Rodzinski was an old friend of Koussevitzky's; he might well have become the first guest conductor at Tanglewood had it not been that, as a union member, he was unable to appear with the still nonunionized Boston orchestra.* By now Koussevitzky had decided to make Tanglewood an important part of his musical life; in some ways *the* most important part. Although he still was content to rent a home in Brookline,** he determined to own one in the Berkshires; henceforth this part of the world was to be his most beloved residence and later his final resting place.

The house that Koussevitzky bought was a lordly mansion high on Bald Head Mountain, just beyond the entrance to Tanglewood, with a magnificent vista including not only the concert grounds but the shimmering Stockbridge Bowl and the blue mountains beyond. The purchase was made from the Art Institute of Chicago, which had received the estate as a bequest from a Berkshire resident, Miss Kate Buckingham. Koussevitzky reputedly paid $25,000 for the property and house, including the china, silverware and linen on the premises—a fabulously low price even by prewar standards. He named the estate Seranak, an anagram derived from "Serge and Natalie Koussevitzky."

Previously Koussevitzky's contract with the Boston Symphony had stipulated that his annual remuneration include return-fare steamship passage to Europe each summer. Now he demanded a different provision: that the orchestra build a blacktop road leading from the county highway up the mountain to Seranak. George Judd used to complain half-jokingly that the cost of Koussevitzky's road was higher than that of his house. In any event, Koussevitzky left no doubt that he and his orchestra had come to the Berkshires to stay.

The Berkshire Music Center

"Little did I think," said Serge Koussevitzky in 1940, "that my own early dream of a Music and Art Center in Moscow, in the heart of Russia, would find its realization in the heart of New England a quarter of a century later. Indeed, miracles cannot be accounted for."

---

*Not until 1942 did the Boston Symphony sign its first union contract.
**Later on, during the war years, he purchased the Brookline home in the name of his wife.

According to Olga Koussevitzky, the conductor first broached the idea of establishing some sort of educational enterprise in America in 1929, only five years after he had come to Boston. Harvard University had just given him an honorary LL.D. degree (he already held a Mus. Doc. from Brown, accounting for his title of "Doctor"), and he began to think of setting up a musical center connected with Harvard. He even talked about it to faculty members in the music department, but the only immediate result of these contacts was that the Harvard and Radcliffe choirs began to sing with the Boston Symphony. The stock market crash of 1929 put an end to further thoughts on the subject, but when Koussevitzky arrived in the Berkshires seven years later, the idea revived in his own mind. And the gift of the Tanglewood estate to the orchestra made it seem more feasible than ever before.

Symphonic boards of trustees, usually made up of businessmen, bankers and lawyers, are not noted for their receptivity to new ideas, and Koussevitzky's proposition of establishing an academy on the grounds met with some hesitation. The Boston Symphony, after all, was in the business of running an orchestra, not a school; summer concerts sometimes make money, but educational institutions usually lose it. A few of the trustees had never especially liked the Tanglewood idea altogether; one of them, Richard Paine, was famous for never visiting the site until he was passing it one November day and decided to drop in for a look at the empty Shed out of sheer curiosity.

But Koussevitzky was persistent and persuasive, arguing that a summer school in connection with the Festival would fulfill a vital musical need for America and bring the orchestra new importance and prestige. He also had an unspoken argument on his side: the New York Philharmonic was not having a particularly happy experience with John Barbirolli, who had succeeded Arturo Toscanini on its podium in 1937, and there were rumors that efforts might be made to lure Koussevitzky from Boston to New York. In fact, such talk persisted until 1942, when Koussevitzky actually made one of his rare guest-conducting appearances with the Philharmonic.

Whether out of a desire to placate their brilliant conductor, or because they shared his vision—possibly out of a combination of both—the Boston Symphony trustees put aside any doubts and decided to effectuate the concept of a school at Tanglewood. "Go ahead—we can't afford to lose it," Ernest B. Dane, who had succeeded Bentley Warren as president of the board of trustees in 1939, told Koussevitzky. Nor was the commitment half-hearted, for once launched, the Berkshire Music Center had the full support of the Symphony board, even when the school, like the Festival itself, grew far beyond original expectations and turned into an ever expanding and more costly operation. In fact, the official literature of the Boston Symphony has always made a point of not giving Koussevitzky exclusive credit for the idea of establishing the Center, but of tracing it back to an 1881 statement of Henry Lee Higginson, the founder of the orchestra, that he wished to set up "a good honest school for musicians."

Be that as it may, with the actual opening of the Berkshire Music Center in the summer of 1940 there was no doubt that it was Koussevitzky's school. He chose the faculty, supervised the selection of the students and, once sessions started, was in constant evidence on the grounds. About the locale of the school headquarters there never was any doubt, for the steeply gabled Tappan manor house, with its multiplicity of rooms, its solid fittings and its sheer size made it an ideal school building. Various other structures on the property—barns, sheds and the like—were also pressed into service, and on warm summer days some classes were held out of doors. Baldwin, the Boston Symphony's official purveyor of pianos, supplied twenty-seven instruments for use at the Center that first year.

The faculty assembled by Koussevitzky was a mixture of personal friends and prominent performers with whom he had been associated— without exception musicians of the highest attainments. The composition department was run by Aaron Copland and Paul Hindemith who, as an anti-Nazi, had left Germany several years before. Gregor Piatigorsky had charge of chamber music. Operatic activities were under Herbert Graf, assisted by Boris Goldovsky. G. Wallace Woodworth, the chairman of Harvard's music department, and Hugh Ross, director of the Schola Cantorum, headed choral activities. For instrumental ensemble instruction there were some thirty members of the Boston Symphony Orchestra, including all the first-desk players, headed by concertmaster Richard Burgin. It was a faculty such as few other schools in the world—certainly no other summer school—could boast.

In its first year the Berkshire Music Center was divided into two sections, an Institute for Advanced Study, in which only students bent on a professional career could enroll, and an Academy in which less proficient and committed applicants were welcome. In one form or another, these two basic groupings have persisted through the Center's existence. It was specified that no diplomas, certificates or degrees would be given to any one. However, many scholarships were made available—some through a $60,000 grant from the Rockefeller Foundation—and have always been integral to the Berkshire Music Center operation. For those who were paying, the

This lunch bus used to bring hot food to students from Lenox when Berkshire Music Center opened. But it broke down too often and was replaced by an on-the-grounds cafeteria. Prices included milk: 10 cents, iced tea or coffee: 10 cents, rolls: 8 cents, pat of butter: 1 cent. (Courtesy the *Berkshire Eagle*)

tuition fee was set at $100. Dormitory accommodations, including meals and priced at $12 to $15 a week, were available at several nearby preparatory schools which normally were closed during the summer months. Hot lunches were served on the grounds from an old bus equipped with steam tables which stocked up with food at the kitchen of the Curtis Hotel in Lenox and drove a mile to the Tanglewood grounds. The bus only lasted one summer, suffering too many breakdowns en route.

Word quickly spread through the musical world of the unique new institution backed by the prestige of the Boston Symphony and supervised by its distinguished music director. No fewer than 599 students applied, of whom 312 actually enrolled—153 men and 159 women. Most were in their early twenties.

The Berkshire Music Center formally opened on July 8, 1940, with its sessions scheduled to last six weeks. Inaugural exercises were held in the Tanglewood Shed, and among those sending "hearty best wishes for great success" was President Franklin D. Roosevelt, whom Koussevitzky had met when they both received honorary degrees at the Harvard commencement of 1929 and with whom he had remained on friendly terms. Ernest Dane of the trustees presided and Gertrude Robinson Smith was in the audience. Also on hand was Olin Downes, the *New York Times* critic, who was to be a guest lecturer on the faculty, and Albert Spalding, the violinist, who resided in nearby Great Barrington and was a frequent visitor to the Festival. Koussevitzky, in a speech he had worked over long and carefully, described the project as the fulfillment of his long-cherished dream and, alluding to the war which by then was being fought furiously in Europe, said: "There is hope for humanity, and all those who believe in the value and inheritance of culture and art should stand in the front ranks. If ever there was a time to speak of music, it is now in the New World."

Those first opening exercises established a tradition which has been carried out ever since at every Berkshire Music Center opening. Randall Thompson, the American composer who taught at the Curtis Institute in Philadelphia, had been commissioned to compose a short, unaccompanied choral work which could be sung by the students at the opening exercises. It was characteristic of the school Koussevitzky intended to run that every student was expected to sing in the choir and to sing contemporary music. It so happened that the work Thompson produced was his *Alleluia,* a masterpiece of its kind, set on the one word "Alleluia," which has been performed countless times since by choirs all over the world. The piece was late in reaching Tanglewood, and preparations were made to substitute a

Bach chorale if it did not arrive in time. G. Wallace Woodworth later recalled:

> On Saturday, forty-eight hours before the formal opening, we had not heard from Thompson nor seen the music. Mr. Judd telephoned to Philadelphia; Thompson assured us that the score had just been printed and that three hundred copies would arrive in Lenox Monday morning. . . . At two o'clock on Monday afternoon the students assembled for the first time. . . . In the corner of the barn I had secreted our collection of Bach chorales, for one mail after another had arrived at the Lenox post office during the morning without the package from Philadelphia. But at just five minutes before two, Mr. Judd came in with the music. I tried it over once on the piano, and the chorus of two hundred and fifty, assembled from all over our country for the first time, went to work. By 2:45 it was time to go to the Shed for the exercises, and at 3:30 we had given the first performance of a work which has been heard hundreds of times in choral concerts from Boston to San Francisco. So sure was Thompson's technique, so expert his craftsmanship, and so masterly his grasp of the true genius of choral singing, that despite a blueprint of unique limitations, he had created one of the noblest pieces of choral music in the twentieth century.

Two days later Thompson himself arrived for a visit to the new Center and found that his piece, which he was told "had been sung to perfection," had made him a celebrity among the students. "The Music Center is truly marvelous," he wrote to the composer Douglas Moore, "—a wonderful setup in heavenly country and such a fine group of students and teachers. I was there the first week but already the place had such spirit and atmosphere. Most congenial and stimulating. . . . Most of all I relished watching Koussevitzky sit directly behind the student conductors at all rehearsals, criticizing them at every turn. He has proved himself a fine teacher and— still more surprising—a most skillful administrator of the school. . . . There is no doubt in my mind that he has come out with a permanent institution of the greatest value and importance."

Koussevitzky himself told an interviewer from the *New York Sun* that his purpose at the Center was to develop young conductors, composers and orchestral performers. Speaking of the last he said: "Perhaps you do not know how difficult it has been in the past to find American-trained first-desk men. It has not been because there were no gifted players here, but because it was so hard for these talented ones to obtain the experience for such important posts. . . . When first I came to America I asked, 'Where are the young American musicians? The composers, the conductors, the players?' And they said to me that there weren't any. I would not believe. I said that it was not possible for a country of 130,000,000 people to have fewer than fifty really fine young musical talents, and after a while I found out that there was a Copland, a Piston and others. So I sent for them. I said to Piston, 'Why do you not compose for orchestra?' and he replied, 'Why? No one will play such work.' I said that if he'd compose a good thing, I would play it. Four months later, he brought me a suite for orchestra—very interesting. Then a year later, he gave me a really fine suite, and after that a concerto. It was the same with others. It was my great joy to give these men the hearings they deserved. And when I believed in a work, I played it again and again.''

Besides actively supervising all activities, Koussevitzky himself taught two classes in conducting. To the larger, numbering about thirty, he mainly lectured on technique and interpretation, but the students never actually worked with an orchestra. It was to the smaller class to which he was most devoted and in which he most spectacularly carried out his expressed purpose of passing the wisdom and experience of the older generation to the new. Five students were enrolled in this class, all selected by Koussevitzky himself. The oldest, Gaylord Browne, twenty-nine-year-old head of the music department of Evansville College in Indiana, was the only member of the class who did not go on to a major conducting career. The other four were Richard Bales, Leonard Bernstein, Lukas Foss and Thor Johnson.

They had learned about the school in various ways, made application to Koussevitzky, undergone interviews and received acceptances. Johnson, twenty-seven, later to become music director of the Cincinnati Symphony, had heard about the Center early and actually was the first student at any level to send in his application. Bales, twenty-five, later the conductor of the National Gallery Orchestra in Washington, had studied at the Eastman School and Juilliard. Bernstein, who tells his own story of his coming to Tanglewood later in this book, was twenty-two and fresh out of the Curtis Institute in Philadelphia after four years at Harvard. Foss, the baby of the class at seventeen, had also been at Curtis, after coming to the United States with his German parents only three years previously. Considering the subsequent careers of its members, this was the most remarkable conducting class ever assembled at Tanglewood and perhaps anywhere else in the world.

Lukas Foss says he was ''born'' at Tanglewood. His experience was typical of what close contact with Koussevitzky at the Berkshire Center could mean to a young musician of talent.

''I applied both for the composition class with Hindemith and the conducting class with Koussevitzky," he recalls. "Koussevitzky said: 'You can't take both. It's not allowed; besides, you're too young—you are seventeen and you look fourteen.' So I said, 'All right, I'll take composition, but I'd like at least an audition with the orchestra.' So he let me conduct the student orchestra in *Till Eulenspiegel.* But he repeated: 'You still can't do both. Take conducting.' I said, 'Maestro, I still want both.' So he said: 'You want to do both? All right, do both.'

"I was there for three summers of very hard work. It was terribly exciting—the years when Tanglewood was trying itself out. There was excitement among the teachers as well as the students. It was as if Koussevitzky had suddenly acquired children.

"I remember once going to the barber in Lenox. He had just been up to Seranak to trim Koussevitzky's hair. He said that Koussevitzky had told him, 'There are two students I believe are geniuses. One is Dionysian, his name is Bernstein; the other is Apollonian, his name is Foss.' It was the Nietzschean distinction. I was happy to accept it, though I hope we both have a little of each.

"Koussevitzky decided I didn't have nice clothes. So he gave me his—things that he had worn four or five times and that was it. They didn't fit me, but he dressed me in his clothes.

"He made me his assistant, and the official pianist of the Boston Symphony Orchestra—to give me a chance to compose. It did just that. There would be four or five weeks when I wouldn't have anything to do, and I also learned a lot sitting in the orchestra. I did it for four years. And he played many of my works."

For the young would-be conductors there was something even beyond the privilege of Koussevitzky's tutelage; there also was the opportunity of conducting the student orchestra at concerts with an audience. The orchestra coalesced in a remarkably short time into a skilled and sensitive ensemble; in his letter to Douglas Moore, Randall Thompson reported hearing a "really fine performance" led by Bernstein after only one week of preparation. He modestly forbore to mention that the work played was his own Second Symphony. At the same concert Bales led two of Debussy's *Nocturnes,* "Nuages" and "Fêtes," and Thor Johnson directed Brahms' *Academic Festival* Overture. Two weeks later Foss conducted Walter Piston's Concerto for Orchestra, and at still another student concert Bernstein conducted Haydn's Sinfonia Concertante in B-flat, in which four young instrumentalists had the opportunity to step forward into solo roles. Best of all from the standpoint of the players, Koussevitzky himself decided to rehearse and conduct the student orchestra at a concert. The principal work

Bernstein's warm relationship with Koussevitzky began at Tanglewood in 1940, the first year of the Berkshire Music Center, when the young conductor was twenty-two and his mentor sixty-five. (Courtesy the Boston Symphony Orchestra)

on his program was to be Berlioz' *Symphonie Fantastique,* but the students, having learned that Koussevitzky's birthday fell a few days later—on July 26—decided to surprise him at a rehearsal in the Shed. When he brought down his baton for Berlioz' opening notes, they played instead "Happy Birthday." Failing to recognize the tune he glared at the young players and said: "Come, we do again." The orchestra repeated the "Happy Birthday" melody, and this time other students sitting in the audience area joined in, singing loudly enough for Koussevitzky to understand the words. Visibly moved, he made a little speech with all his characteristic fervor, accent and syntax, urging them to work hard and do their best at all times. "Study as more as you can," he concluded. The birthday was his sixty-sixth.

Triumphs . . .

While the Berkshire Music Center was beginning its operations, the Berkshire Symphonic Festival, of course, continued unimpaired. As a matter of fact, in 1940, its seventh summer of operations, it was expanded from two weekends to three—a total of nine concerts. They were timed to coincide with the last three weeks of the school's operations, with the first concert on August 1 and the last August 18. One of the privileges of being a student at the Center was to attend all concerts of the Festival without charge, so a new element was added to the Berkshire audiences in 1940—young musicians following the music attentively, often with score and pencil in hand as they sat in benches placed at the sides of the Shed. Koussevitzky regarded attendance by students at all concerts less as a right than an obligation; he was always there, and he expected everybody else at Tanglewood to be there too.

But Koussevitzky had resolved that the students be more than observers at the Festival; he wanted them to be participants. For him the Berkshire Music Center and the Berkshire Symphonic Festival were one. Accordingly on August 15 the 200 best vocalists among the students were selected for a "Berkshire Festival Chorus," which sang in Bach's B Minor Mass with Koussevitzky conducting the Boston Symphony. A complete performance of the B Minor Mass was a rare event in those days, particularly at a summer festival, and this was an especially powerful one, with the four vocal soloists consisting of Elisabeth Schumann, soprano, Viola Silva, mezzo-soprano, William Hain, tenor, and Alexander Kipnis, bass. Seven thousand listeners turned out for the Mass, overflowing the Shed onto the lawn behind it; one member of the audience said he had traveled all the way from Salt Lake

City, Utah, to hear the work. Because of the length of the Mass, the starting time was advanced to 7 P.M., which meant that the music began with the sun slanting into the Shed and ended under a full moon. A one-hour intermission was held between the Gloria and the Credo, to give the audience a chance to take other than musical nourishment. A "hot New England supper" was sold on the ground for 50 cents, and draught beer was also available. Actually, many people had arrived by midafternoon carrying their own food and drink.

On the following day, a Friday, Koussevitzky made the public really aware of the existence and accomplishments of his student corps by staging an "Allied Relief Fund Benefit" to help the embattled people of Britain who were being battered by the Luftwaffe bombers following the collapse of France in the spring of 1940. At this event, or rather series of events, for the first time the Boston Symphony Orchestra and the Berkshire Music Center Orchestra, as the student "Institute" orchestra became known, actually combined forces, with Koussevitzky conducting them in Elgar's *Pomp and Circumstance* March No. 1, and his English-born assistant, Stanley Chapple, taking over for the "Jupiter" section of Holst's *The Planets*. But the evening's music included much more than Koussevitzky's concert in the Shed, for each department of the Center had an opportunity to perform, starting at 6 P.M. with Copland's *An Outdoor Overture* played by the student orchestra. The opera department put on brief scenes from *Aida, The Bartered Bride, Lohengrin* and *Rigoletto,* and the "Second Orchestra," made up of students in the "Academy," also had a chance to play.

The main Shed concert opened with Woodworth conducting the student body in Thompson's *Alleluia,* which by now had become the Berkshire Music Center's musical signature. Kipnis, Piatigorsky and Albert Spalding all appeared as soloists in the course of the evening, and once again "hot New England suppers" were available at intermission time. The last number was a sequence of Strauss waltzes played by Arthur Fiedler and the Pops Orchestra—that is, the Boston Symphony without its first-desk men— and for a final salute, everyone was asked to join in singing the "Hallelujah" Chorus from Handel's *Messiah.* Although it wasn't yet called by that name, this farrago of musical events was the forerunner of "Tanglewood on Parade," that delightful and sometimes daffy annual musical celebration of the Festival and all its works. But in this first year, the war in Europe inevitably produced a somewhat somber undercurrent to all the festivities, and there was a brief speaking program, presided over by Archibald MacLeish, the poet and Librarian of Congress, with addresses by newspaper columnist Dorothy Thompson and New York State's Gov. Herbert H. Lehman.

If the Berkshire Music Center drew strength and solidity from its proximity to the Berkshire Symphonic Festival, the process also worked in reverse. With young musicians flocking to Tanglewood from all over the country—eventually, from all over the world—it became a far more important, talked-about and prestigious operation than it ever had been previously. The addition of another weekend of concerts to the 1940 Festival season was one sign of its growing stature, and it was assumed that Koussevitzky and the Boston trustees contemplated further expansion in the future.

Most, but not all of the Berkshire populace was happy about such a prospect. To some of the old-time inhabitants, the weekend crush of visitors was an intrusion on their placid way of life. A few of the summer residents grumbled at the necessity of providing extra parties and entertainments as the season was lengthened. But the majority, of course, loved it. From the start, the Berkshire Festival to a considerable extent had been a high-society affair, and many of the local gentry in that prewar era took such obligations seriously. In fact, an early report in *Time* magazine characterized the Festival as "swanky," and even today Tanglewood maintains a measure of elegance not associated with many other summer festivals. Back in 1940 *The New York Times* solemnly listed the names of some of the boxholders who were giving dinners before the opening concert, at which Koussevitzky was to play the First Symphonies of Beethoven, Schumann and Sibelius—Mrs. Norman H. Davis, Mrs. Woodrow Wilson, Mrs. John Clarkson Potter, Countess Giovanni Cardelli, Princess Diane R. Eristavi, Count Roman Michalowski and others presumably equally worthy to conjure with.

To bring more commonplace listeners to the concerts—including those without automobiles of their own—buses ran from Pittsfield and Stockbridge one hour before concert time. For New York music lovers, the New Haven Railroad offered low-fare Sunday excursions on a special train leaving Grand Central at 7:55 A.M. and returning the same night. However, most concertgoers continued to arrive in their own cars, with the American Legion and other local auxiliaries assisting local and state police officers in regulating the parking lots—for which no admission has ever been charged—and keeping traffic moving on the two county roads that run by the grounds. In the Shed itself, new chairs were installed, replacing the old wooden benches which dated back to Dan Hanna's horse ring, whence they had been transported intact. Miss Robinson Smith's organization which, as proprietor of the Shed, had raised the funds for the chairs, decided to paint them red and blue, with ticket colors to match.

Musically, Koussevitzky continued his Festival policy of interspersing a few contemporary works in otherwise standard programs. Since the year marked the centenary of Tchaikovsky's birth he scheduled that composer's Fourth, Fifth and Sixth Symphonies during the summer. He also played such music as Prokofiev's *Lieutenant Kije,* Hindemith's *Mathis der Maler* and Roy Harris' Symphony No. 3. Altogether, some 70,000 persons attended the nine concerts, nearly one-third of them from outside New England. Many made repeated visits, among them Mrs. Eleanor Roosevelt, who began to make a practice of driving over from Hyde Park, about an hour away.

Far from being satisfied with the Festival and school, thriving though they both were, Koussevitzky kept pushing for expanded facilities. Herbert Graf's opera department, for example, lacked a proper setting. They rehearsed in a garage on the grounds, and to get scenery for a performance of the Act I duet between Rodolfo and Mimi in Puccini's *La Bohème* borrowed a stove, a table and two chairs from the nearby home of Tanglewood's superintendent of grounds, Ward J. Gaston.

Lacking a proper theater, Graf decided to perform an opera out of doors in the daylight, thus obviating the need for scenery or lighting. The work selected was Handel's *Acis and Galatea,* a pastoral "masque" about nymphs and shepherds set against a background of grottoes and groves. The scenario fitted admirably into the formal gardens on the Tanglewood expanse, especially when Graf induced the designer Richard Rychtarik to come to Lenox and plan the production in return for his travel expenses. The students themselves built the stage and made their own peasant costumes, and the opera, conducted by Boris Goldovsky, was given with the student orchestra concealed from the audience's view behind the garden's hedges.

Although the Handel opera, presented on August 16, was by any standard a success, the need for some sort of theater was obvious. Mrs. Mary Louise Curtis Bok, founder of the Curtis Institute, who happened to be in the audience, pledged $10,000 toward construction of a Theater-Concert Hall, and with this as a start a total of $40,000 was raised to build a 1,200-seat structure near the formal gardens at the opposite end of the grounds from the Shed. Eliel Saarinen, by now recovered from his pique over the revision of his Shed plans, was employed with his son Eero for the architectural work and at the same time designed a 400-seat Chamber Music Hall for the grounds. Both buildings were made of wood and severely functional and, in the manner of the Shed, both opened out onto the lawns permitting out-of-doors audiences far larger than the seating capacity. Several smaller studios, little more than primitive cabins, were also added to the school's facilities.

Koussevitzky himself presided over the inaugural of the Theater-Concert Hall as the 1941 season opened, conducting thirty members of the Boston Symphony in an all-Bach program. For the opening concert in the Shed on July 31, the climactic number was Beethoven's Fifth Symphony, which with its V-for-Victory opening motif had become a symbol of Allied determination in the war against Hitler. Also on the program were Haydn's Symphony No. 88, Debussy's *Nocturnes* and Villa-Lobos' Chôros No. 10.

For the first—but not the last—time in Tanglewood's history, some grumbling began to be heard from the newspaper critics about the preponderance of standard classical and romantic works on the summer programs. Robert Lawrence complained in the *Herald Tribune* about the number of "chestnuts"—"even beautifully roasted chestnuts"—that were included in the season's prospectus. Nevertheless, the huge crowds that turned out— total attendance for 1941 was 95,000—responded warmly to such works as Mozart's G minor, Beethoven's "Eroica," Brahms' First, Tchaikovsky's Fifth and Mendelssohn's "Italian" Symphony. And an antichestnut critic might well have noted that the programs also included Copland's *Quiet City* and Hindemith's Cello Concerto, both of which had been composed at Tanglewood the previous summer, as well as Howard Hanson's "Romantic" Symphony, Shostakovich's Fifth, Vaughan Williams' *A London Symphony* and Samuel Barber's Violin Concerto, in which Ruth Posselt, Richard Burgin's wife, was soloist. Also performed during the summer were Beethoven's *Missa Solemnis,* with student choristers participating, and Mozart's *Così fan Tutte,* put on by the opera department in the new Theater-Concert Hall with Goldovsky again conducting, Graf handling the staging and Rychtarik doing the designs. *Così,* given twice with different casts, was described by one critic as "amazing." As if to allay suspicions that he might be succumbing to anti-Wagner feelings stirred up by the war, Koussevitzky scheduled the preludes to *Lohengrin* and *Die Meistersinger* on one program.

The European conflict—this was four months before Pearl Harbor— was again responsible for a Tanglewood-on-Parade type of gala for the joint benefit of the United Service Organizations and British War Relief. Once again, Thompson's *Alleluia* was sung and several British works were played. Koussevitzky opened his Shed program with the first movement of Beethoven's Fifth, this time listed in the program as the "V Symphony." He concluded it with Tchaikovsky's "1812" Overture, which seemed a highly appropriate work since Adolf Hitler had sent his invading armies into

Wartime visitors to the Shed were the musicians of the Yankee Division from Camp Edwards, who found Koussevitzky ever ready to conduct them in military marches. (Courtesy the *Berkshire Eagle*)

A British War Relief concert in 1940 brought out a huge crowd. Eventually these benefit galas developed into the annual Tanglewood on Parade. (Courtesy the Boston Symphony Orchestra, photo by Ellsworth Ford)

the Soviet Union barely two months before. For the "1812" the Boston Symphony and Berkshire Music Center orchestras were again combined, and this time they had a new partner, the military bands of the 26th (Yankee) Division, up from Camp Edwards on Cape Cod. The visit by 250 bandsmen constituted a return call on Koussevitzky, for earlier in the year he had gone down to the Cape to conduct the nine bands stationed there. The GIs traveled to Tanglewood in a motorized column, bringing their own mobile kitchens with them, since it seemed rather unlikely that the Thursday Morning Club of Great Barrington, which operated a refreshment tent on the grounds, would be equal to providing adequate rations. The army musicians bivouacked on the shores of Lake Mahkeenac, and before heading back to their base entertained the Tanglewood crowds with a program of Sousa marches.

The second summer of the Music Center was as productive as the first. This time 338 students, selected from 796 applicants, were on hand—169 men and 169 women. They came from thirty-four states, the District of Columbia and Hawaii, and eight foreign countries—Argentina, Brazil, Canada, Chile, Colombia, Mexico, Scotland and Switzerland. Copland had been on a Latin-American tour sponsored by the United States State Department and met many young Latin-American composers and listened to their music. He also told them about Tanglewood, with the result that five enrolled there in the summer of 1941, all on scholarships from the Boston Symphony. Other musical institutions, appreciating the value of the intensive summer course at Tanglewood, also offered scholarships for outstanding students to go there—among them the Academy of Vocal Arts of Philadelphia, Curtis, Eastman, Juilliard and the New England Conservatory. Most of the students arriving there were already students or graduates of colleges or conservatories.

Entrance to the Berkshire Music Center was at once a process rigorous and informal, the objective being not to register students who had met specified tests or requirements but those who had the talent to benefit from the work. Forty-six young composers applied for the master classes under Copland and Hindemith; sixteen were accepted. Among them were Norman Dello Joio, Ulysses Kay, Gardner Read, Sam Morgenstern and Barbara Pentland, a Canadian girl.

Hindemith invariably held his classes out of doors, setting up a blackboard on the grass. "He never used instruments, or let us use them," recalls Morgenstern. "You wrote your music on that blackboard and you sang it. You didn't have to sing it well, but you had to sing it. Only at the end was it played on instruments at a concert. He would also hand out sheets of old music, like Gabrieli, Gesualdo and Salomone Rossi, and we would have to sing that and analyze it. We talked and sang music with him all summer.''

Among the piano students that year was Carlos Moseley, a soft-spoken young South Carolinian who had been studying privately in New York. In the Berkshires to visit friends, he was introduced to Jesus Maria Sanroma, the Boston Symphony's official pianist. Sanroma listened to him play and promptly signed him up for the school. During the six weeks, he worked both with Sanroma and with Stanley Chapple and for the first time met Leonard Bernstein, who was back for a second summer along with Lukas Foss and Thor Johnson. Koussevitzky's conducting class also included three new-comers of talent, Walter Hendl, Richard Korn and Robert Whitney. Expert listeners increasingly marveled at the quality of the student orchestra, whether led by one of its young conductors or by Koussevitzky himself. A report in *The New York Times* dated August 1, 1941, read: ''The young conductor who has made the biggest splash among Mr. Koussevitzky's group of hand-picked students is Leonard Bernstein, who tonight directed a movement from Brahms's Second Piano Concerto with Carlos Moseley as the student soloist. Walter Hendl, Richard Korn and Thor Johnson were the other stu-dent conductors, and their efforts met with the approval of their fellow stu-dents and invited listeners.''

Assuredly nobody who attended that concert could have imagined that twenty years later Leonard Bernstein and Carlos Moseley would once again be teamed up, this time at the New York Philharmonic, one as its music director, the other as its managing director.

. . . and Troubles

Koussevitzky's pleasure in the work of his young disciples was tempered by a growing personal tragedy, for his wife Natalie, his companion and bulwark through so many years in Russia, France and now the United States, suf-fered from a circulatory ailment, and her health began to fail. Even now she continued to be as helpful as she could, rehearsing him, for instance, in the little talks he loved to give. Natalie Koussevitzky attended only a few con-certs that summer; Margaret E. C. Downs, a Lenox nurse who often stayed with her at Seranak while Koussevitzky was conducting, says that on some nights Natalie went to the open windows so she could hear faintly the music being played in the Shed far below.

Clouds of a different sort also began to appear in 1941, involving the very future of the Festival itself. What had started in 1934 almost casually as a pleasant weekend pastime had somehow developed into an institution of international import. The Boston Symphony, which had first come into the area merely to play a few dates, now found itself committed to one of the most important continuing projects it had ever undertaken. And the Berkshire Symphonic Festival, Inc., a group made up mostly of amateurs, dilettantes and clubwomen, now was struggling to cope with a big-business enterprise involving hundreds of thousands of dollars, not to mention some of the world's leading musical personalities. Obviously the potential of Tanglewood as it now existed was something that had been foreseen neither by the officials of the orchestra or the Festival, and each group was determined to direct its future course to its own advantage. The Boston Symphony had one tremendous weapon on its side: thanks to Mrs. Brooks' gift, it owned the ground on which the Festival was held. However, the Berkshire Symphonic Festival, Inc., also had a sizeable weapon: thanks to its own fund-raising efforts, it owned the Shed in which the concerts were given. To help bring matters to a head, the five-year contract between the orchestra and the Festival, under which the concerts had been held all along, was due to expire in February, 1942.

Miss Robinson Smith was especially concerned lest the Festival be saddled with the costs of Koussevitzky's new school and of the far-reaching expansion plans he loved to talk about to newspapermen. As early as January, 1941, she was inquiring anxiously of the Boston board of trustees as to what was going to happen to her once comfortably sized, almost personally run Berkshire Festival. For the trustees, Jerome D. Greene wrote her a perhaps overly soothing letter dated January 17, 1941:

> Ever since the astonishing interview attributed to Dr. Koussevitzky in *The New York Times* some months ago . . . the Trustees of the Boston Symphony Orchestra have had to exercise what I may mildly call a slightly restraining influence on the exuberance of Dr. Koussevitzky's vision of a future center of all the Fine Arts in the Berkshires. . . . For the Trustees of the Orchestra, Dr. Koussevitzky's vision is not even a programme for the future, near or distant, for we have to think of ways and means; and we shall consider ourselves more than fortunate if Tanglewood can be made permanently useful on a scale not materially larger than that of last year. . . .
>
> Let me add, with reference to Dr. Koussevitzky, that while he has been somewhat exuberant, we do owe a tremendous lot to his enthusiasm and vision. These are qualities of the artistic temperament with-

out which he would not be the great man he is, and I will say for him that he has taken in very good part the restraining influence which we hard-boiled trustees have sometimes had to exert. I have the strongest liking and respect for him.

Whatever Miss Robinson Smith might have thought of Mr. Greene's reassurances (it is interesting to speculate what Koussevitzky might have thought of them, had *he* seen them!) she was soon to undergo another unpleasant surprise. For early in 1941 it developed that Koussevitzky wanted more money for conducting at Tanglewood. Under the five-year agreement negotiated in 1937, the conductor's pay, like other expenses of engaging the Boston Symphony, was chargeable to the orchestra. It had been set at $1,000 a concert, the same fee that Hadley had been paid in his second year. Now, however, Koussevitzky indicated that he wanted more to conduct the nine concerts of 1941—in fact, he wanted twice as much. On March 10 Ernest B. Dane, president of the board, wrote to Miss Robinson Smith:

> I enclose herewith the estimate for the 1941 season of the orchestra in the Berkshires.
>
> You will note that there is an increase of about $11,000. $2,000 is because last year we under-estimated the expenses by $2,000, and this year the conductor has insisted upon a payment of $2,000 per concert as conductor, which accounts for $9,000 extra. He makes this request very definite, even going so far to say that if it is not granted there will be no concerts in Tanglewood. We feel that an increase in his compensation is just, on account of the extra concerts.

Koussevitzky's demand caused consternation among the Berkshire Symphonic Festival trustees, who argued about it for weeks. At a meeting on July 8, it was branded as excessive, and there was some dark talk of trying to engage a "guest conductor." Miss Robinson Smith reported that Koussevitzky had told her he wanted any profits from the Festival to go to his school, and that he expected the Berkshire people to contribute to the cost of the new Theater-Concert Hall. At one point she denounced his request for more money as "a pretty high-handed holdup" and said it shouldn't be accepted without "very careful consideration and possibly . . . a counterproposition." Eventually the dispute was settled with an agreement to pay Koussevitzky $500 extra per concert with the proviso that the Berkshire Symphonic Festival had a sufficient profit at the end of the season to cover it. But all these quarrels seemed trivial compared to the open struggle which developed with the end of the 1941 season over whether the Boston

Symphony or the Berkshire Festival people would henceforth assume the dominant role at Tanglewood. As shown in the letters exchanged between the contending parties, and in the minutes of the Berkshire Symphonic Festival, it was a bitterly fought battle, at times ignoring even the surface amenities of ordinary boardroom disputes.

For its part, the Boston Symphony argued that, essential as the initiative of Miss Robinson Smith and her associates had been in establishing the concerts, it was the participation of the orchestra that had set the standards of excellence that had raised the Festival to its present eminence. As for the Berkshire Music Center, Mr. Greene informed Miss Robinson Smith in a lengthy oral statement at a specially called meeting, rather than being "a casual and unrelated activity of Tanglewood," it was "a highly strategic contribution to what should always be the aims of both the Festival Corporation and the Boston Symphony Orchestra."

Greene told the Berkshire people that divided control of the orchestra was no longer a viable arrangement, and urged that "a simplified and efficient administrative setup" be instituted, whereby "physical control of the whole establishment" would be "unified" in the hands of the orchestra. Under this new set-up, the Berkshire Symphonic Festival, Inc., would continue its "sponsorship" of the concerts and receive reimbursement for promotion and advertising costs plus "a percentage of the gross receipts for the promotion of music in the Berkshires during the whole year." Financial control of the entire operation, it was made clear, was to pass to the Boston Symphony Orchestra.

Miss Robinson Smith, however, affirmed that she had no intention of yielding control of the Festival to the orchestra. She insisted that any profits arising from Tanglewood should be shared by the two organizations, rather than going to the orchestra "for support of the Berkshire Music Center or for other corporate purposes." She estimated that on the basis of the 1941 season, the orchestra corporation would derive "between $15,000 and $20,000" from the Tanglewood concerts "in addition to an equal sum which the Boston Symphony Orchestra is receiving under our present contract." Finally, Miss Robinson Smith asserted that having raised well over $100,000 for construction and upkeep of the Shed, the people of the Berkshires were not about to turn it over to the Boston Symphony.

With characteristic directness, Miss Robinson Smith carried her case directly to Koussevitzky, with whom she had had many conversations over the last five years. They happened to meet at Saratoga, New York, and afterwards Koussevitzky felt impelled to write her the following letter:

BOSTON SYMPHONY ORCHESTRA
Symphony Hall
Boston

Lenox, Mass.
Sept. 22, 1941

Dear Miss Robinson Smith:

When you asked me: could Tanglewood exist without you, I took your question jokingly, and answered in the same light vein. But later my thoughts returned to your question time after time, and I wondered whether you meant it seriously. In this case, my answer to a seriously put question will be serious, too.

Could Tanglewood exist without you?—if asked in joke, the answer is, of course, no. If meant in earnest, then my answer will be thus.

In the artistic field, the part of the Organizer is an ungrateful one. Only a few realize it and are really interested in the Organizer. If tomorrow you decide to give up organizing the Berkshire Festival concerts, true regret will rest with just a few and your personal friends. The masses will be hardly conscious of it. With the masses, the importance lies in what takes place on the platform and what the stage can offer: if they are attracted, they will come; if not, they will stay away.

I do not intend, however, to explain what the part of the Organizer is—you are well aware of it. What I want to say is that your question becomes important if you put it seriously, because it then means that your personal part and efforts in the enterprise overshadow the aim, that is, Art, as it is created in Tanglewood. Yet you must realize that Tanglewood occupies today such an outstanding place in the world of music, that each and every one connected with it should feel a responsibility toward the nation and, particularly, toward American youth, who come to learn and to listen to great Art in the making.

For that reason, everything personal should fall back: every effort should be centered on the Aim and its development, striving to uphold as well as to constantly further the achievements of an organization which is now regarded by the entire world as a Musical Sanctuary. And any one who, being connected with this work, introduces a feeling of contention will bear a heavy responsibility.

This is what I wanted to tell you as an afterthought and in addition to our conversation at Saratoga.

Yours,
Serge Koussevitzky

Miss Robinson Smith sent a copy of Koussevitzky's letter to a Boston friend, with this covering note:

The enclosed from Koussey may interest you. I don't have to tell you that I did not ask him if he thought Tanglewood could exist without me but, rather, if he thought "the Festival would be as successful without our group." He can always twist things especially to my disadvantage. This particular conversation took place at the time he was telling me how the musicians backed him and that they would do whatever he wanted. And that *he* could give the Festival himself and engage the orchestra, etc., etc. I think I told you all this.

I'm surprised he didn't ask me to call a meeting of our Board and propose to them that we should turn over all the profits to the school.

He's a queer man and thoroughly unreliable!

The acrimonious discussion about the future of the Festival carried over into the councils of the Berkshire Festival trustees, some of whom, led by George Edman, were fairly conciliatory to the prospect of a Boston Symphony take-over. Edman expressed the view that the Festival was "at the cross roads" in its development. "It isn't a question of loyalty to Berkshire County," he said. "I think we should take the broad point of view." But Edman ran into unflinching opposition from Miss Robinson Smith and eventually resigned from the trustees. Another opponent of Miss Robinson Smith was Mrs. Andrew H. Hepburn—the former Mrs. Gorham Brooks—who had donated the Tanglewood property to the orchestra. Rather testily, Miss Robinson Smith asked her why she had given her estate to the Boston rather than the Berkshire people in the first place.

"I thought about it," replied Mrs. Hepburn, "and since the Berkshire trustees are a more or less changing group of people and the Boston Symphony is a thing that had been established for fifty years then, I thought they were a capable conservative crowd, and I thought their motives were entirely uncommercial and entirely to further art. I thought they were more fitted to own a musical project and that they were more musicians. My instinct was to give it to the people I had known the longest and who I thought would be excellent administrators."

"What do you mean 'changing group'?" Miss Robinson Smith demanded.

Mrs. Hepburn explained that she only meant she thought the Boston Symphony officials were more experienced in administration, and that they should now take over the Festival "just as when a child reaches a certain age it is wise to afford him the proper advantages away from his parents."

"Yes," snapped Miss Robinson Smith, "but you don't want him kidnapped."

"Lord pity us if the Boston Symphony Orchestra takes this thing over," added Mrs. Carlos de Heredia.

Negotiations with the orchestra continued all that summer and autumn, with various proposals and counterproposals set forth. In September the Berkshire Symphonic Festival offered to purchase from the orchestra for $10,000 the land on which the Shed stood plus the parking lots, thus permitting the local people to run the concerts while the Boston Symphony ran the school—an offer which was politely but positively declined.

Aside from the terms of a long-term contract, there was an immediate issue concerning the 1942 concerts, which both sides wished to hold while the underlying dispute was being resolved. Since a 50-50 split of any surplus had been ruled out by the orchestra, various other formulas were proposed—80-20 by the Boston board, and 66 2/3–33 1/3 by the Berkshire board. "They have put the screws on us pretty bad," Miss Robinson Smith wrote to a friend. Finally agreement was reached upon a formula whereby 72 1/2 percent of any profits were to go to the orchestra, and 27 1/2 percent to the Berkshire Symphonic Festival. The question of what kind of new contract could eventually be worked out was left in abeyance. Then, on December 7, 1941, came the Japanese attack on Pearl Harbor which plunged the United States into war and, among many more pressing problems, raised the question of whether there would be any Berkshire Festival at all the following summer.

Summer of '42

No one who was associated with it has ever forgotten the summer of 1942 at Tanglewood. In some respects it was the Berkshire Music Center's finest hour, and perhaps Serge Koussevitzky's as well. It represented a valiant and astonishingly successful effort to keep music alive in a world that seemed, at least for the moment, to have little heart for it.

The year began tragically for the conductor, for on January 11, Natalie Koussevitzky died at Brookline after a lingering illness. They had been married for forty years. Characteristically, Koussevitzky arranged that music be her memorial, for the following month he set up the Koussevitzky Music Foundation in her honor with the announced purpose of commissioning and bringing to performance new works by new composers. The first three commissions went to Nicolai Berezowsky to write a symphony, and Samuel Barber and Benjamin Britten to compose operas.

As if to lower Koussevitzky's spirits even further, it began to be evident that wartime restrictions and shortages were bound to affect the 1942 Tanglewood operation. Miss Robinson Smith's Berkshire trustees were determined to carry on the concerts uncut and unimpaired, citing the example of major league baseball, which was to continue in business with the government's blessing. But baseball was played in urban centers within reach of public transportation, while Tanglewood was out in the country, accessible mainly by automobiles which utilized two severely restricted consumer commodities, gasoline and tires.

Nevertheless, in February the Berkshire Symphonic Festival announced plans for a business-as-usual, nine-concert season, with Koussevitzky conducting the Boston Symphony. By March one-third of the seats had been subscribed and by May over 40 percent. There was talk of providing bus service and special New Haven Railroad trains for those unable to attend by car. Letters of congratulations began to pour in. "Tanglewood and the good doctor's music are among the things really worth fighting for," wrote one subscriber sending in his check. Another wrote: "We are delighted, and only hope frightful Harold Ickes* doesn't go on another spree along about August. But if the boys play, we'll be there if we have to come on a scooter."

The Boston Symphony trustees were considerably less enthusiastic about holding the Festival under wartime conditions. Back in 1941 Jerome D. Greene, he of the "hard-boiled trustees," had warned Miss Robinson Smith that "the possibility of a disastrous season . . . is not to be ignored," and now, with gas rationing reducing the size of the audiences, the Boston Symphony management feared a financially calamitous summer. Henry B. Cabot, newly elected treasurer of the board, wrote to Secretary Ickes in Washington, asking his advice and mentioning the possibility of moving the entire summer festival to Symphony Hall in Boston. Ickes, acting on an estimate that Tanglewood audiences traveled "900,000 automobile miles" each summer, "regretfully" advised that the move to Boston be made. Even the *Berkshire Eagle,* that loyal supporter of the Festival, urged that it be canceled as a patriotic as well as a practical move. Miss Robinson Smith briskly replied: "People look to us. I feel it would be patriotic to continue."

In her campaign to carry on the Festival Miss Robinson Smith had one unexpected and formidable ally—Serge Koussevitzky. However they had differed in the past, he now joined forces with her against his own board of trustees. "Let me say," he wrote, ". . . that the pulse of artistic and cul-

*Secretary of the Interior and also Petroleum Administrator.

tural life cannot be suspended." He contended that it was the "patriotic duty of the trustees of the Boston Symphony Orchestra and Berkshire Symphonic Festival to preserve the continuity—even if on a smaller scale—of the Festival and Berkshire Music Center, which stand high and unique in all the world." Even the prospect of a move to Boston did not satisfy him, because while he enjoyed the Festival concerts, his real concern was the school. On April 30 he even talked about resigning unless the Boston Symphony trustees agreed to continue the Festival. He had periodically made similar threats in the past, presumably never intending to carry them out, but his statement was unmistakable in its feeling of honest indignation:

> I have had no other communication from the Trustees except that they intended to discontinue the Berkshire Symphonic Festival, giving as their motive their patriotic concern to save gasoline. My answer to this is that the question of gasoline is the concern of the Government. The true and patriotic duty of the Trustees of the Boston Symphony Orchestra is to maintain the activities of their institution, to preserve its artistic values, and to protect musical art. This is the true manifestation of patriotic duty and patriotism.
>
> No different word has reached me about the result of the Trustee's conference. A rumor is spreading here that the Boston Symphony Orchestra board has refused to carry on the Festival and the activities of the Boston Symphony Orchestra at Tanglewood. If this rumor is correct, I consider it an act of vandalism on the part of the new president of the Boston Symphony Orchestra.* It bespeaks his profound misunderstanding of the fundamental duties and aims of a musical institution. In this case I could not collaborate with the Trustees of the Boston Symphony Orchestra any further and would immediately hand in my resignation, because I cannot participate in a premeditated destruction of cultural and artistic values or even remain as a passive witness of such an act.

For a time, the Berkshire Symphonic Festival, Inc., considered running the concerts themselves, assuming full financial liability. However, the risks seemed too great and Miss Robinson Smith was finally forced to announce that the Boston Symphony would not give any concerts at Tanglewood that summer. Washington had refused to cooperate in easing transportation restrictions, she said, so the programs were being canceled completely and

---

*Jerome Greene, who had been elected to succeed Dane as president in 1942 at the same time that Cabot was named treasurer. In 1945, Cabot became president of the board.

refunds sent out to subscribers. Koussevitzky commented: "The two boards of trustees could not agree on two points: patriotism and high expenses. It is not for me to judge who is or is not responsible for this action."

Then, on May 27, in a letter to the Boston Symphony Orchestra trustees, Koussevitzky made a startling proposal: "If you will permit the Koussevitzky Music Foundation, Inc., a membership corporation which is now being organized under the laws of the State of New York and of which I shall be President, to use the facilities at Tanglewood during the period June 20 to and including August 20, that corporation will carry on the summer session of the Berkshire Music Center and I will personally guarantee the payment by it of all expenses in connection with such summer session other than the salary of the superintendent and maintenance of the grounds and building."

Koussevitzky's decision to subsidize the 1942 Berkshire Festival himself must surely be accounted the most generous single act of a lifetime devoted unstintingly to the cause of music. Once he understood that the Boston Symphony management would not participate, he determined to keep the Berkshire Music Center open and to organize an orchestra from its students. Classes would be held for six weeks, and starting August 1, three series of weekend concerts would be given in the Shed, in addition to operatic and chamber music performances. At a press conference he held in New York on June 4, Koussevitzky estimated that the cost of maintaining the school during the summer would run to $40,000. Only $10,000 could be expected in tuition fees, since most of the students would be on scholarships. "I hope that my friends will help me out with the deficit of about $30,000," he said. "If they don't, I shall meet the deficit myself." Koussevitzky said he had moved "to rescue" the Festival to keep the school, "the vision of my life," alive, and to help preserve the nation's music and art treasures in a time of war and crisis. "America has a great responsibility toward the agonized European world," he said. "America . . . has been given the flaming torch of all the suffering and suppressed people to carry, to keep burning until the time of peace."

Koussevitzky repeated the same motif in an address to the 260 young people (the average age that year was twenty, and half were women) at the opening exercises of the school on July 5, saying: "If there ever was a time to speak of music it is now, in America. It is during the troubled periods in history that those who believe in the values and inheritance of culture stand in the front ranks, battling to save an endangered humanity." Talking of the Koussevitzky Music Foundation he said: "This is an unusual Foundation because none of its directors are millionaires. But, for a music association, it has the inestimable advantage of being directed exclusively by musicians." Then he named the members of his own board of trustees: Mrs. Clarence E. Mitchell, Aaron Copland, Richard Burgin, Gregor Piatigorsky, Howard Hanson and himself.

The Berkshire Music Center faculty that summer included Burgin, Stanley Chapple, Copland, Olin Downes, Boris Goldovsky, Herbert Graf, Ifor Jones of the Bach Bethlehem Choir, Piatigorsky, Rychtarik, Hugh Ross and Bohuslav Martinu, replacing Igor Stravinsky, who had been originally announced as composer-in-residence. Thirty members of the Boston Symphony were also invited by Koussevitzky to work with the young instrumentalists. Far from being in any way curtailed, the activities of the Center reached a new pitch of intensity. Says Leonard Bernstein: "That was maybe the greatest year of Tanglewood. The orchestra rehearsed forty hours a day." By now Koussevitzky had appointed Bernstein his assistant and referred to him affectionately by the Russian diminutive of "Lenushka."

The Berkshire Center Orchestra that Koussevitzky organized that summer consisted of 105 players about equally divided between men and women. When it gave its first Shed concert on August 1 after working together for nearly a month, with a program consisting of Haydn's Symphony No. 88, Beethoven's *Leonore* Overture No. 3 and Shostakovich's Fifth Symphony, the critics marveled at its excellence. The following day Koussevitzky led the orchestra in a special War Bond concert that opened with two Sousa marches, "Semper Fidelis" and "The Stars and Stripes Forever." Later concerts included Martinu's Concerto for Two Pianos with Pierre Luboshutz and Genia Nemenoff, and Beethoven's Ninth.

But the major event of the summer, one which drew critics from all over the Northeast, was a Russian War Relief concert on August 14 featuring Shostakovich's Symphony No. 7, Op. 60, the "Leningrad," composed the previous year while that city was under siege by the Nazis. The symphony had been widely discussed in musical circles for months, and several orchestras vied for the right to perform it first. Ultimately, Arturo Toscanini played it first on a radio broadcast, but Koussevitzky and the Berkshire Music Center Orchestra gave it its first concert performance in the Western Hemisphere, before an audience that included Russian Ambassador Maxim Litvinoff and Crown Princess Juliana of the Netherlands. Although critics differed on the quality of the work itself there was unanimous acclaim for the brilliance, power and polish of the student orchestra's performance of the difficult score. Koussevitzky himself was quite enamored of the music—at least temporarily. Walter Trampler, a young refugee from Germany who later became one of

In 1942, with the Boston Symphony's participation canceled by war conditions, Koussevitzky personally underwrote Tanglewood's activities, and built the Festival around the student orchestra (above) assembled from young musicians throughout the country. Among the summer's highlights was the United States concert premiere of Shostakovich's "Leningrad" symphony. (Courtesy the Boston Symphony Orchestra)

America's leading viola players, was then a violinist in the student orchestra. As a matter of fact, at the end of the Tanglewood season Koussevitzky engaged him for the Boston Symphony, placing him at the last desk of the second violins.

Trampler says he has never forgotten that performance of the Shostakovich Seventh. "We heard Toscanini was going to do it first with the NBC Symphony," he remembers, "but we resolved to play the hell out of it anyway. Koussevitzky had this marvelous way of going around elegantly in a white suit, cape and cap. One day on the porch of the main house he said to us: 'The Beethoven Ninth and the Shostakovich Seventh are the two greatest symphonies.' It was one of his typically extravagant statements. But all through the war, he played it repeatedly with the Boston Symphony. Then I remember one night we were in Buffalo winding up a tour and waiting at the railroad station for the train back to Boston. There was a little group, Richard Burgin, Louis Speyer, the English horn, and one or two others. Koussevitzky came over to us and Burgin asked him quietly: 'Dr. Koussevitzky, was tonight the last time we play the Shostakovich?' And Koussevitzky answered in that haughty way: 'Yes.' And then he paused and added: 'Just as well.' He'd had enough of it, too. But while he was playing it, it was the greatest symphony."

Throughout the summer the reviews of the student orchestra were ecstatic. *Time* magazine headlined its report "Miracle in the Berkshires," and Robert Lawrence wrote in the *Herald Tribune* after a concert that included Roy Harris' Third Symphony and Brahms' Fourth: "By the results that he has achieved with a student orchestra exactly five weeks old, this conductor must be accounted one of the greatest cultural figures of our times. . . . Never yet . . . have I heard such a thrilling concert here as that of last night . . . it had the spark that can only come from youth—the enthusiasm and receptivity of the young players, who have their careers fresh before them and have not slipped into the deadening ways of routine, and the eternal youth of a conductor whose flame for music has never burned low."

Operatically, too, 1942 was a notable summer, for Graf and Goldovsky decided to give two performances of Nicolai's *The Merry Wives of Windsor*. Among the students in the opera department was a young tenor from Philadelphia born Alfredo Arnold Cocozza. According to one frequently reprinted story, which may even be true, Cocozza had been tipped off that Koussevitzky was conducting at the Academy of Music in Philadelphia and, in order to gain an audition, helped some friends move a piano from a U.S.O. club in the building's basement to a rehearsal room adjacent to the conductor's room, all the time singing at the top of his voice. Sure enough, Koussevitzky heard him, asked who he was and arranged an audition. The youth, who had learned most of his music from listening to phonograph records, sang "Vesti la giubba" from Leoncavallo's *Pagliacci,* and Koussevitzky, with his customary enthusiasm for a gifted newcomer, exclaimed: "That's a great voice. You will come with me to the Berkshires."

The tenor later recalled: "I didn't know what 'the Berkshires' was, but I figured it must be something big." He forthwith adapted his mother's maiden name, Mary Lanza, into a stage name for himself, Mario Lanza, and went to Tanglewood on a scholarship.

Some of Lanza's fellow students that summer remember him as doing more beer drinking than studying. But he also did a great deal of singing. Boris Goldovsky recalls him singing a duet from *La Bohème* with a young Mexican soprano, Irma Gonzales, to such effect that Koussevitzky wept and cried out: "Caruso redevivus!"—Caruso reborn! Then he excitedly told Goldovsky: "You must teach him the Ninth Symphony."

"After two sessions," says Goldovsky, "it became obvious that one could not teach him the Ninth Symphony. I had lunch with Ifor Jones and said, 'Please tell me what to do. I have a young tenor named Lanza and Koussevitzky wants me to teach him the Ninth Symphony,' Jones said 'Oh, I know Lanza. It can't be done. You can't teach him *anything.*'"

"So I went to Koussevitzky and told him, 'Uncle Serge,* it can't be done. Pick out something else.'" So we decided to teach him Fenton, a small role in Nicolai's *The Merry Wives of Windsor.* He had only one thing to sing, the Serenade. But how he sang it! Afterwards Koussevitzky said: 'Hah! *That* you taught him!' I think that Fenton was the only part Lanza ever learned to sing on stage. He was a poor musician and simply couldn't remember things. But my God, that sound!"

In his report in the *Herald Tribune,* Lawrence, after praising Mack Harrell for his singing of Ford in *The Merry Wives,* wrote: "Another outstanding member of the cast was a young tenor, Mario Lanza, in the part of Fenton. If Lanza's natural abilities are directed in the proper direction, he will own a splendid dramatic voice." As it turned out, it was a big "if."

Attendance at Tanglewood in the summer of '42 was somewhat smaller than the two previous years, but substantial enough that the season ended with only a modest deficit of $6,000. Koussevitzky's confidence that "the masses" would come out for the concerts was more than justified. Not even

*For an explanation of Goldovsky's use of the avuncular form, see page 117.

a war, it seemed, could keep people away. An effort was made to run buses right to the Festival grounds, but transportation officials in Washington declined to give clearance for the creation of a route not on a previous schedule, so passengers were deposited in Lenox to travel the remaining long mile as best they could. Some formed car pools, others hitchhiked, still others walked. A haywagon and a milk truck were among the conveyances pressed into service. Wrote one soldier to Koussevitzky: "I hitchhiked on my weekend pass and went to Stockbridge. I really consider it one of, if not the high spot of my still brief Army career. At least I felt I was actually doing one of the things we are fighting for."

The War Years

Although Koussevitzky closed the 1942 Festival with an announcement that he intended to keep the Berkshire Music Center going throughout the war, the problems involved proved insuperable. Perhaps audiences might still be found, but there simply were not enough quality players available to justify opening the school. Everyone was in the service.

But Koussevitzky did not allow the Festival to lapse into complete inactivity. For the benefit of the American Red Cross he put on a modest series of chamber events in Sedgwick Hall, a little building adjacent to the Lenox Public Library on the main street of Lenox. He himself gave a lecture, for which he invited Leonard Bernstein to come to Lenox and play musical illustrations at the piano. Jennie Tourel also gave a concert, at which she introduced a new cycle of "kid songs" which Bernstein had composed, entitled *I Hate Music*. The young composer, of course, accompanied her.

It was during this visit to Lenox that Bernstein took the first giant stride in his professional career. He was staying at Koussevitzky's home, and while there received a telephoned invitation to visit Artur Rodzinski on his farm near Stockbridge. Rodzinski had just been named music director of the New York Philharmonic and was in the market for an assistant. As a summer resident of the area, he had been following Bernstein's work closely for the last three Tanglewood seasons. When Bernstein arrived at his farm, Rodzinski greeted him with the words "I asked God who I should take as my assistant, and He said I should take you." Bernstein went to New York with Rodzinski and three months later, at the age of twenty-five, stepped in for an indisposed Bruno Walter to conduct a regular Philharmonic subscription concert and become an overnight nationwide celebrity.

In 1944 and 1945 it still was impossible to open the school or to give concerts with the full Boston Symphony. But Koussevitzky, restive at the thought of a totally nonmusical summer, wanted to do *something* at Tanglewood. He had given with success a series of Bach-Mozart programs with small orchestra in the New England Mutual Hall in Boston. Now he saw no reason why he should not undertake a similar series at Tanglewood, utilizing instead of the huge Shed the Theater-Concert Hall which had opened in 1941. Accordingly in the summer of 1944, Koussevitzky gave a four-concert Mozart Festival, spread over two weekends, with thirty members of the Boston Symphony. At the first concert Dorothy Maynor was soloist, singing several arias and receiving a tremendous ovation. Koussevitzky also conducted such works as the Divertimento in B-flat for Strings and Two Horns, K. 287, and the Symphonies Nos. 29 in A and 34 in C. Other soloists during the brief summer season were Luboshutz and Nemenoff, playing the E-flat Concerto for Two Pianos, Ruth Posselt in the Violin Concerto No. 4 in D, and Robert Casadesus in the "Coronation" Concerto, K. 537.

The miniature festival was repeated in 1945, but this time music by Bach as well as Mozart was played, the number of musicians was increased to forty, and a third weekend with a pair of concerts was added. Soloists invited during this second summer included pianists Alexander Brailowsky and Alexander Borovsky, the two-piano husband-wife team of Abram Chasins and Constance Keene, and Lukas Foss, who was the pianist in the Bach Brandenburg Concerto No. 5. The previous winter Foss had become the youngest composer ever to have a work performed by the Boston Symphony when Koussevitzky played his *The Prairie* at Symphony Hall.

For all these concerts the Theater-Concert Hall was filled beyond its capacity of 1,200, with audiences overflowing onto the lawn beyond the open rear, just as at the Shed. Most who attended were local people or summer vacationers, but there also were military personnel including a large delegation of Waves stationed at Northampton, Massachusetts. A group of Mount Holyoke students bicycled over from South Hadley. Total attendance for the six concerts in 1945 was 16,400—more than twice the seating capacity of the theater.

On July 26, 1944, three days after the first Mozart Festival had started, Koussevitzky celebrated his seventieth birthday. During the years of the Berkshire Music Center, the maestro's birthday had always brought forth a student celebration. One year Bernstein conducted a specially concocted version of Stravinsky's *L'Histoire du Soldat,* transformed to depict Koussevitzky's years in Russia. For another celebration Foss composed a birthday Ode for chorus and piano, very contrapuntal and lasting six minutes, which Bernstein conducted at Seranak. In later years there were to be such musical tributes as a "Koussevitzky Blues" and an "Also Sprach Koussevitzky."

Now, with no students around, the Town of Lenox finally decided to recognize its most distinguished resident. In a ceremony at Seranak, J. Joseph McCabe, chairman of the Selectmen, presented the conductor with a box of flowers and a formal resolution expressing the wish that he would "continue to dwell in our midst for many years to come." Gravely accepting the document on the terrace overlooking Tanglewood and the lake and mountains beyond, Koussevitzky replied: "I am very happy to be a citizen of Lenox." He had already been a citizen of the United States for more than three years, since April 16, 1941.

The approaching end of the war both in Europe and the Pacific brought an inevitable renewal of the conflict between the Berkshire Festival trustees and the Boston Symphony trustees over who was to control the Festival when it resumed full-scale operations in 1946. At one point the orchestra proposed that control be vested in an eleven-member board—six from Boston, five from the Berkshires. At another, the Berkshire trustees offered an experimental three-year lease of the Shed to the orchestra, without giving up title to it. Both sides kept arguing over questions of expenses, tax payments, attorneys' fees, and costs arising from the wartime suspension. The struggle grew more heated, irreconcilable and futile.

Finally, at a meeting at Miss Robinson Smith's home, the Berkshire Symphonic Festival's Finance Committee simply decided to give up. They voted to make a gift of the Shed and all its "rights, title and interest" therein to the Boston Symphony Orchestra. It must have been difficult for Gertrude Robinson Smith to frame the telegram, but on October 4, 1945, she wired the news of her board's decision to the symphony officials in Boston, concluding with the words: "Our best wishes to your great conductor and your fine musicians for many years of happy and successful festivals."

The following day Henry Cabot replied, saluting Miss Robinson Smith for her "generosity and vision." He also assured her that her role in creating the Festival—it had been ten years since Hadley gave his first summer concerts in the Berkshires—would always be remembered. Cabot also invited her to take over, for her permanent use, Box No. 1 in the Shed with the compliments of the Boston Symphony Orchestra. "You said that it was the official box," he wrote, "but nevertheless I would not feel that it was proper for anyone to have it except you. I sincerely hope that you will continue to enjoy it for a long time to come."

However, despite these polite exchanges, a certain residue of bitterness persisted for years. The Berkshire Symphonic Festival decided to remain in existence as a corporate entity to make certain that the Boston Symphony maintained Tanglewood in the best interests of Berkshire County. Not until 1950 did it finally wind up its affairs. When it did so, it still had a few thousand dollars left in its treasury. A proposal was made that the sum be given either to the Boston Symphony or the Berkshire Music Center. But Miss Robinson Smith objected, and it was voted that the money instead be donated to the American Red Cross in Washington, D.C.

"Tanglewood, U.S.A."

Koussevitzky reopened the Berkshire Music Center in 1946 with a speech reaffirming his belief in the power of art, specifically music, to transcend times of crisis and unite men everywhere. He also spoke out—one of the first musicians of his stature to do so—in favor of state support of music and the other arts. "Is there a law preventing democratic governments to support the fine arts?" he asked. "In ignoring the arts the state will inevitably lose the sustaining interest and influence of the foremost minds and creative spiritual forces of the nation."

From now to the time of Koussevitzky's death the patterns of the Berkshire Music Center and the Berkshire Festival became firmly established and inextricably intertwined. Tuition at the school went up from $100 to $120— the first sign of post-war inflation—but some 400 students were enrolled, over one-quarter of them on the newly enacted GI Bill of Rights. As Koussevitzky had foreseen, the direction of international musical traffic had reversed, and over the next few years the numbers of foreign students coming to Tanglewood rose steadily. The faculty was solidified and strengthened with succeeding summers: Copland became assistant director under Koussevitzky; Ralph Berkowitz, a fine pianist who was Piatigorsky's accompanist and assisted him with chamber music classes, was named dean of the school; Thomas D. Perry, Jr., was administrator, being succeeded later by Leonard Burkat; Robert Shaw, with a growing reputation for a fresh approach to choral performance, worked with the singers. Says Copland: "Titles didn't entail much. Everybody took care of his own classes and his own work. The place was made by the quality of the students."

Koussevitzky was inordinately proud of the student orchestra. A society of Friends of the Berkshire Music Center had been organized, and he expansively told an audience of 600 members gathered at the Berkshire Museum in Pittsfield that his students had one of the best orchestras in the country— "as good as Cleveland or Cincinnati." Koussevitzky's remarks did not endear him to the musical citizens of those two cities, and several wrote him indignant letters, but he stuck to his publicly expressed opinion. He never tired of sitting in on the rehearsals and learning sessions of the orchestra, and of trying to impart both to the players and the young conductors the instinctual qualities he himself brought to symphonic music. Louis Lane, a student who later became assistant conductor of the Cleveland Orchestra, once told the writer Joseph Wechsberg of a Tanglewood rehearsal at which Koussevitzky watched a young conductor attempt to get the players started on the first movement of Beethoven's Symphony No. 2 in D, a tricky opening in which a thirty-second note is followed by a longer sustained note. The student vainly tried several times to get a coordinated attack, making indecisive gestures with his baton. Finally Koussevitzky shook his head and asked in wonderment: "What's the matter? It's so simple." He stepped in front of the orchestra, lifted his arms, let them fall in a powerful gesture, and the players came in with absolute precision. "He had an imperious will, and he was able to communicate his command," said Lane.

Koussevitzky could also show keen understanding of the problems faced by the student conductors. Howard Shanet, in later years the chairman of the music department of Columbia University, came to Tanglewood in 1946 and 1947 as a composition student, switched to conducting in 1948 and later joined the faculty. He was conducting the student orchestra in a Shed concert whose program included Arcady Dubensky's *Fugue for Eighteen Violins*. At one point in the intricate piece a violinist anticipated a cue and came in too soon, another violinist made a similar misstep, and in an instant the performance had become a shambles. Shanet desperately tried to plow ahead, but seeing it was hopeless, stopped the orchestra, turned to the audience and said: "It's useless to pretend there's nothing wrong, so we'll start again at the beginning and try to do it better." This time the piece went off without a hitch, bringing an ovation. Shanet motioned the orchestra to rise, turned around to bow and, as he did so, saw Koussevitzky hastening down the aisle toward the backstage area. The young conductor, uncertain whether he had acted properly in halting a performance at a public concert, tried to slip out but was caught by Kossevitzky at the door. "Exactly right!" Koussevitzky cried out to him. "We are here a school. We are not here only a concert hall. If something is not done right, we do again and again until is done right!"

At the Center Koussevitzky continued his policy of inviting a composer

Eleazar de Carvalho, Mrs. Koussevitzky, Koussevitzky and Bernstein in a 1949 gathering at Tanglewood. Note white gloves being carried by Koussevitzky. (Courtesy the *Berkshire Eagle*)

from abroad every summer to work with Copland in the composition department. Arthur Honegger came from Paris in 1947, but suffered a severe heart attack two weeks after his arrival, just before he was to conduct his Symphony No. 2 for String Orchestra. He was lodging at the comfortable Lenox home of Margaret Downs, the nurse who had helped care for Mrs. Koussevitzky, so he was in good hands. But he was unable to carry on his work—as a matter of fact, it was several months before he was well enough to return to France—and Samuel Barber replaced him on the Tanglewood faculty for the rest of the season. Three Frenchmen were composers-in-residence for the succeeding years: Darius Milhaud in 1948, Olivier Messiaen in 1949 (he returned in the same role a quarter of a century later, in 1975) and Jacques Ibert in 1950.

Koussevitzky had the idea that every composer at Tanglewood should know enough about conducting at least to lead his own works in performance, and among those accordingly called upon to direct the student orchestra at various times were the late Irving Fine, Peter Mennin and Harold Shapero. Leonard Burkat recalls Fine conducting a not very smooth performance of Brahms' *Variations on a Theme of Haydn* with Koussevitzky listening in the wings. As the conductor walked off after taking his bows, Koussevitzky called out: "Fine! Fine! It was *awful*."

In the postwar years Koussevitzky for the first time permitted some of his conducting proteges to take over the Boston Symphony podium during Shed concerts, though he still never invited an outside guest conductor. Bernstein was the most frequently selected, directing Schubert's great C Major Symphony in 1947, Mahler's Second and Stravinsky's *Petrouchka* in 1948 and playing the solo piano part in his own *Age of Anxiety* in 1949.

Another young conductor who quickly won Koussevitzky's favor was Eleazar de Carvalho, a thirty-two-year-old Brazilian. De Carvalho, born of a Dutch father and an Indian mother, was older than most Tanglewood students but had been recommended strongly by Heitor Villa-Lobos. De Carvalho's English was shaky, but he was able to tell Koussevitzky in 1946 when he walked in: "Villa-Lobos sent me. I'm a conductor and tuba player." An especially brilliant performance he led of *Also Sprach Zarathustra* with the student orchestra so impressed Koussevitzky that he kept him on as his assistant in Boston, added him to the Tanglewood faculty the next summer and permitted him to conduct in the Shed. Virtually every conductor of talent who presented himself at Tanglewood was quickly recognized for his true worth. A rare exception was eighteen-year-old Thomas Schippers who arrived in 1948 from Kalamazoo, Michigan, by way of the Curtis Institute in Philadelphia. Koussevitzky himself actually worked with a small group of three or four conductors each year; the others in the department only sat in on the sessions and observed. Schippers, whose principal previous experience had been as a pianist and organist, was relegated to this secondary group of conducting "auditors" and never actually directed the student orchestra. However, his career on the podium burgeoned over the next few years, and he had the satisfaction of being invited back as a Tanglewood guest conductor in 1954, and returning many times since.

Whatever the accomplishments of the students, the major attraction at Tanglewood continued to be Koussevitzky, conducting with all his old-time brilliance and intensity and expertly sandwiching in modern and difficult compositions among the standard symphonic fare—an art in which he has never been excelled. In 1947 he played Copland's Third Symphony, commissioned by the Koussevitzky Foundation, which had won the New York Critic Circle's award the previous winter, and also a cycle of all nine Beethoven symphonies—the first time this had been attempted at Tanglewood. In 1948 there were Walter Piston's Third, Vaughan Williams' Sixth (in its first performance in the United States), Prokofiev's then-new *Romeo and Juliet* ballet music and Stravinsky's *Oedipus Rex* to go along with works like the *Eroica* and Sibelius' Second. An informal tradition also sprang up, dating from the wartime concerts in the Theater-Concert Hall, of playing a good deal of Mozart at Tanglewood, much of it concentrated in the first two or three evenings.

Whether because of Koussevitzky's skill as a program maker, the quality of his performances with the orchestra, the sheer beauty and tranquillity of the surroundings, or a combination of all three, the Tanglewood concerts in the postwar epoch drew continually expanding audiences. In 1949 a seasonal high to that time of 116,200 was reached, with a single-concert record of 14,700 attained at the final concert of the 1948 season. Guided tours were instituted during the daylight hours, generally led by college students hired for the summer, who solemnly explained to the tourists that the Stockbridge Bowl was a lake and not a football stadium, and that birds really did roost in the rafters of the Shed. Among those who began distinguished careers in musical administration and management by working as summer guides at Tanglewood were George Judd's two sons William and the late George, Jr., and Harry Kraut, who became administrator of the Berkshire Music Center from 1963 to 1971.

With rising attendance it became necessary to expand the parking facilities, and additional fields were taken over. But although the two roads leading to the Festival, Route 183 to the north and Hawthorne Street on the south, were kept in good condition, no attempt was ever made to widen or straighten them, let alone turn them into superhighways. On some nights it took nearly two hours after a concert to gain the Pittsfield–New York highway a mile and a half off. For years a little card was distributed reading: "Tanglewood is a country estate, served by country roads, where we park the automobiles in broad open fields. It's beautiful and we want to keep it that way, without multi-lane highways and asphalt parking fields. But the price we pay is some unavoidable inefficiency in traffic congestion. . . . When you come to Tanglewood we ask you to allow a good deal more time than you would normally expect to be necessary—or bring a picnic supper."

The only one who invariably made good time getting to the Tanglewood

The Shed, the grounds, and Lake Mahkeenac, or Stockbridge Bowl.
(Courtesy the Boston Symphony Orchestra)

grounds was Koussevitzky. Ward Gaston, the grounds superintendent, had the assignment of escorting the conductor from Seranak down Bald Head Mountain to the Shed on concert nights. Gaston remembered: "He wouldn't leave the house until the final bell was ringing. I had arrangements made ahead of time so that when the State Police heard me coming, they would stop all traffic." To help identify the conductor's car, Gaston had a three-note musical horn installed. Koussevitzky loved it. In recognition of the police, traffic and other services provided by the towns of Lenox and Stockbridge, the Festival has always paid local taxes voluntarily, even though, as a cultural nonprofit enterprise, it is legally exempt from such obligations.*

With the economic health of the nation growing ever more robust after World War II, the Berkshires had gone beyond the stage of regarding the annual music festival as a panacea for its ills. It had become something even more significant—the centerpiece of the region's summer and touristic activities. Hotels like the Red Lion Inn in Stockbridge and the Curtis Hotel in Lenox found their rooms filled and their dining halls crowded every summer; restaurants did by far their best business of the year; and townspeople who had never taken in lodgers before began putting up "Rooms Available" signs. In 1947 it was estimated that 10,000 rooms in the area were bringing in $100,000 a day. Although few visitors complained about the Tanglewood concerts themselves, not everybody was pleased with other facets of a Berkshire weekend. Edmund Wilson, the literary critic, paid a visit in the summer of 1948 and, after praising the Festival and all its musical aspects, went on to write in *The New Yorker:*

> The invasion of Lenox and Stockbridge by this flooding of musical life has in some quarters been welcomed by the inhabitants, but in general one gets the impression that the natives as well as the summer residents are rather put out by the appearance of so many strange people, so much busier about what they are doing than rural New Englanders usually are, and evidently enjoying the stimulus of some source of inspiration which the townspeople do not understand. The rapacity with which the hotelkeepers and others attempt to exploit these outsiders is amusingly combined with an instinct to make things uncomfortable for them and to give them less-than-money's worth in as grudging a way as possible.

*The Festival pays taxes to both towns because the line between them runs through the Tanglewood property. The Shed itself lies on the Stockbridge side, although the town center of Lenox is nearer.

In a way, the high prices of accommodations represented one more in-dication of a fact of American vacation life: Tanglewood had become one of the country's best-known touristic attractions, visited even by people who never went to concerts anywhere else. A *Time* magazine correspondent in 1946 found that Koussevitzky, jauntily clad in gray flannel trousers, blue flannel jacket, white wool beret and white shoes, did not even regard it as a compliment to hear the Festival described as ''an American Salzburg.''

''Why a Salzburg?'' he asked. ''Let's have the courage to say it. In the early stages, Salzburg was an ideal place—now it is the most commercial-ized thing you can imagine. Most people who come to Salzburg are snobs who come to say they have been in Salzburg. . . . Why not a Tanglewood, U.S.A.?''

It was a typical response from a musician who in addition to being a great conductor had turned into one of the most productive and creative personages on the American cultural scene. When Koussevitzky's final citizen-ship papers came through in 1941 he said: ''This is where I have carved out my career in life. . . . I have great hope for the future of America and am proud to be adopted and accepted as one of its citizens. . . . I'm sorry I didn't do this earlier.'' In 1944 he became a supporter of President Roosevelt in his reelection campaign. With the establishment of the State of Israel in 1947 he openly began evincing interest in Jewish affairs. On August 15, 1949, the Pittsfield Jewish community honored him at a reception in the Berkshire Museum ''in recognition of his musical contribution to Israel.'' Leonard Bern-stein and Pittsfield Mayor Robert T. Capeless were among the speakers, and Jay Rosenfeld of the *Eagle* presided. Music was provided by musicians from Tanglewood—including Israelis studying at the Berkshire Music Center.

Around this time a significant change occurred in Koussevitzky's personal life. Among the important members of the Koussevitzky household, both in Brookline and at Seranak, had long been Mrs. Natalie Koussevitzky's niece, Olga Naumoff, who had acted as the conductor's secretary for the last eight-een years. After the close of the Tanglewood season in 1947, Koussevitzky was driven to New York by his valet Victor Sakharoff to board the Queen Elizabeth on his way to his first postwar European vacation. Olga was at his side as he stood on deck amid a crowd of well-wishers. Not knowing who she was, an Associated Press photographer asked innocently: ''Is your wife accompanying you on your trip?'' Koussevitzky hesitated a moment, then answered: ''Yes.'' It was the first that even the friends at the going-away gathering knew that they had been married a few days before, on August 14, at a ceremony at Seranak. The marriage was performed by the Reverend

J. Herbert Owen, pastor of the Congregational Church-on-the-Hill in Lenox, with concertmaster Richard Burgin and his wife Ruth Posselt the only attendants. Koussevitzky was seventy-three, Olga forty-six. Her devotion to him henceforth shone brightly to the end of his life, and beyond.

Opera's Golden Age

Opera had been an integral part of the Berkshire Music Center from the start, even though no theater was available until construction of the Theater-Concert Hall in 1941. Koussevitzky was deeply interested in musical theater; in Russia he had been a friend and admirer of the great Konstantin Stanislavski and he believed that opera, like symphonic music, could be made more understandable to "the masses." On the operatic repertory he held strong if somewhat unconventional ideas. In a speech in 1946 he expressed some of them: *Carmen* was the greatest of all operas; only Bizet, Wagner and Moussorgsky belonged in the topmost rank of operatic composers; Puccini and Mascagni were guilty of composing "banal" music. Koussevitzky reiterated that he regarded opera as essential to Tanglewood and added: "We want to avoid the banal, the routine. We need the opera in America, the real opera." He expressed the hope that Tanglewood would eventually have a "Greek amphitheater" sloping down to the Stockbridge Bowl and seating 25,000, at which great musical and dramatic pageants could be staged. He even talked to Bernstein, who by now had acquired theatrical experience, about putting on these "pagans," which was the Koussevitzkian pronunciation of "pageants." Bernstein recalls him saying: "At the end of the season a great pagan ve vill have. And Lenushka, you vill do, you vill make."

For the 1946 season Koussevitzky scheduled an operatic event of prime importance—the American premiere of Benjamin Britten's opera *Peter Grimes.* This was Britten's first opera; the composer, still in his twenties, had started work on it in 1942 after receiving a commission from the Koussevitzky Music Foundation. Completed in Britain during the war, it was dedicated to the memory of Natalie Koussevitzky and was hailed as a masterpiece by British critics at its premiere at London in 1945. Koussevitzky was tremendously excited by *Grimes* and by its success abroad, and he wanted to give its American premiere at Tanglewood—by far the most important such event the Festival had yet witnessed. Britten and his stage director Eric Crozier were brought from England to make revisions in the opera and assist in its preparation. They labored long into the nights, turning down the social invita-

Bernstein—who also has been known to wear his coat like a cape—with Mrs. Olga Koussevitzky. (Courtesy the *Berkshire Eagle*)

tions that poured in on them from the local gentry, leading to some complaints that they were a pair of "British snobs."

For one of the few times in the Berkshire Music Center's history, the cast of student singers was judiciously strengthened with the addition of a few young professionals. Bernstein was selected to conduct and the important choral preparation was entrusted to Hugh Ross. All three scheduled performances—with alternating casts—in the Theater-Concert Hall were sold out. Naturally critics from all over the country were on hand.

The premiere of *Peter Grimes* on August 6, 1946, was a tremendous popular success. It left the music critics impressed, but reserved. Francis D. Perkins, never one to throw caution to the winds, wrote in the *Herald Tribune*: "The work as a whole is English opera of a new kind, nationally as well as personally individual, and its future in this country is to be awaited with much interest." Downes commented in the *Times* that "it is nearer a dramatic oratorio with stage settings than it is to a living, breathing music drama." However, Downes went on, "the score is astonishing . . . this is more music than theater." Downes' conclusion, not unlike Perkins', was that Britten, at thirty-three, was "a young composer . . . to be watched respectfully." Such hemming and hawing was not for Koussevitzky; he pronounced *Peter Grimes* as the opera that came "first after *Carmen*," and when Britten, flushed with the applause after the first performance, told him, "This opera belongs to you," Koussevitzky replied, "No, it belongs to the world."

Audience enthusiasm was fervent throughout the three performances, not only for Britten's music but for the student orchestra and for the singers of both casts who sang the parts of the various inhabitants of a bleak North Sea fishing village: tenors William Horne and Joseph Laderoute; sopranos Florence Manning and Frances Yeend, alto Eunice Alberts; baritone James Pease. Two of the smaller parts, the "Nieces" of the Boar Inn, were sung by two students, Mildred Miller and Phyllis Smith—later Phyllis Curtin—who wound up as Metropolitan Opera singers.

The *Peter Grimes* performances marked the opening of what might be called Tanglewood's Golden Age of Opera, a period that lasted a decade and a half. Herbert Graf, who had launched the program, was not around to see it develop, for prior to the 1946 season he informed Koussevitzky that he had accepted a summer engagement in Hollywood. This was not the sort of tidings that Koussevitzky accepted lightly, and Graf was never asked back to Tanglewood. In 1946 Boris Goldovsky became head of the opera department, with Koussevitzky in close supervision of it.

Goldovsky, born in Moscow in 1908, came to this country as a young

The Maestro arrives. Koussevitzky, ready to conduct another concert. (Courtesy the *Berkshire Eagle*)

Benjamin Britten's opera *Peter Grimes,* commissioned by the Koussevitzky Music Foundation, had its American premiere at Tanglewood in 1946. Here bows are being taken at the conclusion by Britten (left), librettist Eric Crozier, and Bernstein (white jacket, center). The cast, mostly of students, joins in the applause. (Courtesy the *Berkshire Eagle*)

man and began training singers at the Curtis Institute in 1932, later heading the opera departments at the Cleveland Institute of Music and the New England Conservatory. His mother was the violinist Léa Luboshutz and his uncle the pianist Pierre Luboshutz. Like Gregor Piatigorsky, Goldovsky could literally speak Koussevitzky's language, called him "Uncle Serge," and helped form a comfortable little Russian émigré coterie at Tanglewood. Says Aaron Copland: "Goldovsky and Koussevitzky spouted Russian together, and that made an opera department."

Goldovsky led an active career as a commentator and lecturer, and also as director of his own touring opera company, which developed many fine singers and brought live opera to remote corners of the land. But it is as a teacher that he has left his greatest imprint on the American opera scene, and much of his most important activity took place at Tanglewood. A pretty good opera company could be staffed from among Goldovsky's singers there over the years: sopranos Adele Addison, Mildred Allen, Phyllis Curtin, Mattilwilda Dobbs, Saramae Endich, Ellen Faull, Heidi Krall, Evelyn Lear, Lynn Owen, Leontyne Price, Regina Sarfaty and Margaret Willauer; mezzos Betty Allen, Rosalind Elias, Mildred Miller, Shirley Verrett, Nancy Williams and Beverly Wolff; tenors Richard Cassilly, Paul Franke, David Lloyd, Robert Nagy, David Poleri, Robert Rounseville, George Shirley and Luigi Velucci; baritones and basses McHenry Boatwright, Justino Diaz, Donald Gramm, Frank Guarrera, Spiro Malas, John McCurdy, Robert McFerrin, Sherrill Milnes, Thomas Paul, James Pease and Thomas Stewart.

Goldovsky's method was to emphasize opera as theater as well as music; to get singers to address themselves on the stage to one another rather than to the audience or the conductor; to dispense with outmoded and foreign conventions; and to perform whenever possible in a good English translation—even if this meant preparing one himself. Tanglewood's opera department was a pioneering operation if for no other reason than that so few comparable workshops and companies for young singers existed elsewhere in the late 1940s and early 1950s. Only later did such professionally oriented educational centers begin to flourish.

In 1947 Goldovsky staged Mozart's *Idomeneo, Rè di Creta,* which for all the respect accorded it in musical history books, had never had a performance in the United States. No adequate English translation being available, the work was performed in its original Italian, with Joseph Laderoute as Idomeneo, Anne Bollinger as Idamante, Paula Lenchner as Elektra and Frank Guarrera as Arbace. The newspaper critics regarded Mozart's stately yet dramatic score as a revelation, and several urged in their reviews that either the Metropolitan or the then-new New York City Opera produce it—a suggestion not realized until 1975 when Julius Rudel conducted three performances by the New York City company. In 1948 the opera department put on Rossini's *The Turk in Italy,* which had gone unperformed in the United States for a hundred years; in 1949 there was the American premiere of Britten's comedy *Albert Herring* and also Gluck's rarely heard *Iphigenia in Tauris.* Subsequent years brought forth such works as Mozart's *La Clemenza di Tito,* sung in English in what was believed to be its first complete presentation in this country; Jacques Ibert's *Le Roi d'Yvetot,* a United States premiere with student singer Rosalind Elias in a starring role and the composer looking on; Grétry's *Richard the Lion-Hearted,* Copland's *The Tender Land,* and other works seldom heard in a conventional opera house. No wonder that opera lovers, no less than concertgoers, began making regular pilgrimages to the Berkshires.

Tanglewood's opera program not only represented a vital outlet for young singers, it also offered a unique opportunity for young directors. No one profited more from it than a heavyset girl from Missouri named Sarah Caldwell. Born in Maryville, Missouri, in 1928, she grew up in Fayetteville, Arkansas, where her father was a professor at the University of Arkansas and her mother a music teacher and pianist. She came to Boston to study violin and viola at the New England Conservatory but found herself attracted to Goldovsky's courses in opera production, stage design and conducting. "Those classes lit a match under her," says Goldovsky. "Goldovsky taught me what I wanted to do and made me do it," says Caldwell.

Sarah came to Tanglewood in 1946 as a student, enrolling in the opera department. From the day of her arrival she impressed everybody as the most talented, ambitious and industrious student on the premises. She had an insatiable appetite for working in the theater and learning her craft. "She did everything," recalls Leonard Burkat, then on the administrative staff, "—scenery-pushing, lighting, translating, directing—everything. She had a gigantic ambition and the talent to go with it."

Each summer at least one major production was staged, a kind of showpiece which attracted large audiences to the Theater-Concert Hall and which the metropolitan critics reviewed. But there also were a number of smaller undertakings—single acts and even short scenes from operas which while more modest in their staging nevertheless afforded valuable ensemble experience to singers, instrumentalists, conductors and designers. In 1946, the year of *Peter Grimes,* the Tanglewood opera department gave a second seafaring opera, Ralph Vaughan Williams' *Riders to the Sea,* based on the John

Mozart's *Cosi fan tutte* is staged by students in the Theater-Concert Hall. Here the supposed doctor Despina successfully applies her therapeutic magnet to two expiring suitors. (Courtesy the Boston Symphony Orchestra; photo by Richard Davis)

Millington Synge play. Sarah Caldwell, then eighteen years old, was assigned to stage and conduct it. The result was a performance that not only pointed up the musical impact of the opera but that recreated the stark and somber atmosphere of Synge's original play.

Koussevitzky, always quick to sense the presence of a gifted and promising newcomer, was so impressed with Caldwell's capabilities that he appointed her to the faculty—one of its youngest members—for the following season as Goldovsky's assistant. Instead of relaxing in her new status, Caldwell characteristically redoubled her efforts and began taking on more tasks than ever.

"Koussevitzky gave everybody the feeling that Tanglewood was the most important thing in the world," she says, "and to those of us who were there, it was. When they put me on the faculty I was convinced they had made a tremendous mistake, but I wasn't going to let them find it out. I worked so much in the opera department, day and night, that I didn't go to the Boston Symphony concerts. Koussevitzky, of course, wanted everybody to attend those concerts, and there were rumors that he knew who went and who didn't—that he kept a secret roll.

"At the next to the last concert I finally went, and afterwards when I went backstage to the green room Koussevitzky kissed me and said: 'How *nice* to see you at a concert!'

"I was worried, because he always said he wanted everybody at Tanglewood to give 200 percent, and that he would fire anybody who gave less. So I went to the last concert, too, and he said: 'Oh, you came to *another* concert? How nice!'

"I figured I was done for.

"In those years every summer after the last concert Koussevitzky gave a farewell dinner for the faculty and staff in the dining room of the Curtis Hotel in Lenox. I decided I'd better talk to him. So I went up to him and said: 'Dr. Koussevitzky, this is my first faculty dinner, and I want you to know that it is an honor to be here. There is just one thing I find wrong with Tanglewood.'

"He kind of bridled and said: '*W-r-r-ong* with Tanglewood?'

"'Yes,' I said, 'I simply cannot find a way to give 200 percent and still go to concerts.'

"There was a long silence, then he looked at me with a smile, hugged me, and said: 'I never want to see you at another concert!'"

Caldwell stayed on at Tanglewood as Goldovsky's principal assistant for five summers, gaining a variety of operatic experience she could have

Rehearsals for Leonard Bernstein's opera *Trouble in Tahiti* went on far into the night. Here, at 1:30 A.M. , are (left to right) the composer, Sarah Caldwell, and Boris Goldovsky. In the pit is conductor Seymour Lipkin. (Courtesy Whitestone Photographers)

Latin-American composers began to flock to the Berkshire Music Center after World War II. Here a group of them pose with young composers from the United States. Top row, left to right: Lukas Foss, Hector Tosar, Juan Orrego-Salas, Irving Fine. Bottom row: pianist Raoul Spivak, Antonio Estevez, Leonard Bernstein, Julian Orbon, Oscar Buenaventura, Alberto Ginastera. (Courtesy the Boston Symphony Orchestra)

Koussevitzky cuts the cake on his seventy-fifth birthday. At extreme right are
Howard Shanet (in white suit) and Eleazar de Carvalho. (Courtesy Whitestone Photographers)

found no place else in America. At the time, she was the only female conductor on the premises. "Students in an orchestra are never wild about being conducted by another student," she says, "and they could be rough on the young conductors working with them. I always felt they were more courteous to me than to the others out of chivalry, and I appreciated it."

In 1973 Winthrop Sargeant wrote an article about Sarah Caldwell in *The New Yorker*, quoting an unnamed former student as depicting her as an "earnest and humorless" girl with few friends at Tanglewood. Caldwell says that is not the way she remembers it. "My memory is that I had a grand time," she says. "I had plenty of friends among the opera people. The greatest year for me was 1950, the summer of Mozart's *La Finta Giardiniera* with Jimmy Pease, David Lloyd and Phyllis Curtin. We worked on it from 9 A.M. to 10 P.M. every day."

Caldwell continued her association with Goldovsky at the New England Conservatory and later became head of the Opera Workshop at Boston University. She and Goldovsky, from whom she had learned so much, eventually went their own ways. Goldovsky had his own opera company, and Caldwell wanted hers. There remains a residue of some feeling between them, though each professes nothing but admiration for the other's talents.

Caldwell's group, launched in 1957, eventually grew into the Opera Company of Boston and won national recognition for resourceful and imaginative productions of works like Rossini's *Semiramide,* Berlioz' *Les Troyens,* Schoenberg's *Moses und Aron* and Sessions' *Montezuma.* As at Tanglewood, she was intensely involved in every aspect of her productions, doing everything but singing in them. Obviously Boston, as important a musical center as it is, eventually had to share her talents with the rest of the country. In recent years Caldwell has become a kind of national cultural heroine, with frequent engagements—mostly as a conductor—in other cities. In 1976 she became the first woman ever to conduct at the Metropolitan Opera, just as in 1946 she had become the first woman ever to conduct at Tanglewood.

But Sarah Caldwell's unique achievement is not her talent as a conductor, or for that matter as a stage director, a scenic supervisor, an operatic producer or a musical researcher. What sets her apart is her capacity to put all these things together, to build an opera literally from the ground up by sheer dint of ability, insight, labor and personal forcefulness. She is one of the most complete musical persons in America today, and she became that way at Tanglewood.

"I Will Never Give It Up"

In April of 1948 it was announced that Serge Koussevitzky would retire the following year, at the age of seventy-five, as music director of the Boston Symphony Orchestra, and that Charles Munch would come from Paris to succeed him as of October, 1949. Thus the 1948–49 season became both Koussevitzky's Silver Jubilee and his farewell season at Symphony Hall.

At Tanglewood the summer of 1949 was a particularly brilliant year. Modern works abounded: Shostakovich's Seventh, Bernstein's *Age of Anxiety,* Britten's *Spring Symphony,* Roussel's Suite in G, Messiaen's *Ascension,* Villa-Lobos' *Mandu-Carara,* William Schuman's Symphony for Strings. Jascha Heifetz made his first Tanglewood appearance, playing the Tchaikovsky Violin Concerto and donating his $3,000 fee to the scholarship fund. Janice Moudry and David Lloyd sang Mahler's *Das Lied von der Erde* with the orchestra. The United States State Department made a twelve-minute film about Tanglewood for distribution to fifty foreign countries. The Berkshire Music Center was filled to capacity, with 460 students from thirty-six states and nineteen foreign countries. Attendance records hit new peaks all season long, with the overall total reaching 116,200. Koussevitzky was as buoyant as ever, and his seventy-fifth birthday party at Seranak was particularly festive. He conducted all except three of the summer's concerts himself, turning two over to Bernstein and one to de Carvalho. Right to the end, his mind was on music. At the closing concert of the Tanglewood season—the last he would give anywhere under the title of music director of the Boston Symphony Orchestra—he played Beethoven's Fifth Symphony. With a valedictory feeling in the air, a tremendous crowd turned out and at the end gave him an endless ovation. Finally, after waving his arms and taking countless bows, Koussevitzky signaled concertmaster Richard Burgin to leave and told the chief electrician to put out the lights. Then, turning to Leonard Burkat who was standing nearby, he remarked: "These days it is not so easy to make a success with the Fifth Symphony."

The announcement of Koussevitzky's resignation as music director of the Boston Symphony left up in the air—either accidentally or by design—his future role at Tanglewood. Relations between Koussevitzky and the orchestra's trustees—he always pronounced the word "trustys," with the accent on the first syllable—were not overly cordial at the moment; it was an open secret that he wanted Leonard Bernstein, not Charles Munch, chosen as his successor. It also soon became obvious that whatever happened in

Mrs. Eleanor Roosevelt was a frequent visitor to Tanglewood and acted as narrator of Prokofiev's *Peter and the Wolf* in 1950. This picture of her on the stage with Koussevitzky was made after that performance. (Courtesy the Boston Symphony Orchestra; photo by Howard S. Babbitt, Jr.)

Boston, in the Berkshires Koussevitzky was determined to remain in charge indefinitely. He had no intention of resigning from Tanglewood. What complicated matters was that Munch, like Koussevitzky himself twenty-five years before, had been engaged as music director on a year-round basis—presumably including the Tanglewood months. To further complicate the picture, the orchestra management announced on May 31, 1950, while Koussevitzky was abroad on a tour that included concerts with the Israel Philharmonic, that it had invited the Italian conductor Victor de Sabata to guest-conduct two concerts at Tanglewood on August 3 and August 5.

The first inkling the public received of a falling-out between Koussevitzky and the "trustys" over Tanglewood came on a Columbia Broadcasting System radio program, "Your Invitation to Music," during which James Fassett interviewed the conductor soon after his return to the United States on June 14. In response to a question about guest conductors, Koussevitzky said:

"This year is something happen unexpected for me. Some of the guest conductors like my pupils, Leonard Bernstein and Eleazar de Carvalho, they are considered by myself and by the faculty the best of my pupils. Therefore I invite them to conduct the Festival concerts. And I considered always that this school is for the Americas and for America's gifted people.

"But it happened this season that the trustees, without my knowledge, without to ask me, they invited themselves a guest conductor. So this year I take off any responsibility for the programs of the Festival."

"Except your own?" Fassett asked.

"Except those of my pupils and my own."

Koussevitzky referred to de Sabata as "my old friend," and said that while he did not object to his having been engaged as a guest conductor, "I do object to the manner in which it was done"—that is, without his being consulted. Then he said emphatically: "I do not want any responsibilities apart from Tanglewood. Tanglewood, it is my child. It is my creation. It is my blood and tears. I will never give it up."

A few days later Koussevitzky revealed to a reporter from the *Berkshire Eagle* who came to see him at Seranak that he had discovered in February that his name wasn't to be carried in the Boston Symphony programs during the summer of 1950 as musical director at Tanglewood. "I have never resigned from Tanglewood," he told the reporter. "If any agreement has been signed by the president of the Boston Symphony Orchestra with anyone else as musical director at Tanglewood it was done without consulting me and without my knowledge. I strongly believe that the institution I created and developed at Tanglewood should have a strong leadership

Bernstein, Copland, and Koussevitzky. Observe the blood vessel in Koussevitzky's temple. Some musicians said it pulsated according to the music. (Courtesy the Boston Symphony Orchestra)

and artistic authority and the traditions I established should be carried on."

From the board of trustees' standpoint, the transition between the Koussevitzky and Munch regimes, which was simple enough in Symphony Hall, was inevitably complicated by Koussevitzky's special relation with Tanglewood. Back in February, the board hinted to Koussevitzky its desire to separate the administration of the Berkshire Music Center and the Boston Symphony concerts. Munch would technically be in charge of the entire Festival, although he would share the actual conducting of Shed concerts with Koussevitzky. However, Koussevitzky then hinted back that he might not be able to conduct one set of concerts which had been designated for him, at which point de Sabata was engaged. Explained Henry B. Cabot for the trustees: "We invited Mr. de Sabata, an international figure, to replace another international figure, Dr. Koussevitzky." Amid the flurry of statements and explanations, the most sensible decision of all was made by Charles Munch: to remain in France for the summer.

So when the 1950 Tanglewood season opened, Koussevitzky was still very much in charge. De Sabata, having been engaged, came to the Berkshires to conduct his two concerts and, as a matter of fact, scored a huge public success. On August 3 his program included Respighi's *Pines of Rome,* Schubert's "Unfinished" Symphony, Morton Gould's Spirituals for String Choirs and Orchestra, and the Prelude and Liebestod from Wagner's *Tristan und Isolde.* On August 5 he played Ghedini's *Pezzo Concertante,* Mozart's Symphony No. 39 in E-flat and Berlioz' *Harold in Italy.* The fifty-seven-year-old Italian thus became the first conductor outside the Koussevitzky "family circle" to conduct the Boston Symphony at Tanglewood. Koussevitzky exchanged amicable greetings with his "old friend" at his first rehearsal, but he did not attend the concerts, his box being pointedly vacant.

One other minor contretemps arose during the summer: the orchestra management had scheduled an outdoor screening of the film documentary on Tanglewood made the previous year by the State Department, to take place on July 27, following a concert at the Theater-Concert Hall. It seemed like a harmless enough project, but Koussevitzky, protesting that he had not been consulted, said that showing a film would "lower the standards of Tanglewood" and that he wanted the audience to leave "remembering the concert and not a movie." He carried his protest to Cabot, who was vacationing in Maine. Cabot said he agreed with Koussevitzky, and the screening was called off. The reason announced by Tanglewood's press office was that "there's a full moon tonight."

These little tiffs aside, the summer of 1950, like the summers before, turned out to be lively and fruitful. Koussevitzky had gathered around him his usual devoted array of faculty helpers—Leonard Bernstein, Richard Burgin, Eleazar de Carvalho and Lukas Foss as his conducting assistants, Hugh Ross in charge of choral work, Piatigorsky directing the chamber music program, Aaron Copland and Jacques Ibert working with the student composers, and Howard Shanet, who had toured Europe and Israel as Koussevitzky's assistant, directing the student orchestra. Goldovsky was on leave, and Jan Popper was acting head of the opera department, assisted by Sarah Caldwell. Aside from de Sabata's two concerts, Koussevitzky and his associates ran the season as they always had. The year marked the 200th anniversary of the death of Johann Sebastian Bach, so both the Shed and the Theater-Concert Hall resounded to his music—all six Brandenburg Concertos, the four orchestral suites, a selection of cantatas. All in all, sixty-one Bach works were performed, including the B Minor Mass in its first Tanglewood presentation since 1940, with an audience of 7,800 overflowing the Shed. The summer was also marked by the first Israeli work ever played at Tanglewood, Manuel Mahler-Kalkstein's Music for Strings which Shanet performed with the student orchestra.

Tanglewood on Parade, by now a solidly established all-day event, was highlighted by the appearance of Mrs. Eleanor Roosevelt as narrator in Prokofiev's *Peter and the Wolf*. Ralph Berkowitz had the assignment of instructing the former First Lady in the niceties of the work and wrote this memo after his first visit to the Roosevelt home in Hyde Park:

> **Mrs. Roosevelt graciously accepted the greetings I brought her from Dr. and Mrs. Koussevitzky and sent hers in return.**
>
> **In regard to "Peter & the Wolf" Mrs. Roosevelt stated that she had not expected that the work would be as complicated as she now found because of her lack of musical knowledge. With a piano score which I had carefully marked in colored pencils to indicate entrances of the speaker, Mrs. Roosevelt soon found that her problem would be considerably simplified.**
>
> **I played through the complete score for Mrs. Roosevelt and she read her part, following perfectly the cues I gave. There will be no difficulty, I feel certain, at the orchestral rehearsal. . . .**

At the performance Mrs. Roosevelt's reading went off without a hitch, with Koussevitzky introducing her to the audience as "a godmother to youth and the First Lady of the world." RCA-Victor, which then had an exclusive

The funeral procession leaves the Church on the Hill after the service. (Courtesy the *Berkshire Eagle*)

Koussevitzky's burial in 1951, with both Russian Orthodox and Episcopal clergy officiating. The red maple tree at the graveside fell after a storm in 1974, the 100th anniversary of his birth. Among mourners are Mrs. Koussevitzky and Bernstein (with handkerchief to face). (Courtesy the *Berkshire Eagle*)

recording contract with the Boston Symphony, seized the opportunity to make a recording of Mrs. Roosevelt narrating the work with the orchestra.

The last concert of the 1950 Tanglewood season was held on Sunday afternoon, August 12, with Koussevitzky conducting the Boston Symphony in two symphonies, Prokofiev's Fifth and Brahms' First. The largest crowd of the summer, 12,600, was on hand, filling the Shed and covering the lawn behind it all the way back to the gabled Tappan mansion that for twelve years had housed the Berkshire Music Center. Many in the audience thought that Koussevitzky and his orchestra had never sounded more intense and eloquent than in the two serious, almost somber symphonies that made up the day's program. They summoned the conductor back for seven bows at the conclusion.

No one had any way of knowing it, of course, but this was Serge Koussevitzky's last concert at Tanglewood, and the last time he was ever to conduct the Boston Symphony Orchestra. During the winter that followed he and Bernstein led the Israel Philharmonic on a tour of the United States and Canada. He had become attached to the orchestra, and it to him, during his visit to the new state the previous year, and it seemed fitting that he should be involved in its first visit to the New World. The tour was grueling and the weather wintry, with Koussevitzky and Bernstein alternating in concerts in Washington, New York, Boston and Montreal. When they reached Denver, Colorado, the seventy-six-year-old conductor was suffering from a heavy cold with a fever and was ordered hospitalized for a few days. But he continued on to San Francisco, keeping going, according to his wife, "by sheer force of will." After another brief spell in the hospital, he and Mrs. Koussevitzky went to a house they had near Phoenix, Arizona, and there, through March and April, 1951, he seemed much improved.

Actually, Koussevitzky was suffering, and had been for some time, from polycythemia rubra vera, a blood disease characterized by an overproduction of red corpuscles. But the rest in Phoenix reinvigorated him, and he pushed ahead with an intriguing project he had conceived—to conduct his first opera in America. The work he selected was Tchaikovsky's *Pique Dame,* or *Queen of Spades,* which he had conducted years ago in Russia. Now he wanted to put it on during the summer of 1951 at Tanglewood with Goldovsky's students. He spent hours in Phoenix planning the production and going over the score on the piano. Bernstein, who was en route to Mexico, stopped off, and they discussed the opera and the Tanglewood season ahead.

On May 1 the Koussevitzkys left Phoenix and flew to Boston, going to their home at 191 Buckminster Road, Brookline. There he held further conferences with Goldovsky about *Pique Dame*. But he again began to feel weak and to run a temperature, and his Boston physician recommended that he be hospitalized. So he was taken to the New England Medical Center, and though he rallied from time to time during the next few weeks, his condition gradually worsened. The end itself was sudden and painless. It came at 5 P.M. on June 4, 1951, with Mrs. Koussevitzky and Bernstein, who had been called back from Mexico, at his bedside.

A funeral service was held at the Church of the Advent in Boston, with both the Russian Orthodox and Protestant Episcopal rites. But the final resting place he had chosen was not in Boston but in the Berkshire Hills that had become his real home. He was cremated, and his ashes were taken to the cemetery of the Congregational Church-on-the-Hill in Lenox, barely two miles from Tanglewood. There, at a ceremony attended by his wife, his students and his fellow musicians, Serge Koussevitzky was laid to rest, just as another Tanglewood season was about to begin.

Bernstein on Tanglewood

(Transcript of a conversation between Leonard Bernstein and the author in Lenox, Massachusetts, July, 1975)

H.K.   How did you meet Koussevitzky, Mr. Bernstein?

L.B.   Well, it's very strange. I mean I, a Bostonian, had never met him. I'd gone to the Boston Symphony all through my Harvard days, but it would never have occurred to me to go backstage or anything like that. He was quite far away, so glamorous and remote. In fact I never thought of being a conductor. I graduated from Harvard in '39. I went to Curtis that fall, following the urging and advice of Dimitri Mitropoulos, whom I did know, the only conductor I knew or had ever met. I met him when he was guest conductor of the Boston Symphony in January '37, and I met him by accident and played for him and showed him some of my music and he got all excited and invited me to all the rehearsals.

And then after I had graduated, that summer of '39 I went to New York to look for a job and didn't find one. I didn't know what I wanted to be when I grew up. I knew it would be a musician, which means everything of course in my book. But then I just wanted to have something to live on. My family wasn't very congenial to the idea and I spent that summer of '39 with my tail between my legs just having been not accepted by the draft board on account of asthma. It was the beginning of September '39, which was when Hitler marched through Poland, and I was feeling very low indeed.

It's a very long story and I don't want to tell you long stories. But somehow or other, Mitropoulos, whom I hadn't seen for years, was on a ship that docked in Boston and he ran into a friend of mine, Leonard Burkat, who was there to meet a friend who was getting off that boat. And he said to Burkat, who was introduced to him, "Oh, I know somebody with a name very like yours who lives in this city." And Burkat says, "Oh, he's an old friend of mine; we went to the Boston Latin School together." "Well, give him my regards and tell him I'll be in New York at the Biltmore Hotel for the weekend and I'd like to see him."

From that chance meeting on a gangplank this second of September or whatever it was, when Hitler was marching into Poland and I felt the world was about to end, I was sort of pulled out of my gloom. Leonard Burkat called me up and said, "Guess who I just saw coming off a ship?" So I went to New York and I called Mitropoulos up and saw him at the Biltmore Hotel. I said, "I'm in despair, what should I do?" and he said, "You should be a conductor." It was the first time the idea ever arose. And I said, "How do you know? I mean, why should I be a conductor? I have no qualifications, no ambitions to be a conductor; it never occurred to me." And he said, "I just know, that's all."

So I said, "O.K. How do you get to be a conductor?" He said, "You go to study at a school, like Juilliard." So I called up Juilliard. It's already September, mind you, and they were full. Albert Stoessel was teaching then and his class was full. There was nothing to be done. I said to Mitropoulos, "What do I do now?" He said, "Well, I hear that Fritz Reiner is teaching at Curtis." He was a great master, so I called Curtis and luckily it turned out that Fritz had been delayed in Europe and had not yet returned to form his class, so auditions were about to be held. And I went down and took the auditions, based on what I don't know, but he took me in his class and I spent that year in Philadelphia—something quite marvelous. Reiner was my real introduction to the study of conducting. All this time I still had not met Koussevitzky, and I'm now twenty-one years old. And then I read in the paper that Koussevitzky was opening a thing called the Berkshire Music Center, so I applied, like all the other kids. I mean, I had no particular in or anything.

H.K. You just saw it in the newspaper.

L.B. Yes, I just applied. I got some recommendations. I got one from Roy Harris and one from Aaron Copland and one from Reiner, with whom I'd already studied. He was a very tough customer, he didn't much like the idea of my going off to study with Koussevitzky but he gave me a letter anyway. And I came to Boston armed with these letters and met Koussevitzky for the first time in the green room at Symphony Hall after one of his concerts. We just sat there and talked, there was no audition or anything, and he suddenly said, "But of course, I vill accept you in my class," which was astonishing to me. I jumped for joy.

That was April. And then that summer I arrived here. And the first week of our relationship we became as close as we were when he died. It was instant. We just loved each other very much. He was so good to me. I guess he loved me as a kind of son, not having had one himself, and we became very, very close immediately.

I remember the first week I was up here, very confused, not knowing what to do, never having conducted an orchestra at all, and there was this beautiful student-conductor orchestra ready to be conducted. I was very nervous, as I can tell you. I thought maybe I could get through *The Afternoon of a Faun* with some luck, or something like that. But he announced to me the first day that I would have to conduct Randall Thompson's Second Symphony, because Randall Thompson was up here then, having just written that famous *Alleluia* for the opening exercises which has been sung every year since. And Randall was somebody I had been studying with at Curtis.

H.K. Oh, you had known him then?

L.B. When he was director of Curtis. And I'd studied orchestration with him at Curtis that same year I was with Reiner. Koussy said: "But how apropos! Of course you must conduct Randall's Second Symphony!" And I said, "*All* of it? All four movements?" And he said, "All of it." And I said, "When?" He said, "Well, Friday night. This is Monday—you have rehearsals Tuesday, Wednesday, Thursday." Just like that!

So I got hold of a score and went into the bushes somewhere

and studied till I was blue in the face. The next day I had my first rehearsal with Koussy by my side. We had private sessions in between at which he gave me great long disquisitions on legato . . . and the sun coming out . . . "it must *be varm,* varm . . ." exactly the opposite of what I'd been through with Reiner, which was very technical, and very great teaching. Reiner was the most underestimated guy in the world—a really great master and a great teacher—but the opposite end of the rainbow from Koussevitzky, who was an inspirational teacher. He taught "Be varm, be varm." He was so inspiring, so caring. And I must say I was in the sky somewhere. And I did that symphony on the Friday.

H.K. How did it go?

L.B. It was great. I couldn't believe it. It took a lot of doing. Koussevitzky was so thrilled. And that began a long friendship which, now that I think of it, was all of eleven years long, because that was 1940 and he died in 1951, practically in my arms. The whole relationship was only eleven years.

H.K. In that first year did he say, "Now that you can do Randall Thompson you can go on to Beethoven," or something like that?

L.B. I did all sorts of things. I did something *every* week. I was one of several students, but I did something in every concert, and attended his rehearsals and everybody else's rehearsals and soaked it all up. Hindemith was there that year and that was very instructive and beautiful.

H.K. Do you find that the spirit of the first year has been maintained pretty much or did you have a kind of pioneering feeling in that first year that this was something new?

L.B. Nothing can quite match that first year, of course. But with ups and downs it has remained an extraordinary experience. It can't be the same without Koussevitzky, that goes without saying. He was a unique man. But the spirit remains in one form or another depending on who's around.

H.K. I didn't realize that you'd met Carlos Moseley in that first year.

L.B. I conducted him in the first movement of the Brahms B-flat Concerto. He was very good.

H.K. Carlos told me that Tallulah Bankhead came over here that first year when she was playing in the Berkshire Playhouse.

L.B. Carlos told me he was talking to you about that. He said he had the lines wrong and I should give them to you right.

H.K. All right, let's have them right.

L.B. The great, the key line is "Dahling, those back muscles!"

H.K. That was up here at Tanglewood, right at the beginning.

L.B. Tallulah and I had never met. She was doing *Her Cardboard Lover,* and she had been invited by Koussevitzky to come and visit Tanglewood. And apparently he had taken her to the Shed in which I was rehearsing something for that night's concert—*The Rio Grande* by Constant Lambert, a very difficult piece with chorus and alto solo and one piano solo, a sort of campy, sexy piece which for some reason I had been given to conduct.

This was like the dress rehearsal of it, and I was conducting in a T-shirt or something, and when Koussevitzky brought her into the Shed she went ape, and said: "Who's that? I must meet him at once!" So he brought her backstage, and there I was, suddenly confronted with this glorious creature. She was so pretty back then in 1940, and of course I was a devoted fan. And there she suddenly was, and there I was, all sweaty in my T-shirt, and she said: "I just had to meet you, dahling—those back muscles! What are you doing for dinner?"

And I said, "Dinner? My God, I have a concert at eight o'clock."

"Eight o'clock, yes," she said. "It's only five now. I'll see that you get back on time."

She had a big chauffeured Cadillac and I was whisked away under Koussevitzky's very eye to her lodgings in Stockbridge, where she was staying. It was a boardinghouse. She ordered dinner for me, and as we waited there was a great deal of bourbon in evidence, and I was plied with bourbon. And who knows what happened? All I know is that I suddenly looked at my watch, it was almost eight o'clock and I was roaring drunk. It's the one time in my life that I ever had a drink before a performance.

I said, "This is impossible, I have to go back." And dinner hadn't arrived yet. I rushed out into the chauffeured limousine which brought me back to the Cranwell School, where I was staying, about eight. Luckily I was not the first one on the program. I managed to shower and shave, cutting myself and bleeding. I got into a white jacket and just made it to the stage on time, reeling with bourbon. It was awful. I've never had a drink before a concert since. Not a beer. Nothing.

H.K. In general, how did your Tanglewood experience affect you?

L.B. Some very important things happened both musical and nonmusical at a very critical time of my life. Those years in the '40s at Tanglewood are so connected with the roots of my whole life that I can't really talk about it objectively. It's connected with the war, with anti-Fascism, with love affairs. But through it all runs Koussy. It just didn't occur to me before today that we really knew each other just one decade, eleven years—it seems to me like a whole lifetime of personal relationships.

I think that in those eleven years we had only one quarrel, or one time of tension. Quarrel's not the right word. It was the first time I knew that I was really very important to him. He invited me to dinner at Seranak and began to make me a speech which obviously he had rehearsed in his mind. It had a certain formality about it. He was addressing me. And I remember the words very clearly. He said that he had been thinking a great deal about me and so on, and then he said: "It vill be open to you all the gates from the vorld." It was the first time I ever heard anybody speak in those terms—full of sentences about what I would be and become, and what I would signify for my country, and my people, and music, and at the end of all this he said: "But Lenushka, it vill nothing happen ven you vill not change it the name." Those words are engraved on my brain: "It vill nothing happen ven you vill not change it the name."

And then he began to put me wise to the fact that there was anti-Semitism in the world, which I had never thought of before, of course. And he had my new name all figured out. It was to be Leonard S. Burns. And I winced in horror at the idea of being called such a thing, but I did manage to ask him what the S was for. And of course you know that the Russians always observe the patronymic very fervidly and so S would stand for my father's name Samuel, and thus I'd be Leonard Samuelovich Burns.

H.K.   Quite a choice!

L.B.   Outside of asking him what the S stood for I didn't have a thing to say. I was just awash in silence. And he said: "You think about overnight. It is the most important thing." This would have been in the middle of the war, maybe '42—I was already his assistant. He was so eager and ardent about my being a success and being his creature, his disciple, that he couldn't stand the idea that something like a name would stand in the way. Naturally, I didn't have to think about it very much overnight. I may have lost an hour of sleep. But I had to tell him no. And he was very upset. And when the war ended he came to understand gradually that it didn't matter that much. As a matter of fact, when my relationship with Israel began he became terribly interested in Israel. You know he was converted. They wouldn't have him. And I spent a couple of brutal years there fighting to have him invited. The Israelis would not have a converted conductor. And I succeeded by 1950, whenever it was.

H.K.   I'm interested in that, because just from reading about him I have the feeling that underneath he always had this interest.

L.B.   He was very Jewish. He was incredibly Jewish. The book about Koussevitzky that remains to be written is the book about Koussevitzky the Jew. They tried to deny it. There was a certain period of his life when he was trying very hard to live it down and to be the image created for him by Natalie and the whole Parisian period—the white gloves and the capes. Maybe our relationship did reawaken it.

H.K.   It would be nice to think so, wouldn't it?

L.B.   Not nice; I mean, I don't want to take any credit for it. All I know is—well, I'll give you an example. In 1941 I did for the first time, in my life anyway, with the student orchestra Bill Schuman's *American Festival* Overture. And Bill came up for the occasion. It was a fairly new piece then and very difficult. And it was a smash. I mean, to everybody's amazement the house came down, and there was big screaming, and Bill was asked up on the stage, and Koussy came on the stage to congratulate me, and to congratulate Bill, and there were bows after bows after bows, and as I was walking off Koussy put his arm around me and said: "Lenushka, do you know? He is a Jewish boy!"

   And I was shocked, not by the information, but by the *pride.* I saw a whole thing, and this was the second summer, so already something had happened. It was around the same time, '41, Koussy in the middle of a lesson, suddenly made, out of the blue, a totally incomprehensible statement. He said: "You know, counterpoint is a Jewish idea." What he meant—I think I know what he meant—is that it's a Talmudic idea, that you can balance two apparently contradistinctive notions at the same time, that you could have simultaneity of variety, or you could argue two sides of a case, which is very Talmudic, at the same time. And I had the gall, the chutzpah, to say: "But the great contrapuntalists of music have never been Jewish."

H.K.   What, Bach wasn't Jewish?

L.B.   Bach, Bruckner, *Mendelssohn?* "Vonderful counterpoint!" He didn't last long in that argument. But I remember being so appalled at the thought and so taken with his fervor about it. He suddenly turned Jewish. I wish I could remember what place this was, where this whole awareness seized him.

H.K. Maybe it was the war and Hitler.

L.B. Oh, I know it was; it was obviously the war, but I'm trying to think of the exact place. I remember a lunch at Seranak one day when I heard him discourse for the first time on anything political. He stopped the conversation at the table and he said: "Have you read the papers? Heetler and Muzzolini—two gangsters." And he held up his two fingers. And everybody was terribly impressed. There was nobody there that had to be convinced that Hitler and Mussolini were two gangsters. But he announced it as though he had just discovered this thing. Maybe that was the turning point.

H.K. What turned him away from Judaism?

L.B. Practicality. I don't know too much about these years even though he's told me about them. He's even told me slightly conflicting stories at different times. At one time it was in order to get into the Conservatory, or in order to maintain residence in Moscow. I think his torture about it must have been as great as Mahler's. He maintained his Russian Orthodoxy but also, because he said that was all too fussy and glamorous and caused too much attention to be paid, he joined the Church of the Advent on Charles Street.

He had two priests at his funeral—two services simultaneously. Talk about Talmudic juggling! At his death he had this bearded patriarch from the Russian Orthodox Church whom I had to summon; when the doctor said he didn't have more than an hour or so to live I went to the yellow pages of the Boston telephone book, looked up the nearest whatever it was, and found a Russian Orthodox man who arrived with a portable altar and set it up next to his bed.

At the funeral service there was this Russian Orthodox priest and the reverend from the Church of the Advent. And they sort of alternated, which made it a very long service. And there was a headstone of marble from Jerusalem, which had been sent by the Israel Philharmonic Orchestra.

H.K. Did Koussevitzky ever talk to you about succeeding him?

L.B. Day and night. But it was not meant to be. No. I didn't want it, and he couldn't understand that. He was very hurt, as a matter of fact. He couldn't understand why I didn't want an orchestra. I didn't want to be music director of any orchestra; I wanted to write music and

Koussevitzky with his favorite pupil. His wish to have Bernstein succeed him did not meet with the approval of the trustees. (Courtesy the _Berkshire Eagle_)

Bernstein in a 1949 appearance conducting the Boston Symphony in the Shed. At left is concertmaster Richard Burgin, at right, first viola Joseph de Pasquale. (Courtesy the *Berkshire Eagle*)

be free and be flexible. Maybe he was right. Maybe I made a great mistake. But whatever came, I was committed to the idea of doing various things in music and especially writing it.

He told me one day that he was going to retire. And he said, "You're the only one who could succeed me." And I had to tell him I didn't want that. And his answer was very typical—I remember it like yesterday. He said: "Lenushka, they vill offer you, you vill take." I said: "Well, we'll see about that." The thing that broke his heart was that they did not offer it. He couldn't get over that. Because he submitted a whole plan, on the assumption that I would be so flattered that I wouldn't be able to say no.

H.K.   Well, why do you suppose that they didn't offer it?

L.B.   I've never inquired. There were some intimate enmities between him and the people on the board. He had it all figured out that I could take a third of the season and then the next year we'd share it equally—he had it figured out month by month—and then the next year he would leave comfortably, knowing that I would have the two years of apprenticeship or whatever you want to call it and that he could leave the orchestra safely in my hands.

That was the plan he wanted, and they said no. And he told me with tears in his eyes that the "trustys" have decided, they seem to prefer "Thees freevolous Frenchman," this frivolous Frenchman, who turned out to be Charles Munch, a beautiful and great man. And Koussy couldn't bear the idea that his orchestra was to pass into the hands of a frivolous Frenchman instead of mine. He really sobbed when he told me this, he was so heartbroken. Because it was not only a rejection of me, it was a rejection of *him*. After twenty-five years of giving his all!

H.K.   Well, of course, when Munch came to Tanglewood there was a great change, and I just wonder what might have happened had you come in then. I mean strictly on the Tanglewood end of it.

L.B.   I'm not the person to answer that.

H.K.   How do you see your future relations with Tanglewood?

L.B.   I don't know. I have nothing to say about my future, no predictions to make. Don't ask me about that.

H.K.   Well, I was going to ask if you would continue as an adviser?

L.B.   I don't think adviser is a just term because I'm not around enough to advise. I think I should continue as something—I don't know what. We've all been trying to change that word "adviser" and think of a better one. Maybe you can think of the right word. But I don't ever want to break my relations with Tanglewood, because it's very dear to me.

Charles Munch, who succeeded Koussevitzky at Tanglewood, was content to remain in background. But he took an interest in outstanding students and sometimes sat in on orchestra rehearsals. (Courtesy the Boston Symphony Orchestra)

4. The Munch Years

"A Boy from Alsace"

Charles Munch, who succeeded Serge Koussevitzky as the director of both the Tanglewood concerts and the Berkshire Music Center, was among the most brilliant conductors France has ever produced. In what was surely one of the most remarkable predictions ever made by a music critic, Virgil Thomson wrote in Paris in 1935 that Munch, then forty-four years old and totally unknown in the United States, would someday become conductor of the Boston Symphony Orchestra.

The Boston, of course, had a certain tradition of French conductors, including such men as Henri Rabaud and Pierre Monteux; indeed, Koussevitzky himself had had years of Parisian experience and had invited a number of French instrumentalists to come to America and join the orchestra. Munch himself was Alsatian, having been born in Strasbourg in 1891, when the city belonged to Germany, part of the spoils of the Franco-Prussian War of 1870. He had even seen service in the German Army in World War I, fighting at Peronne and Verdun, but after the war he gladly accepted French citizenship.

Munch began his musical career as a violinist, and after the war was concertmaster of the Leipzig Gewandhaus Orchestra under conductors like Wilhelm Furtwängler and Bruno Walter. The Leipzig orchestra asked him to take out German citizenship papers as a condition of further employment, but Munch preferred to return to France. Like Koussevitzky, he married a wealthy woman, Geneviève Maury. She was an accomplished poet, writer and translator—in fact, she translated the works of Thomas Mann into French. She also was the heiress to the Nestlé chocolate fortune, and her money was important in enabling him to meet the essential expenses of starting a conducting career in Paris in 1932.

Once launched, Munch quickly became the most admired and respected conductor in France. His familiarity with both French and German musical styles, his brilliance on the podium, and his interest in new music all contributed to his reputation. If anything further was needed, it was provided by his personal charm and magnetism, for he became something of a matinée idol and was known in Parisian musical and social circles as "le beau Charles."

In January, 1947, Munch made his United States debut with the New York Philharmonic, scoring an instant success with audiences and critics. His combination of musical and personal gifts made him, as Thomson foresaw, a logical choice for a Boston Symphony conductor. He resembled Koussevitzky in the inspirational, instinctive nature of much of his conducting, yet differed from him in his somewhat relaxed, low-pressure approach to the mechanics of music-making. For one thing, he disliked rehearsals and had a practice of cutting them short, which endeared him to his musicians but did not necessarily guarantee a well-prepared concert. Roger Voisin, for many years the Boston Symphony's first trumpet, and a compatriot of the new conductor, remembers: "Munch was more a painter, a performer, than a teacher, and an impressionist painter at that. He wanted you to play music your way. He needed the atmosphere of an actual concert to be at his best. I remember one rehearsal of Brahms' Second Symphony that he cut short. 'You can't do it at ten in the morning,' he said. 'You can't feel passionate at an hour like that.'"

Although he had already served a year as music director of the Boston Symphony, Munch, as previously noted, had tactfully absented himself from Tanglewood during the summer of 1950, leaving Koussevitzky in unchallenged command of both the Berkshire Festival and the Berkshire Music Center. But in 1951, upon receiving word of his great predecessor's death, Munch canceled his European summer musical engagements, crossed the ocean, and came to Tanglewood—which he had never seen before—to take over direction of the Festival and the school.

Plans for the 1951 season had been virtually completed prior to Koussevitzky's death. He had intended to launch the Festival with a series of six Bach-Haydn-Mozart concerts in the Theater-Concert Hall. For several years now these events had proved enormously popular, and since they utilized a reduced orchestra, they made it possible for some members of the Boston Symphony to perform at Tanglewood while others remained in Boston to give the free Esplanade concerts.* In 1951 Koussevitzky had also scheduled himself to conduct Beethoven's *Missa Solemnis* and, of course, the production of *Pique Dame.*

*Thanks to the annual summer overlap of Tanglewood and the Esplanade, some wits used to say that the Boston Symphony was the first orchestra in the country to have a fifty-six-week season.

Munch, who was fifty-nine when he came to Tanglewood, devoted himself to some of these undertakings. He took over the Bach-Haydn-Mozart series himself and at the opening concert had the student choir sing the final chorus from the *St. Matthew Passion,* "Wir setzen uns mit Tränen nieder" (Here sit we with tears flowing) in remembrance of Koussevitzky. Munch requested that there be no applause out of reverence for "the great leader, the great master." At the first Shed concert, Munch conducted the full Boston Symphony Orchestra in a further tribute, a portion of Mozart's *Masonic Funeral Music,* K. 477. Virgil Thomson, covering the opening for the *New York Herald Tribune,* thought the selection ideally matched Koussevitzky's "own nobility of character and consecration to music's excellence." The performance of the *Missa Solemnis* which Koussevitzky was to have led on August 9 was taken over by Leonard Bernstein and dedicated to the conductor's memory. The soloists were Adele Addison, Eunice Alberts, David Lloyd and James Pease, all Tanglewood veterans who had known and worked with Koussevitzky. A Berkshire storm struck during the performance, with thunder and lightning accompanying the Kyrie and Gloria sections, and a pelting rain driving the crowd on the lawn inside the Shed.

It must not be thought that the entire summer was devoted to memorial concerts or that the shadow of the dead conductor in any way darkened the season of music-making. On the contrary, both in the Festival and in the school, activities continued energetically, as if to demonstrate a universal conviction that a festive and flourishing Tanglewood was the most enduring memorial to Koussevitzky. Munch proved as popular a figure in the Shed as he had the previous winter at Symphony Hall. One of his programs that summer consisted of three symphonies—Beethoven's First, Honegger's Fifth and Tchaikovsky's Sixth, and a record Tanglewood crowd of 15,800 turned out, creating the most monumental traffic jam yet seen along Route 183. The season's total attendance reached 126,700, about 400 less than the previous summer's level, but thanks to increased ticket prices, an all-time high of $249,000 in box-office receipts was registered.

But even as Munch assumed an active role at the Festival concerts, so did he shy away from any deep personal involvement in the educational activities of the Berkshire Music Center. Roger Voisin was not the only Tanglewood veteran who observed that Munch was simply not a teacher. When he wrote his autobiography in 1954, Munch called it *Je suis chef d'orchestre* (I Am a Conductor). The title summed up his range of musical interests. He was by no means unaware of the school Koussevitzky had started and of its unique and essential function. He smiled benignly on the students and moved easily among them. One day, listening to an assistant reading aloud a report on foreign students expected to be present at the Berkshire Music Center call out: "A boy from Italy, a girl from Mexico, a boy from Israel . . ." he interrupted and said, ". . . and a boy from Alsace," meaning, of course, himself.

Nevertheless, despite his friendly attitude, he spent little time with the students. When a reporter, encountering him on the Tanglewood "campus," asked him whether he talked much with the young people he said in his heavily French-accented English, "Oh yes, I talk to them." "And what do you say to them?" he was asked. "Oh," he replied vaguely, "I say 'Ow are you?'" Although Munch continued to be listed throughout his years in Boston as the "director" of the Berkshire Music Center, he actually provided very little in the way of direction, and his connection with the school was largely limited to conducting one or two concerts each summer by the student orchestra.

Opinions vary as to the effect that Munch's nondirection of the Berkshire Music Center had upon its operations. Thomas D. Perry, Jr., who was a member of the Center's first class in 1940, later becoming the Center's administrator and ultimately the executive director of the Boston Symphony Orchestra, believes that Munch's contribution may be underrated. "It was a problem coming in here on the heels of Koussevitzky," says Perry. "Munch knew what was happening in the school. He was strong on solfège, the traditional French training, and was happy to see that we stressed it here. But he also was wise enough not to mess around in the sacred groves—to let the school run as Koussevitzky had set it up. I'd say that so far as the school is concerned, he was a positive force in a general, distant way." Mrs. Olga Koussevitzky also feels that while Munch was not interested in administration himself, he let the school run as Koussevitzky had left it.

Most Tanglewood veterans believe, however, that a certain slackness crept into the school's activities as a whole, however brilliant many of its achievements remained. A separation began to develop between the activities of the school and of the Festival—what Gunther Schuller was later to call the "across-the-lawn feeling." Koussevitzky had been an omnipresent figure, wandering around the grounds in his white cap, stopping to chat with a student practicing under a tree, looking in on classes, sitting in on rehearsals, working with the student conductors. Munch made appearances only infrequently, assuming—perhaps correctly—that everything was running well enough without him. He enjoyed Tanglewood, its concerts and its general atmosphere, and spent every summer of his Boston Symphony career there. But when he wasn't conducting or rehearsing the Boston Symphony

Orchestra in the Shed, he went off to play golf or canasta with cronies—including orchestra members.

Munch was quite candid in indicating that his relations with the orchestra were different from Koussevitzky's. Although he did not mention names, there were many who were sure he was alluding to his great predecessor when he spoke rather disdainfully of a conductor who "made his men repeat the same bars over and over again."

"The last time they did not play any better than they had at first," he went on. "It is not funny when you are told like a schoolboy to repeat over and over again the same passage. After all, it is a job like any other by which you live and keep your family alive. I myself have been playing in orchestras for years, and I know what can make the work pleasant, but I also know what can make it unbearable."

At the school, with Munch providing only nominal leadership, a certain fragmentation developed among the various departments. The Berkshire Music Center attempted a style of operations that amounted to the Koussevitzky system without Koussevitzky. Aaron Copland continued as the Center's Music Director. Bernstein, who had been in Cuernavaca, Mexico, when Koussevitzky was stricken and had hastened to his bedside, canceled his plans to spend the summer of 1951 in the resort and instead came to Tanglewood as head of the student orchestra. At its opening concert he exhorted the young players to cherish Koussevitzky's tradition by following "the central line, the line of mystery and fire, to be followed by dedicated people." Among the conducting students that summer was Lorin Maazel, now the music director of the Cleveland Orchestra but then a young man trying—successfully, as it turned out—to resume his career after a premature and almost disastrous start as a boy-wonder conductor at the age of nine at the 1939 New York World's Fair.

It turned out to be an important summer for Bernstein in more ways than one, for on August 12, three days after he conducted the *Missa Solemnis* in memory of his mentor, he became engaged to Felicia Montealegre. The announcement was made by Mrs. Olga Koussevitzky at a buffet supper she gave for the couple at Serenak. They were married in Boston September 9 at Temple Mishkan Tefila, Bernstein's boyhood synagogue, and for their honeymoon went to Cuernavaca, which Bernstein had left so precipitously the previous June upon hearing of Koussevitzky's final illness. Three years later, when their first son was born, the Bernsteins named him Alexander Serge, in honor of Koussevitzky.

Serving with Bernstein and Copland on the Center faculty were such

A scene from Darius Milhaud's opera *Ariana Abandoned,* given by the opera department in 1955. The singers are Claire Watson and McHenry Boatwright. (Courtesy the *Berkshire Eagle*)

Tanglewood regulars as Richard Burgin, Ralph Berkowitz, Hugh Ross, Piatigorsky and Goldovsky. The year's composer from abroad was Luigi Dallopiccola from Italy. Dallopiccola, whose opera *Il Prigioniero* had been given earlier in the season at the Juilliard School in New York, worked with a picked group of eight students. The apostle of twelve-tone music was deeply impressed by what he saw at Tanglewood, especially by the vigor and creativity of the students.

Koussevitzky's project of performing Tchaikovsky's *Pique Dame* was brought to fruition during the summer by the opera department, though of course without its key figure. Goldovsky, who had visited Koussevitzky and discussed the production with him, took over the direction and put on the opera in English in the Theater-Concert Hall. The role of Lisa was to have been shared by two Tanglewood singers, Phyllis Curtin and Carolyn Long, but Miss Long took ill, so Miss Curtin wound up singing the role at all performances. Others in the cast were Lloyd, Alberts, Pease and Elias.

The same summer the opera department also gave Richard Strauss' *Ariadne auf Naxos,* also in English, with a cast headed by a twenty-three-year-old soprano named Leontyne Price, who had studied at Juilliard. Goldovsky remembers Miss Price's arrival this way: "She came in the first year of Munch's regime and went into the opera department. She impressed us all right off. She was skeptical of her chances, but I pushed her into the opera. Tanglewood always was the haven of the black singer. They acted, sang and worked alongside the whites from the very start."

A slight contretemps involving Price arose in connection with a performance Munch was to lead of Schubert's Mass in E-flat Major. Munch had selected Saramae Endich, another talented soprano in the opera department, to sing the solo passages in the Mass, but through a mix-up in communications Miss Price was informed that *she* had been picked for the role. "But I can't, I have nothing to wear," she told Goldovsky. Further questioning disclosed that she did own one evening gown, but it was at her home in Laurel, Mississippi. She was urged to ask her mother to come to Tanglewood with the dress, with the Festival paying the round-trip bus fare. Miss Price's mother set out for Tanglewood and was already en route when the mix-up was discovered. Miss Endich sang the performance as scheduled, but Miss Price was given the $50 fee she would have received had she sung it—plus, of course, the bus fare. "Later that summer Leontyne sang in *Ariadne,*" says Goldovsky, "though it wasn't a compensation for the Schubert mix-up. We didn't do things that way."

Among the visitors in Munch's first year was Mrs. Roosevelt, who drove over for the annual Tanglewood on Parade festivities and was discovered under a maple tree enjoying a picnic supper with two friends. Other lawn picnickers clustered about or stopped to chat with the former First Lady. When Munch learned she was on the grounds, he called her up to the stage and introduced her to the audience.

Afterwards, Mrs. Roosevelt wrote in her "My Day" newspaper column that she hoped the Festival would be carried on "because it is a fitting memorial to Dr. Koussevitzky." Describing a former Berkshire mansion, Elm Court, which had been turned into a public restaurant, she wrote: "Tastes have changed since these houses of rich people were built, but on the whole, I think taste has improved. There is more simplicity today regardless of the money you may have to spend. Perhaps there is less money to spend, too, and I am not sure that it is not a good thing if it drives us to more study of real beauty of line and simplicity, as well as a better use of our space."

Dress, Guests and Tourists

For Tanglewood the 1950s was an era of consolidation rather than innovation. There was no longer the remotest question of survival; all the old uncertainties, whether created by finances, war or weather, were gone. As a summer concert series the Berkshire Music Festival was solidly established—indeed, it had become part of the Establishment itself—with programs that grew gradually less adventurous or distinguishable from the Boston Symphony's winter fare. But the school was always on hand to inject a dash of novelty or originality into the general musical picture, and certainly the weekend audiences continued to arrive in ever increasing numbers, especially when the opening of the Massachusetts Turnpike in 1957 cut the driving time from Boston from four hours on a crowded, narrow Route 20 to around two.

One Tanglewood regular who found the change in regime very much to her liking was none other than Miss Gertrude Robinson Smith. Since yielding up the Festival to the Boston Symphony board of trustees in 1945 she had had little to do with Tanglewood; in fact, she had taken to spending her summers for the most part in France. But in the early 1950s she returned to her old cabin, The Residence, in Glendale. Now in her seventies, she had lost none of her old tenaciousness and imperiousness. With Munch in charge she resumed her role as a personage very much on the scene.

A Francophile of long standing, Miss Robinson Smith welcomed the arrival at the Berkshires of Charles Munch. (Courtesy the Boston Symphony Orchestra)

After all, she was a Francophile of long standing; many of her activities in New York City had been devoted to promoting French culture. Immediately after the war she was instrumental in bringing over a theater troupe from Paris for several years, installing them in a small hall at the Barbizon Hotel. With Munch as director of the Festival she could feel practically in the presence of a compatriot, and she began to call on him regularly. Up to a point Munch enjoyed her visits; among his intimates he referred to her as "le grand chat"—the big cat—a designation not altogether clear and certainly not very flattering. At times he managed to be not at home when he knew she might be calling. But Miss Robinson Smith once again became a familiar, if somewhat forbidding figure on the grounds. Says Harry Beall, the New York concert manager who at that time was just beginning his musical administrative career working in the Tanglewood press office: "When she swept up in her big car, the gates were always open. You always knew when she was there. I, for one, was always glad to see her drive away."

For all their freedom from the personality clashes of the 1940s, the Munch years managed to engender a few controversies, some of them entirely extramusical. Perhaps the most celebrated and—in retrospect—most intriguing—was the Great Apparel War, which grew out of a typically Bostonian attempt to regulate the garb of all who entered the sacred precincts. A certain New England rectitude has always been in evidence at Tanglewood; even today, virtually all the male office staff members make it a point to see that they wear neckties and, except on the warmest days, jackets at all times.

With the advent of the '50s, however, more and more visitors turned up not only coatless and tieless but actually wearing shorts, halters and similar attire both on the concert grounds and in the surrounding towns. One Lenox resident complained publicly about the "perfectly horrid goings-on" on the Tanglewood lawns, as well as "a lack of clothes" among summer visitors on the village streets. The selectmen even posted signs asking tourists to dress "properly" in town. The same cry was taken up at the Festival itself, led by the redoubtable Miss Robinson Smith. "These people wouldn't think of going to a lawn party in shorts," she said. "Why should they wear them to a concert? After all, there's a certain beauty, a certain charm, a certain dignity in a concert, which should be preserved."

The forces of propriety among the Tanglewood management were prompt to rally. First, all girl students were asked to wear skirts to classes and to concerts rather than shorts or slacks. Then Thomas D. Perry, Jr., the orchestra's assistant manager, announced that women tourists wearing

Primly-dressed usher hands cloth skirts to women visitors wearing shorts during cover-up campaign of the 1950s. Boston Symphony's moralists gave up when recipients kept the wrap-arounds as souvenirs. (Courtesy Whitestone Photographers)

shorts or slacks, and men tourists wearing shorts, would be provided with wrap-around skirts at the gate. An initial supply of eight brightly colored nether garments, four medium and four large, were purchased from England Bros. store in Pittsfield. However, Perry's belief that this would cover the situation proved incorrect. Tourists clad in shorts gladly accepted the skirts, but instead of turning them in as they departed, many of the recipients carried them off as souvenirs.

Understandably the Tanglewood skirt contretemps provoked considerable discussion, not to say hilarity, among moralists, sociologists, fashion authorities and students of Bostonianism in general. The *New York Herald Tribune* editorialized upon the matter on August 6, 1951:

Slack Season at Tanglewood

Perhaps the debate now raging at Tanglewood will never go down alongside such past controversies of musical history as piano vs. harpsichord and aria vs. recitative, but it is interesting enough. The new question is skirts vs. slacks, and the musical traditionalists, as they very often do, hold the upper hand.

We take no position on the substance of this question ourselves. Listening to music is a highly subjective pastime. Some prefer it in formal wear in Carnegie Hall, others favor an old bathrobe near a radio. The Tanglewood Festival evidently has varying types of listeners, too. Perhaps those in charge of the concerts could make a survey of the correlation of musical and sartorial tastes. Do those who prefer shorts also prefer Stravinsky? Is there a relation between long skirts and long symphonies? The Festival makes no report on such matters, yet obviously there is material for a statistical study. So far, all we know is that ushers are presenting wrap-around skirts to all female visitors clad in shorts and slacks, and that these skirts come in only two sizes—large and medium. There is no small size. Obviously there are more cellos at Tanglewood than piccolos.

The Festival's attempt to establish clothing standards dragged on for several years; eventually it was given up not because the Boston Symphony's taste-makers had decided that the female thigh had become an integral part of the summer landscape, but because it had become too expensive to maintain the supply of disappearing skirts.

During the spring of 1952 the Boston Symphony had made its first tour of Europe, a completely triumphant affair, and it opened its Tanglewood season with its international reputation higher than ever before. Before the concerts started Mayor Capeless of Pittsfield presented the orchestra with a certificate expressing the pride of the Berkshire Region in the "unparalleled adulation" that greeted the Boston Symphony Orchestra on its tour abroad. Thirty-two Berkshire County towns joined Capeless in expressing their own adulation.

In the musical sphere, Munch began more and more to put his own imprint on the performances, the programming and the choice of guest soloists. His own conducting approach, which involved putting together a performance at the actual concerts rather than during the rehearsals, contained a built-in factor of excitement and suspensefulness; programs could range, in the words of one constant listener during the 1950s, "anywhere from glorious to awful." The men adored Munch—the quickest way to a musician's heart is through a canceled rehearsal—and they played for him with enthusiasm, but the results could be wildly variable. Sometimes one felt Munch was holding things together with his sheer personal warmth and charm as much as with his musical insight and conductorial skill. There is no doubt that everyone led a considerably more relaxed life at Tanglewood under Munch than they had previously. One joke at the time even said that the birthrate in the musicians' families rose during his regime; under Koussevitzky nobody had dared take time out for procreation.

Munch's particular affinity, quite naturally, was for French music, and a great deal of it turned up during his dozen years. To hear Munch conduct the Berlioz Requiem or *Damnation of Faust* or *Symphonie Fantastique* was to recall Heinrich Heine's description: "Berlioz' music in general has something primeval about it if not something antediluvian: it reminds me of extinct species of animals, of fabulous kingdoms and fabulous sins, of sky-storming impossibilities, of the hanging gardens of Semiramis, of Nineveh, of the wonderful constructions of Mizraim." In 1954 Munch devoted much of the Festival to a commemoration of the 150th anniversary of Berlioz' birth (actually on December 11, 1803). He also introduced Rameau and Couperin to the opening series of concerts hitherto devoted to Bach and Mozart; he looked on with approval while the opera department gave Grétry's opera *Richard Coeur-de-Lion* its first American performance in over a century, and when he conducted the annual Koussevitzky Memorial Concert in 1959 he performed Fauré's Requiem.

For the most part, however, Munch seldom strayed far from standard repertory, remaining content to repeat works he and the orchestra had played the previous winter at Symphony Hall. In 1956 there was a splurge of modern pieces by Walter Piston, Aaron Copland, Howard Hanson and others; but even these were repeats, for all had been commissioned for the orchestra's seventy-fifth birthday celebration, and already given in Boston.

One element of novelty Munch did introduce was in the area of guest conductors. The only "outside" conductor to appear in the Koussevitzy years had been de Sabata, but now a steady stream of visitors began to ascend the Shed podium. None was more overdue for an invitation than Pierre Monteux, now seventy-seven years old and about to retire as music director of the San Francisco Symphony. Monteux had been the last conductor of the Boston Symphony prior to Koussevitzky; whether for that reason or for some other Koussevitzky had never asked him back to guest-conduct at Tanglewood. Munch, however, quickly made amends to his fellow Frenchman, and in 1952 invited him to conduct several Shed concerts, including performances of Schubert's C Major Symphony, an all-Wagner program and Stravinsky's *Rite of Spring,* whose notorious world premiere he had led in Paris in 1913. Monteux's reception from both the audience and the orchestra was warm and spontaneous; so much so, in fact, that he remained a Tanglewood "regular," returning each summer until his death in 1964.

Leonard Bernstein also made regular appearances. By now Koussevitzky's favorite protege of the 1940s had gone on to a glamorous career, climaxed by his appointment to head the New York Philharmonic in 1957— the same year, incidentally, that his *West Side Story* had its Broadway premiere. Not only in New York but in European musical capitals as well Bernstein had become perhaps the world's most eagerly sought-after conductor. It was no secret to Munch or to anyone else that Koussevitzky had designated Bernstein as his successor, and many people believed—Bernstein's protestations to the contrary—that he would have leaped at the job if the trustees had offered it to him in 1951. Nevertheless, in a profession notorious for its jealousies and rivalries, Munch and Bernstein developed a warm mutual regard and respect, and the older conductor generously welcomed the younger whenever he came to Tanglewood. To Munch, Bernstein was not a legacy left over from Koussevitzky's time but the most brilliant American conductor of his time and an embodiment of the rising generation.

Because of his own tight schedule and extensive travels, Bernstein's appearances at Tanglewood through the 1950s and 1960s tended to be fast and fleeting. Often he was scheduled as the big attraction at Tanglewood on Parade, the one-day midweek fiesta which served as a benefit for the Berkshire Music Center. Some summers he stayed for a weekend, often drawing the largest crowds of the season. He directed such unusual events

Grétry's opera *Richard the Lion-Hearted* was given with a student cast, conducted by Boris Goldovsky and staged by Sarah Caldwell in 1953—its first American performance in a century. Caldwell and Goldovsky collaborated on the translation. Left to right are singers Christine Cardillo, John McCollum, and Lee Cass. (Courtesy the *Berkshire Eagle*)

Choral director Hugh Ross and Charles Munch confer during a break in a rehearsal of Beethoven's *Ninth Symphony*, for the closing performance of 1955. (Courtesy the Boston Symphony Orchestra; photo by Gus Manos)

Charles Munch (left), Thomas D. Perry, Jr., and Pierre Monteux with a facsimile of a score of Beethoven's *Ninth Symphony*, presented to Monteux on his eighty-fifth birthday at Tanglewood on Parade in 1960. (Courtesy the Boston Symphony Orchestra)

as a concert version of Act IV of Bizet's *Carmen* in 1952 and excerpts from Gershwin's *Porgy and Bess* with Leontyne Price and William Warfield in 1953. He conducted Mahler's Symphony No. 2, the "Resurrection," at a time when performances of it were still rare, and one year appeared as a triple-threat man—conductor, pianist and composer, directing Copland's *A Lincoln Portrait,* playing the piano solo in Gershwin's Concerto in F and presenting the world premiere of his suite *On the Waterfront.* His opera *Trouble in Tahiti* was performed two summers under Goldovsky. In addition to his appearances, Bernstein kept a close eye on the young conductorial talent being developed at Tanglewood, recommended likely candidates for scholarships and also assisted promising alumni to find jobs.

Along with the gradually changing policies of the Munch years went a gradually changing administrative setup. In 1954 George E. Judd retired after nearly forty years as manager of the orchestra; his successor was forty-year-old Thomas D. "Tod" Perry, Jr., a native of Grand Rapids, Michigan, and a Yale graduate. Leonard Burkat became administrator of the Center. The length and scope of the season were gradually extended. In 1953 the Thursday-night concerts by the Boston Symphony were transferred to Friday night, thus producing a concentrated three-day sequence and making the "Tanglewood weekend" a literal reality. In 1960 the Bach-Mozart opening concerts were transferred from the Theater-Concert Hall to the Shed, meaning that the full six weeks of performances were now held in the larger auditorium. In 1961 a seventh week was added and in 1962 an eighth, bringing the current season to its present length. In 1959 a new acoustical canopy was installed in the Shed with the financial aid of Mrs. Edna Betts Talbot, replacing the old shell around the orchestra, which had lasted for twenty-five years, ever since the first season of the Berkshire Symphonic Foundation.

To accommodate the throngs that descended on the grounds every weekend, Tanglewood began to expand its parking areas. A relatively new phenomenon, tour and excursion buses, began to make their appearances. With the Festival itself flourishing, various other cultural—and some not-so-cultural—enterprises began functioning in the area. Jacob's Pillow, which actually antedated the Berkshire Festival, remained firmly established at nearby Lee, and many visitors turned their excursions into a combined weekend of music and dance. In 1955 the Berkshire Music Barn, a summer music hall devoted to "concert jazz," opened about a mile down the road from Tanglewood, offering a first-season roster of Thelonius Monk, Dizzy Gillespie and the Modern Jazz Quartet. The Berkshire Playhouse in Stockbridge, even without a Tallulah Bankhead to enliven its stage, was successfully running a ten-week season. At Williamstown, less than an hour away, there was another playhouse, and the new Sterling and Francis Clark Art Museum had opened. Various other artistic and entertainment ventures came into being over the years. Few other areas in the United States offered as much cultural variety as the northwestern corner of Massachusetts, and Tanglewood was its hub.

New Music, New Musicians

Of the sixty or so concerts presented at Tanglewood during the Munch regime, none were more important to the Festival's future than two modest programs of chamber music given in the Theater-Concert Hall in 1956. What made them unusual was they were devoted exclusively to contemporary works, and what made them significant was that they were the beginning of a commitment to the music of today that was to expand and deepen in the years ahead.

The concerts served to introduce to the Tanglewood scene one of the most generous but reticent benefactors of new American music, a fifty-year-old German-born immigrant named Paul Fromm. In 1952 Fromm, a Chicago importer of European wines, had established the Fromm Music Foundation, devoted to commissioning new works and getting them performed, published and recorded. Fromm, who had come here as a refugee from Hitler's Germany, began by sponsoring concerts in Chicago and in succeeding years extended his activities elsewhere. He had never met Koussevitzky, but admired his activities on behalf of new music, and Tanglewood, with its young performers and huge audiences, seemed like an ideal site for Fromm-supported concerts. In 1956 he approached Copland and suggested "we do something to help contemporary music and also to end the alienation between contemporary composers and performers." To this end he offered to underwrite two concerts, the forerunners of what later became the Fromm-supported "festival-within-a-festival" of contemporary music at Tanglewood.

The composers represented in the first Fromm concerts were Goffredo Petrassi, Samuel Barber, Leland Smith and Julian Orban; the performers were mainly instrumentalists of the Boston Symphony. In 1957 two more Fromm concerts were given, with the audience again invited gratis. The most imposing works were Irving Fine's Fantasia for String Trio, which re-

Tour buses added to the traffic tangle at the main gate in the 1950s.
(Courtesy the *Berkshire Eagle*)

ceived its premiere, and Easley Blackwood's String Quartet No. 1—the latter commissioned by the Fromm Foundation. From then on every year brought forth at least two Fromm concerts, and these gradually began to be augmented by lectures and seminars on modern music. Fromm himself, a benign-looking man with a Henry Kissinger accent, came to Tanglewood in 1956 to listen to the music he helped bring to life, and has since been back every season, usually sitting in the audience of the Theater-Concert Hall unbeknownst to most of the people around him.

From the very start Fromm has been aware that the music he commissions is controversial, and that its detractors very probably outnumber its admirers. Yet he is convinced that if music itself is not to die out, it is essential to assist in the creation and performance of new works. No other aspect of his campaign does he consider more important than his Tanglewood concerts, which marked their twentieth anniversary in 1976.

"Look," he says, "I never think of the compositions we commission as successes or failures. We do whatever we have to do to create a nucleus of musical culture. We can play Beethoven year after year. It's like looking at the beautiful trees around here—they're beautiful but we have to plant new ones. We have seen Stravinsky, Hindemith, Milhaud, and others all accepted in time. We have to develop perspective and patience. In this country we're always in a hurry, but some things can't be done in a hurry. Who knows what music will be like in the twenty-first century? All we know is that we try to support composers who have individuality and are masters of their craft. You can never be in search of masterworks; somehow the masterworks emerge by themselves."

One outcome of Fromm's activities at Tanglewood was the formation of groups of young performers, the Fromm Fellowship Players, who made a specialty of playing contemporary chamber music. Starting in 1957 fellowships at the Berkshire Music Center were given to students specifically for the purpose of reading and performing contemporary works. In 1957 there were ten Fromm Fellows, a number which gradually increased to an average of forty a year.

In 1959 four young Berkshire Music Center veterans, violinists Peter Marsh and Theodora Mantz, violist Scott Nickrens and cellist Donald McCall, formed a string quartet whose major interest was in the modern field. At first they wished to call themselves the Fromm Quartet, but when Paul Fromm asked them "not to honor me posthumously in my lifetime" they took the name Lenox String Quartet. After playing at Tanglewood they made their New York debut on November 23, 1959, at the New School for Social Research, with an all-modern program consisting of music by Roger Ses-

The Dorian Wind Quintet is one of the performing organizations that grew out of the Fromm contemporary music series. Bassoonist Jane Taylor has been a member since its inception. (Courtesy Lyra Management, Inc.)

William Warfield, Leontyne Price and Leonard Bernstein after *Porgy and Bess* performance. (Courtesy the *Berkshire Eagle*)

sions, Leon Kirchner, Milton Babbitt and Ernst Křenek. With some changes in personnel, the Lenox Quartet has flourished ever since.

In 1961 a second permanent group, the Dorian Wind Quintet, grew out of the Fromm Players in Tanglewood. It consisted originally of John Perras, flute; David Perkette, oboe; Arthur Bloom, clarinet; Jane Taylor, bassoon; and William Brown, horn. Once more, time has produced changes, and Miss Taylor is the only original member still left, but the Dorian Quintet continues to perform widely in the United States, records extensively and has made several tours abroad.

Jane Taylor's experience is typical of what Tanglewood could mean to a young instrumentalist in the 1950s. A music and arts major at Queens College in New York City, she had gone to the Berkshires to visit friends in 1952 and decided to enroll in the Center in 1953. She studied in a chamber music group headed by Sherman Walt, who shortly before had been appointed first bassoon of the Boston Symphony. After her summer at Tanglewood Miss Taylor managed to get a job as second bassoonist of the Orlando, Florida, Symphony Orchestra. "They were desperate and I was available," is the way she puts it. "I had free-lanced some in New York, but for them my claim to fame was that I'd been at Tanglewood."

Jane spent four years in Orlando, then returned to New York for more free-lancing. Early in 1960 she heard that Tanglewood was recruiting young musicians for the year's crop of Fromm Players—specifically to perform works that would be written by students in the composition department, which that summer was to have Luciano Berio as guest teacher. Wind players were in particular demand, so Jane and a group of friends, several of whom were also Berkshire alumni, applied en masse for Fromm Fellowships. Not only were they accepted, they were invited back as a unit for a second summer, during which they worked with, among others, Elliott Carter.

"We weren't an ideal quintet, musically or personally," Jane Taylor says, "and we made some changes. But we had seen the Lenox Quartet and how well they had functioned, so we thought we could do it. We made our debut in Carnegie Recital Hall on October 17, 1961, and we've been playing, traveling and even commissioning works ourselves ever since."

The decade of the 1950s was also productive of an impressive batch of important new conductors who learned their trade and launched their careers at Tanglewood. The conducting class of 1958 was especially reminiscent of the fabulous crop of 1940, for it included three students who went on to major careers—Claudio Abbado, Zubin Mehta and David Zinman.

Abbado had met Bernstein in his native Italy some years before and had been encouraged by him to study conducting, which he did at the Verdi

Conservatory in Milan and later at the Vienna Academy of Music. In Vienna he became friendly with Mehta, a twenty-year-old Indian Parsee from Bombay, who had gone to the academy to study under Hans Swarowsky. The two young men continued their friendship at Tanglewood; at the annual award-giving which concludes every Berkshire Music Center season, Abbado won the Koussevitzky Prize for conducting while Mehta won the runner-up Gertrude Robinson Smith prize.

Mehta says he cannot remember who in Europe first told him about Tanglewood. "I just knew about it," he says. "I wrote to them, I told what I had done, they accepted me. De Carvalho was running the conducting program. For me, one of the nicest parts of Tanglewood was the first impression it gave me of America—such a beautiful place. It wasn't like starting out in New York, which is rather a jolt. That, and listening to the Boston Symphony Orchestra playing under Munch and Monteux—such a repertoire, and such playing! The standard of the student orchestra was very high, too. It was exhilarating."

Even as a student at Tanglewood, Mehta exhibited the dash and flair that became his hallmark as a conductor. Nobody yet called him "Zubi baby," which later became his nickname in Los Angeles; but when he conducted works like Richard Strauss' *Don Juan* and Schoenberg's *Chamber Symphony* with the student orchestra, it was obvious that he was a young man of both talent and temperament. Munch, who always took an interest in the more outstanding students no matter how neglectful he was of the school's administrative workings, recommended Mehta for a guest-conducting stint with the Montreal Symphony, whose own conductor had resigned because of ill-health. Mehta was soon appointed permanent conductor in Montreal, and by 1962, at the age of twenty-six, he became head of the Los Angeles Philharmonic. Although he has not guest-conducted at Tanglewood, he retains sentimental ties; when a bassoon student of Sherman Walt applied for a job in Los Angeles, Mehta said to him nostalgically, "If you see Mr. Walt, ask him if he remembers me." In 1976, having overcome his original aversion to New York, Mehta was named to succeed Pierre Boulez as music director of the New York Philharmonic, effective in 1978. In the twenty years since Tanglewood, Zubi baby has come a long way.

Equally meteoric has been the career of another young conductor, who was first called to the attention of the Tanglewood administration by a letter to Olga Koussevitzky from a music-loving Finnish diplomat she had met some years previously when both served on a committee planning to honor Jan Sibelius on his ninetieth birthday. The letter was written from Munich, where the diplomat was stationed, in October, 1959:

Dear Mrs. Koussevitzky:

In September I attended a contest for young conductors held at the Besançon Music Festival. There were forty-eight participants from seventeen countries. In the professional class (i.e., those who had ever earned money for conducting) the winner was a twenty-three-year-old Japanese, Seiji Ozawa.

While talking with him afterwards Mr. Ozawa told me that his scholarship from Japan lasts until the end of this year and that he would then like to leave Paris and go to the United States for further study. I write to you to ask if there would be a possibility that he be invited next summer to Tanglewood, to study conducting.

If I say that I was very much impressed by the performance of Mr. Ozawa, it means next to nothing because I am not an expert. I will therefore list the reasons why I think it would be worth while trying to help him. First of all, the seven-man jury *unanimously* considered him best and I was told that M. Eugène Bigot, the chairman, was very enthusiastic about him. Next, I discussed Mr. Ozawa for over an hour with Lorin Maazel, a conductor who has a very good name here and who was a member of the jury. He said that as far as he could judge from one twenty-two minute performance he thought that Mr. Ozawa was particularly talented and that he definitely is worth helping. Mr. Maazel said that he knows of no better place anywhere to learn conducting than at Tanglewood, particularly if one can be one of the three or so who have a special chance to conduct daily.*

Knowing that Mr. [Charles] Munch was coming to Besançon I tried to arrange that Mr. Ozawa would have an opportunity to speak with him. Since I had to leave earlier I do not know if he succeeded.

As a person Mr. Ozawa is both extremely charming and modest. He thinks that he needs still much study, particularly of western music. I understand that he has very little money and that his scholarship from Japan is just enough to permit him to live in Paris. As an indication of his modesty and eagerness to learn more I will mention that he told me the day after his victory that he had heard that it was easy to get a job in the United States as a "dishwasher or playing the organ in a church." . . .

Sincerely,
Piltti Heiskanen

*Maazel, as previously noted, had been a conducting student at Tanglewood in 1951. Subsequently he conducted and recorded extensively in Europe before returning to the United States to succeed George Szell as music director in Cleveland.

A youthful Seiji Ozawa at Tanglewood. (Courtesy Whitestone Photographers)

Ozawa's triumph at the Besançon competition in 1959 was his first major European success. He was born in 1935 in Hoten, Manchuria, the third of four sons of Kaisaku Ozawa, a dentist, and his wife Sakura Ozawa. In 1944 his family moved to Tokyo, where he first studied piano privately. At the age of sixteen he entered the newly established Toho School of Music. There he quickly developed an interest in Western musical styles. An injury to a finger during a soccer game forced him to give up any idea of a piano career, so he turned instead to composition and conducting. He won first prizes in both subjects at his graduation in 1959. He also conducted the Japan Radio Orchestra (NHK) and the Japan Philharmonic Orchestra. A Japanese music magazine, *Friends of Music,* named him the outstanding young talent of 1959.

Ozawa decided to go to Europe for further study, and to help pay his way there he persuaded the Honda motorcycle company to let him promote its vehicles. Supporting himself by various odd jobs, he traveled by motor scooter from Italy to France and entered the Besançon contest. His victory there suddenly opened up to him the possibility of study in the United States, even though he knew scarcely any English. Piltti Heiskanen recalls that Ozawa's entire English vocabulary at the time consisted of three words, which he kept repeating when asked how he felt about winning the competition: "Oh so wonderful! Oh so wonderful! Oh so wonderful!"—each time with rising emphasis. He also kept repeating to the Finnish diplomat, in French, which he did speak, that he was ready to wash dishes to finance his studies.

In her reply to Heiskanen, Mrs. Koussevitzky advised him to have "your young Japanese conductor" get in touch with Burkat, the administrator of the Berkshire Music Center, and apply for a Tanglewood scholarship the following summer. Meanwhile Heiskanen's attempts to arrange a meeting between Ozawa and Munch at Besançon had been successful, and Munch added his endorsement to the application. As a result Burkat wrote to Ozawa informing him that he could have a full fellowship for the 1960 Berkshire Music Center session, though he would have to pay his own transatlantic air fare.

The young Japanese accordingly arrived one summer day at Logan International Airport in Boston carrying a piece of paper with the words LENOX, MASS. A kindly bystander managed to help him board a bus bound for Lenox. It happened to be a local bus, with frequent stops, so Ozawa got a prolonged look at the Massachusetts countryside the first day.

At Tanglewood Ozawa quickly established himself as the most dynamic

In his student days at Tanglewood in 1960, Seiji Ozawa was shy and short-haired. Here he is with Eleazar de Carvalho (center) who headed the conducting department, and Munch, who took an active role in furthering his career. (Courtesy Whitestone Photographers)

Boris Goldovsky (center) with technical director Thomas de Gaetani (left) and scenic designer David Hayes work on operatic staging in 1959. Picture was made at 4 A.M. during an all-night session. (Courtesy the *Berkshire Eagle*)

of de Carvalho's conducting students that year. Munch took a keen interest in the young man he had met at Besançon, and was particularly impressed by a reading he gave of Fauré's *Pelléas et Mélisande* Suite. All this time, Piltti Heiskanen had had no word from Ozawa, and did not even know he had gone to America. But on August 13, 1960, he received a cable reading: GRATEFUL FOR YOUR HELP. SORRY I COULD NOT WRITE. WON KOUSSEVITZKY PRIZE. SEIJI OZAWA.

The Koussevitzky Prize carried with it a $500 cash award. Ozawa promptly invested $90 of it in an ancient Oldsmobile with which he took a brief motor trip through upstate New York and New England. Then he returned to Europe for further study. But few who had heard him in Tanglewood the summer of 1960 doubted that he would be back.

The Roof Falls In

Charles Munch spent his last two seasons at Tanglewood with his successor looking over his shoulder. His retirement as music director of the Boston Symphony, at the age of seventy, was set for September, 1962, but it was announced in April, 1961. At the same time, Erich Leinsdorf, some twenty years younger, was designated as his successor. The trustees invited Leinsdorf to spend the entire summer of 1961 in the Berkshires, familiarizing himself with the Tanglewood situation, and he also returned for a shorter period the following year. As it turned out, there was quite a lot for him to observe.

The first untoward incident occurred before Leinsdorf's arrival when the roof caved in on the Theater-Concert Hall during a March snowstorm. James F. Kiley, who had succeeded Ward Gaston as superintendent of grounds in 1958, was eating Sunday dinner in his house, located just beyond the fence opposite the Theater-Concert Hall when he heard a loud, explosivelike report. The wooden top of the empty structure had buckled under the weight of the snow, and the ensuing crash had blown out all the doors. The roof had been supported by wooden girders fastened together at the joints by riveted steel braces—this combination of materials being the best available in the immediate post-World War II era, when the structure was erected. It now became necessary to redesign the building, using steel trusses and girders, as in the Shed. The job was entrusted to Prentice Bradley, a Pittsfield architect, and swiftly completed.

But two months later the roof fell in in a more significant, even if fig-

James F. Kiley, head of operations, surveys collapsed roof of Theater-Concert Hall after snowfall early in 1958. Repairs were completed in time for that year's Festival. (Courtesy the *Berkshire Eagle*)

urative, manner when *The New York Times* ran a Sunday article by Harold C. Schonberg severely criticizing Tanglewood's programs and policies under Munch. Watching the ever-increasing crowds pour through the gates for their regular allotment of Beethoven and Tchaikovsky symphonies, with an occasional dash of Berlioz or Richard Strauss, the Festival officials had paid little attention to such critical complaints in the past. But the *Times* blast was too emphatic and comprehensive to ignore. Entitling his article "Warmed Over," Schonberg wrote:

> How festive should a festival be? Should the idea of a music festival imply something out of the ordinary? If so, the programs of the oncoming Berkshire Festival are about as festive as a ballroom after the ball is over. It was with a sinking feeling that we looked over the recently announced programs—programs with no unity, no theme, no adventure, hardly any novelties; programs with the same conductors and soloists as of yore. . . .
>
> From July 7 to Aug. 20, sixty-seven pieces of music will be played. The first two weekends will once again be devoted to Bach and Mozart. The other five will contain popular symphonies, many of them taken from the regular Boston Symphony season in Boston and New York. Three important contemporary pieces of music, the Poulenc "Gloria,"

Schuman's Seventh Symphony and the Foss "Time Cycle" will be conducted by Charles Munch and Leonard Bernstein, both of whom were responsible for the premieres last season. Mr. Bernstein will be doing the "Symphony of Psalms" by Stravinsky. He has conducted it with the New York Philharmonic. About the only major work not heard during the regular winter season will be Mahler's "Resurrection" Symphony and Bartok's Viola Concerto.

The conclusion seems inescapable that neither the conductors nor the sponsors of the festival are going much out of their way. Perhaps they figure that what has worked so well in the past should work equally well in the future, and why trifle with a good thing? One hesitates to accuse these good gentlemen of cynicism. But certainly the Berkshire Festival programs, which year in and year out repeat the same material, make a sorry showing for what is commonly supposed to be the most important music festival in America. . . .

Schonberg's article produced consternation in Boston and impelled Tod Perry to fire off a letter of reply on behalf of the orchestra.

"Mr. Schonberg indicates in his opening sentence," wrote Perry, "that a festival should imply something 'fresh and out of the ordinary.' He may believe so, but this is his own addition to the definition by Webster, who says a festival is 'a periodic seasonal entertainment of a specific sort; as a music festival,' or the Oxford dictionary: 'a musical performance, or series of performances, at recurring periods, e.g., the Handel Festival.'"

Perry's letter went on to say that Tanglewood had always, from the start, intended "to offer music from the orchestra's recent repertoire, at the highest level of performance." He explained that it was the orchestra's established policy to select from music already played in New York or Boston, to freshen it up through rehearsals—"to wed the festival offerings to the winter repertoire." Since this had so long been the policy, Perry said he was surprised that "so knowledgeable a reviewer . . . would argue this practice is shabby, sleepy, base, unworthy or otherwise reprehensible. . . . We are quite aware of what we are doing and we offer no apologies for the course we follow."

The 1961 Shed season, accordingly, ran along its predestined course, with such war-horses as the Franck D Minor Symphony, Beethoven's *Eroica,* Tchaikovsky's Fifth and Sixth, Rachmaninoff's Piano Concerto No. 2 played by Gary Graffman, and the Schumann Piano Concerto by Eugene Istomin. Eugene Ormandy of the Philadelphia Orchestra made his first Tanglewood appearance directing one of the summer's more venturesome programs—Strauss' *Don Juan,* Roy Harris' Symphony No. 3 and Albert

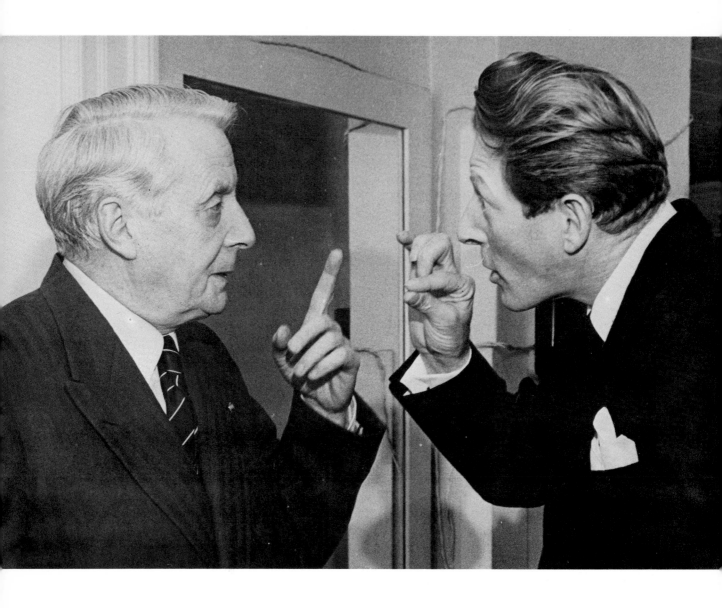

Danny Kaye, a guest artist at a 1961 benefit concert, discusses conducting technique with Charles Munch. (Courtesy the Boston Symphony Orchestra)

Roussel's *Bacchus et Ariane*. Another new "conductor" was Danny Kaye, who directed a special benefit program on July 13.

Goldovsky's opera department, however, continued its penchant for the unusual, staging such rarely heard works as Busoni's *Arlecchino* and Donizetti's *Il Campanello*. But 1961, as it turned out, also represented the swan song of the opera department, and the cessation of Goldovsky's long and fruitful work at the Berkshire Music Center. Actually, opera had always been something of an exotic growth at Tanglewood, if only because the institution was run by a symphony orchestra. Doubts about opera's place at the Festival had long been harbored by some of the trustees, who objected to its cost. But Koussevitzky had wanted opera, and in this, as in most other matters, his wishes prevailed. After Koussevitzky's death, questions about the opera department's deficits became more frequent and pointed.

"The trustees began to have doubts about the need for this kind of thing," Goldovsky says, "and in a way they were right. All the other departments were useful for the Festival. To the trustees the Festival was always Number 1 and the school Number 2—which wasn't true, of course, of Koussevitzky. The opera department related only minimally to the Tanglewood concerts; there was very little contact between them. So in 1956 or '57 I was told they didn't have the money for opera."

Goldovsky's response was, essentially, to provide for his own financing. In 1946 he had established his New England Opera Theater (later called The Goldovsky Opera Institute) which in 1951 began touring nationally, often employing singers he had trained at Tanglewood or at the New England Conservatory. For years the Goldovsky company was one of the more important outlets for young American singers. Much of its work was supported by outside funding. When the cost of maintaining opera began to prove too burdensome for Tanglewood, Goldovsky made arrangements to use part of his Opera Institute grants for the purpose. Thus in his last years at Tanglewood he was not only directing the opera department but raising money for it himself.

The announcement of Leinsdorf's appointment as Boston Symphony and Berkshire Music Center director was the final blow to Goldovsky's department. Leinsdorf himself had an operatic background; equally important, he had strong ideas about how Tanglewood should be run. Goldovsky says that he began packing up as soon as he heard Leinsdorf was coming; and Leinsdorf leaves no doubt that Goldovsky's semi-independent operation did not fit into his plans.

Considering the many notable achievements of Goldovsky's fifteen

Olga Koussevitzky and Charles Munch.
(Courtesy the Boston Symphony
Orchestra; photo by Joe Petrovec)

summers at Tanglewood, it would have been fitting for his final offering to be a triumph. Unfortunately, it turned out to be his solitary fiasco. In line with his policy of selecting rare works, he had decided to give the first American performance of as obscure an opera as exists in the history books—*Il Re Teodoro in Venezia* (King Theodore in Venice) by Giovanni Paisiello, known to posterity as the composer whose *Barber of Seville* was almost totally effaced by Rossini's masterpiece on the same subject. To compound the difficulties of mounting so recondite a piece, it was discovered—after many hours of rehearsal—that the orchestral parts being used by the student orchestra were so poorly copied and semilegible as to be virtually unusable. In the end *King Theodore* had to be given with an accompaniment by two pianos. Leinsdorf says he wondered at the time why a work like Paisiello's opera was being presented by students supposedly being prepared for a professional career.

King Theodore or not, Goldovsky's years at Tanglewood had provided invaluable, not to say unique, training for a generation of opera singers; had uncovered and fostered some remarkable talents including the ineffable Sarah Caldwell; and had brought alive worthy works from *Idomeneo* to *Albert Herring.* Operatic activities have flickered from time to time at Tanglewood since Goldovsky's departure, but they have yet to reach a similarly significant level.

A general air of departure hung over Munch's final season at Tanglewood in 1962, with concertmaster Richard Burgin, who had joined the orchestra in 1920—five years before Koussevitzky—also retiring. His successor, promoted from the orchestra's ranks, was Joseph Silverstein.

Whether in answer to the criticisms of his programming or simply by coincidence, Munch's Shed concerts in his last season contained a somewhat larger proportion of contemporary works than the summers immediately preceding. Among the relatively new pieces he conducted were works by Piston, Honegger and Alexei Haeiff, as well as the Symphony of Irving Fine, who died that year at the untimely age of forty-eight. Guest-conducting appearances were made by two composers—Leon Kirchner—who directed his own *Sinfonia,* and Lukas Foss, playing his *Time Cycle.*

For his own final concert, Munch selected for his first offering another modern piece, Copland's *Quiet City.* But the feature of his last Tanglewood program was the same symphony that had provided other farewells before his, Beethoven's Ninth. The overflow crowd responded with a tremendous final ovation, and when the attendance for the summer was totaled up, it was found to have reached a new high of 217,642. So much for critics.

Innovative programs were a hallmark of Erich Leinsdorf's productive but controversial regime. His presentation of Mendelssohn's *A Midsummer Night's Dream* in his first summer included the vocal parts and employed a spectacularly garbed narrator, Patricia Peardon. (Courtesy Whitestone Photographers)

5. The Leinsdorf Regime

Reform Movement

Erich Leinsdorf's regime at Tanglewood—paralleling his tenure with the Boston Symphony—lasted only seven years, from 1963 through 1969. It was a hectic and eventful time. His departure from Boston, while maintaining the polite forms of resignation and acceptance and mutual expressions of regret and esteem, was anything but amicable. Even today mention of his regime both in Boston and Tanglewood brings forth expressions of opinion of equal vehemence whether pro or con. The orchestra members are divided. Some admired Leinsdorf for his musicianship and technical mastery. Others—a substantial number of others—found him too much of a martinet and disciplinarian, especially after the easygoing Munch. Even his adherents acknowledge that he was something less than a perfect administrator. Perry, who as manager was often at odds with Leinsdorf on policy matters, says: "He had a lot of ideas, but many of them didn't work." Whatever the reasons, Leinsdorf's years with the Boston Symphony, especially toward the end, engendered considerable tension on both the administrative and orchestral levels.

Yet so far as Tanglewood was concerned, Leinsdorf's was a time of tremendous productivity, ferment and change. There still are some associated with the Festival in both managerial and musical capacities who look back on those days longingly. Leinsdorf, who has gone on to a busy and varied career conducting symphony and opera all over the world—without any administrative burdens—says: "I have never for a minute missed Boston. But for Tanglewood I have a soft spot. It was such a beautiful, wonderful place."

Leinsdorf's appointment to head the Boston Symphony at the age of fifty—the same age that Koussevitzky took it over—had seemed at the time to climax a remarkable music career that had been marked both by spectacular successes and curious reverses. Leinsdorf was one of the many middle-European musicians who enriched American cultural life in the 1930s when they were forced to emigrate from their own countries by the rise of Adolf

Hitler. Leinsdorf, Viennese by birth, came to this country in 1938. He had been working summers as an assistant to Arturo Toscanini and Bruno Walter in Salzburg, and winters as an operatic conductor in such secondary musical centers as Bologna, San Remo and Trieste. He was engaged by the Metropolitan Opera in New York as a member of its musical staff with the idea that he might occasionally spell Artur Bodanzky, the supreme Wagnerian conductor of the house, who was showing signs of weariness. Although Leinsdorf was regarded as bright and promising, nobody expected him to take over the entire Wagnerian repertory at the Metropolitan. But that is just what he was called upon to do at the age of twenty-six when Bodanzky died four days before the opening of the 1939–40 season.

Leinsdorf's first reviews were extraordinary. Lawrence Gilman appraised him thus in the *Herald Tribune:* "Mr. Leinsdorf seems to have a cool head on his shoulders—he must have, or he could not conduct with the authority and poise he displays. If he retains his modest self-effacement and his obvious reverence for great music, heaven will look out for him. . . ." In 1943 Leinsdorf left the Metropolitan to succeed Artur Rodzinski as conductor of the Cleveland Orchestra—one of the youngest men, at thirty-three, ever to take command of a major American orchestra. A month later he was drafted into the United States Army, and although he received a medical discharge eight months afterwards, the Cleveland job, through some combination of circumstances never fully explained, was no longer his. Eventually it went to George Szell. After a number of return engagements at the Metropolitan Opera Leinsdorf accepted in 1947 the conductorship of the Rochester, New York, Philharmonic, a respected though second-rank orchestra. He remained in Rochester nine years, then was named director of the New York City Opera. His first and only season, devoted largely to modern works, was a financial failure, and Leinsdorf was left free to accept guest-conducting engagements from Tel Aviv to San Francisco. Eventually he resumed his affiliation with the Metropolitan Opera, where he became the chief musical consultant to general manager Rudolf Bing as well as one of the house's busiest conductors.

Leinsdorf also developed into one of the most versatile recording conductors in the business. At the time of his appointment to Boston he was embarked upon a number of ventures for RCA-Victor, and it was widely assumed that his recording connection influenced his selection for the job. It certainly worked out conveniently for all concerned, since the orchestra had long been one of the label's bulwarks, and remained so until 1970, when it switched its affiliation to Deutsche Grammophon. Said Tod Perry, talking to a reporter shortly after Leinsdorf's appointment was announced: "Dr. Munch is a be-

Erich Leinsdorf became deeply involved with all phases of Tanglewood activities during his tenure. Here he has an outdoor meeting with a class of conducting students. Seated on bench at far right, in shirtsleeves, is Richard Burgin, associate conductor of the Boston Symphony. (Courtesy Whitestone Photographers)

nign, convivial, and charming man, but he doesn't enjoy going in with a group of strangers, and he's not really comfortable unless he's speaking French. Leinsdorf, on the other hand, likes to talk, discuss, argue and listen. Munch's leadership was always there, but it gave few external signs. Leinsdorf's executive ability will be visible to the naked eye." As it turned out, it was perhaps a little too visible.

Although Tanglewood may not have been a primary factor in the appointment of Leinsdorf, the Boston Symphony trustees very much wanted their new conductor to assume an active role in its affairs. Of especial concern to them was the Berkshire Music Center. The school, now well into its third decade, was an integral part of the Tanglewood operation. But it was also becoming increasingly expensive to maintain, and it no longer stood alone as a place where ensemble training was available to young players. Other summer schools from Marlboro, Vermont, to Aspen, Colorado, came into being during the 1960s, and while they might not have matched the stature or the depth of the Berkshire faculty, they nevertheless introduced a new competitive element.

The trustees were prompt to direct Leinsdorf's attention to Tanglewood, as attested by their invitation to him to spend the summer of 1961 there prior to taking over the orchestra the following year. Furthermore, Henry Cabot took Leinsdorf aside and told him, in effect, that the Center was a costly operation and there was no point in continuing it unless it remained an outstanding institution. "He said that the Boston Symphony was in fine shape, but that the school needed new ideas" is the way Leinsdorf recalls the conversation. In any case, Leinsdorf proceeded to give not only the Berkshire Music Center but the Berkshire Festival itself the most thorough revamping they had undergone since Koussevitzky resumed the operation of both in 1946 after the World War II interregnum. And while some of the reforms he instituted have faded over the summers, an impressive proportion of them remains in effect to this day.

Leinsdorf's first priority was reorganization of the school. His summers of observation had led him to the conclusion that the Berkshire Music Center no longer had a "central idea" and that during the Munch years the various departments had become too independent of one another. To his way of thinking, the semiautonomous opera department was the prime example of a lack of any central administrative control, and he replaced it with a vocal department whose activities, he felt, would blend better with the rest of the Tanglewood operation.

Leinsdorf also concluded that the school had become too slack in its admissions policies. "I like the concept of a master class lasting eight weeks," he recalls. "But we had no business taking beginners for that period. I wanted an elite student corps, and I felt that we couldn't expect tuition; talent, not ability to pay, should be the only criterion for admission. We instituted a complete fellowship program, with no tuition at all for orchestral and conducting fellows."

As a result of Leinsdorf's new policy, the Berkshire Music Center program for 1963 had an enrollment of around 300—about 100 fewer than the previous average—and 60 percent of them were there tuition-free. He said his objective was to provide concentrated training in the basics of the profession, including the ability to read scores quickly and securely. Too many young musicians, he contended at the time—and still contends today—aim for solo stardom while neglecting to acquire a thorough musical education. Addressing the students at the opening ceremonies of his first Berkshire Music Center class on June 30, 1963, he declared: "We will certainly try to to make you more fully aware of what is involved in a total commitment to music. . . . Our faculty members are determined not to encourage sluggish minds or mediocre ability. That group is unfortunately more than sufficiently represented within our profession."

With the actual start of sessions Leinsdorf put his ideas into practice. He arranged for a series of seminars and symposiums, including one on the problems of string players. He emphasized chamber music practice and instruction to expose the students to the needs and niceties of ensemble performance. When rising young pianists like Malcolm Frager or Lorin Hollander were scheduled for guest appearances with the orchestra, Leinsdorf brought them across the lawn to meet and talk with Center students. Eugene Ormandy, who made two guest appearances in the Shed, obligingly agreed also to conduct the student orchestra. Leinsdorf himself was on the scene everywhere, visiting classes, overseeing rehearsals, even sitting in the ranks of the student orchestra to observe the young conductors close up. A reporter attending one such session heard him stop a student conductor in midbeat and ask: "Why didn't the orchestra play for you there? Are you taking the orchestra's tempo or are they taking yours? Be honest with me."

There was no doubt that such blunt questioning sometimes shook up the student musicians, or that the Berkshire Music Center became a more competitive and demanding institution than it had been during Munch's tenure. "Leinsdorf stripped the place down to the musical essentials" is the way Harry Kraut, the Center's administrator from 1963 to 1971, sums up the change. Boston Symphony concertmaster Joseph Silverstein, who played an increasingly important role at the Center over the years and eventually became its chairman of faculty, is among those who believe that Leinsdorf's changes left a lasting beneficial effect upon the school. "Whatever his differences with the trustees over the orchestra itself," says Silverstein, "at Tanglewood he was allowed to do what he thought necessary. The present prosperity and status of the Berkshire Music Center is due as much to him as anything else."

In Search of a Theme

Leinsdorf's revamping of the school's operations were paralleled by an equally thorough reorientation of the Festival concerts themselves. For the more than 200,000 visitors who now came to Tanglewood annually, these changes were, of course, the most visible and important of those wrought by the new director. With the Festival, as with the school, Leinsdorf left no doubt of his intentions. He wanted, he said, to give Tanglewood's concerts a coherence, thrust and freshness that they had lacked for many years. To this end he announced that each summer's Festival would, when possible, be built around a "theme." For 1963 he selected a celebration of the music of Serge Prokofiev, who had died ten years previously on March 5, 1953. Fourteen works by Prokofiev were scheduled, including the Piano Concertos Nos. 1, 2, 3 and 5 (with Frager, Hollander and Jorge Bolet the soloists), the Symphonies Nos. 5 and 6, *Alexander Nevsky,* and various other works new to Tanglewood audiences. Altogether there were thirty-seven compositions by nineteen contemporary composers to be heard in the summer's orchestral and chamber concerts.

Leinsdorf also arranged for Tanglewood to be the scene of its most important premiere since *Peter Grimes* in 1946. Once again the work given was by Benjamin Britten, this time his *War Requiem,* a majestic score combining the standard Latin liturgical text with the World War I poems of Wilfred Owen. Britten's *War Requiem* had first been presented at the rededication of the bombed-out St. Michael's Cathedral in Coventry, England, in May, 1962. Several American orchestras had vied for the privilege of giving it its first American hearing, and Boston had won out. Leinsdorf might easily have performed it in Symphony Hall, but he saw the opportunity of presenting it in the far more spacious Tanglewood Shed, where it would attract a large audience, bring the out-of-town critics flocking and once again make the Berkshire Festival a focus of national interest. He was right on all counts. A

Leinsdorf directs the student choir at a nighttime rehearsal. (Courtesy Whitestone Photographers)

throng of 10,811 attended—four times the capacity of Symphony Hall—and the Boston and New York critics turned out, as did many from more distant cities. Leinsdorf conducted the premiere on July 27, 1963, and a performing force of 200 was onstage, including, besides the orchestra, the Chorus Pro Musica of Boston, the Columbus Boychoir and soloists Phyllis Curtin, soprano; Nicholas di Virgilio, tenor; and Tom Krause, baritone. The performance, dedicated to the memory of Koussevitzky, brought an ovation that lasted twenty minutes.

The *War Requiem* by no means exhausted Leinsdorf's capacity for innovation. In his first Tanglewood season he also gave the first all-Haydn program in the Festival's history; presented Mozart's Requiem in memory of Pope John XXIII; directed a memorable performance of Mendelssohn's *A Midsummer Night's Dream* including the usually omitted vocal portions.

In succeeding seasons Leinsdorf continued his search for a central theme. In 1964 he found it in the 100th anniversary of the birth of Richard Strauss, and scheduled thirteen of his works, winding up with *Ein Heldenleben*. In 1965 his centerpiece was an uncut performance of Wagner's opera *Lohengrin,* spread out over a single weekend, one act at a time. It was the first time that an entire weekend had ever been devoted to one work; it also was the closest that Tanglewood ever came to being Bayreuth. Such a piecemeal venture seemed peculiar both artistically and commercially, the only possible explanation being that Leinsdorf was later making a recording of the opera with the orchestra and singers—Lucine Amara, Rita Gorr, Sandor Konya, William Dooley and Jerome Hines. In 1966 Leinsdorf built the Festival around "The Romantic Concerto," a "theme" that had considerable box-office appeal and also allowed for the engagement of a formidable array of soloists headed by Van Cliburn who played the Rachmaninoff Piano Concerto No. 3 in D Minor.

The theme approach eventually was dropped, but throughout his regime Leinsdorf managed to schedule works seldom or never performed in the Berkshires. Such selections were marked in the printed programs with daggers, and some seasons fairly bristled with them.

No one welcomed the advent of Leinsdorf more warmly than Paul Fromm, the businessman who had been financially supporting contemporary music activities at Tanglewood since 1956. At the outset Leinsdorf indicated his desire to integrate these more fully into the annual operation. The Juilliard String Quartet was invited to give a series of Tuesday-night contemporary chamber recitals. The Fromm Fellowship Players performed other new works in a Monday-night series. Roundtables and seminars were held on contem-

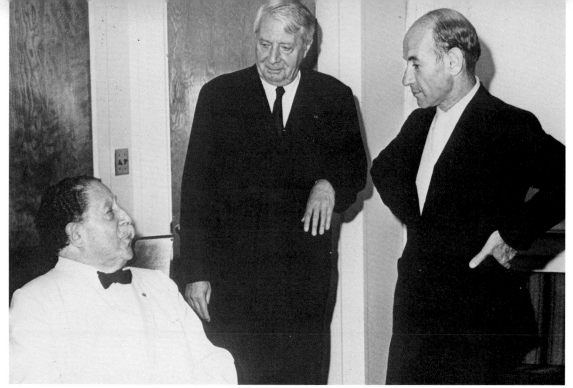

Boston Symphony conductors of three eras gather at Tanglewood. From left, Monteux, Munch, and Leinsdorf. (Courtesy Whitestone Photographers)

Mrs. Koussevitzky, Paul Fromm, and Michael Tilson Thomas photographed during Fromm Week in 1973. (Courtesy Whitestone Photographers)

A concert version of Wagner's opera *Lohengrin,* uncut, is conducted by Erich Leinsdorf in the Shed. With one act at a time, the performance took a whole weekend in 1965. (Courtesy Whitestone Photographers)

porary music, with Yannis Xenakis, Lukas Foss, Gunther Schuller and Arthur Berger among the participating composers.

In 1964 contemporary music activities at Tanglewood were systematized into a five-day "festival within a festival," during which the entire energies of the Berkshire Music Center were concentrated on performances of contemporary works. The "Fromm Week" has remained a Tanglewood fixture ever since; a sometimes stimulating, sometimes exasperating interlude for the performers no less than for audiences. Sometimes the Fromm concerts have also served to focus attention on a promising conductor, as in 1968 when *Elephant Steps,* a madcap "electronic opera" by Stanley Silverman, was conducted by Michael Tilson Thomas, a student from Los Angeles. Thomas won the Koussevitzky Prize, returned to Tanglewood the following summer and subsequently went on to a brilliant career, including an appointment as associate conductor of the Boston Symphony and later the musical directorship of the Buffalo Philharmonic.

Among the portents of changing times at Tanglewood was the arrival on the scene of Gunther Schuller. Originally invited by Leinsdorf as a guest member of the faculty he actually embodied the new generation of composers whose philosophy, for better or worse, was to take the place of the school of thought represented by Aaron Copland and his followers, which for so long had dominated the Berkshire Music Center. Henceforth the Center was to be more attuned to the avant-garde, the electronic, the experimental.

Schuller came of a musical family reaching back several generations. His father, Arthur E. Schuller, had been a violinist and violist with the New York Philharmonic Symphony Orchestra and had actually been one of the musicians who traveled with Henry Hadley to the Berkshires for the very first Festival in 1934. Gunther, who was born in 1925 in New York City but who spent four years of his childhood in Germany, became a French horn player, serving as an extra musician with the Philharmonic under Toscanini while still attending classes at Jamaica High School in Queens. Eventually he became the first horn of the Metropolitan Opera Orchestra, which is where he met Leinsdorf.

Schuller's interests extended to jazz as well as to symphonic music; it was he who coined the term "third stream" to indicate the confluence of the two styles he found developing in modern music. His range of talents was formidable, and he soon found himself in demand as a composer as well as a performer. Eventually he left the Metropolitan orchestra to work on some of the commissions that poured in on him. When Leinsdorf moved to Tanglewood, he immediately invited Schuller to join him. Eventually Schuller's edu-

Contemporary music conference: from left, Foundation head Paul Fromm, composer Elliott Carter, Erich Leinsdorf, Aaron Copland. (Courtesy Whitestone Photographers)

Among changes made by Leinsdorf was the addition of "third-stream" composer Gunther Schuller (right) to the faculty. Schuller eventually replaced Aaron Copland as mentor of young composers at Berkshire Music Center. (Courtesy Whitestone Photographers)

cational work at Tanglewood led to his being appointed president of the New England Conservatory of Music in Boston.

Schuller began to shoulder increasing responsibilities at the Berkshire Music Center although Copland remained as its official head for several years after Leinsdorf's advent. In 1963, his first year, he led a jazz concert by the Center's musicians one Friday afternoon. He also became involved in the Fromm Foundation concerts; indeed, he later became one of the Foundation's directors.

By now Tanglewood had attained an age, though not a solemnity, that entitled it to begin celebrating anniversaries regularly. In 1965 it marked the twenty-fifth anniversary of the establishment of the Berkshire Music Center, and in 1966 the thirtieth year since the Boston Symphony joined the Berkshire Festival. The major celebratory event was the unveiling of a plaque on the Shed in honor of Henry Hadley, who had hitherto not been accorded such an honor. The plaque was contributed by the National Association of American Composers and Conductors, which Hadley had founded, and his widow was among the participants in the ceremony.

The Berkshire Music Center's celebration of its first quarter-century was a gala affair at which Bernstein (Class of '40), de Carvalho (Class of '46) and Leinsdorf all made conducting appearances. Bernstein's contribution, as at Tanglewood on Parade twelve years previously, was Act IV of *Carmen* with leading roles taken by Rosalind Elias ('51) and George Shirley ('60). De Carvalho led the student orchestra in Aaron Copland's *Outdoor Overture,* a tribute to a faculty member who had been with the school ever since its inception, even though he was now gradually loosening his ties with it. Leinsdorf directed Dvorak's "New World" Symphony. Ozawa ('60) also made an appearance connected with the Center's anniversary conducting Isaac Stern, Leonard Rose and Eugene Istomin in Beethoven's Triple Concerto in C.

There also were commemorations to observe. Pierre Monteux died on July 1, 1964, at the age of eighty-nine, a few weeks before he was scheduled to make one of his regular Tanglewood guest-conducting appearances. Leinsdorf accordingly dedicated the first concert of the year, an all-Mozart program, to his memory, with the audience standing in silent tribute after Helen Boatwright and the student choir sang the Kyrie from the Mass in C Minor. The concert Monteux was to have conducted, consisting of Beethoven's *Egmont* Overture, Ravel's *Alborado del Gracioso* and Elgar's *Symphonic Variations,* was taken over intact by Ormandy. The same summer a performance of Schubert's Mass in E-flat was dedicated to the memory of

Gertrude Robinson Smith. The woman whose energy and perserverance had done so much to bring the Berkshire Festival into being had died in New York City the previous October. She had seen three conductors—Hadley, Koussevitzky and Munch—come and go, and to the end regarded Tanglewood, with some justification, as "her" Festival, even though she had long since been cut off from any participation in its affairs. The plaque in her memory on the Shed and the conducting award that bears her name constitute a modest recognition of her great contribution.

During the 1966 season Leinsdorf instituted a change in his weekend scheduling that proved so successful that it has remained a Tanglewood custom ever since. Rather than starting the Friday-night concerts at 8 P.M. he moved them back to 9, thus permitting weekend travelers an extra hour to complete their trip to the grounds. However, for those who preferred to arrive early, he scheduled a weekend "Prelude" each Friday at 7 P.M. —a preliminary concert in the Shed, usually involving a chamber ensemble or even a solo performer in a program of unusual musical interest, sometimes allied in spirit to the symphony concert that followed, and sometimes totally independent of it.

Thus, preceding the all-Mozart orchestral concert of July 8, early arrivals could hear a selection of the composer's rarely performed "Scatological Canons" sung by the Tanglewood Festival Choir, and his two-piano Sonata, K. 448, played by Claude Frank and Lilian Kallir. On July 22 a Chopin Piano Trio and part-songs by Mendelssohn and Rachmaninoff preceded an orchestral program led by Ozawa, and on August 5 Mozart songs and an organ fantasia served as an introduction to a program by the full orchestra devoted to Prokofiev, Saint-Saëns and Schumann. The Weekend Preludes, during which the audience is permitted to sit anywhere in the Shed regardless of their ticket locations for the concert to follow, have on many occasions proved among the most rewarding aspects of a trip to Tanglewood.

Still another seasonal attendance mark was reached in 1966, with a total audience of 236,196 and box-office receipts of $625,994.50. These figures were especially heartening to Tanglewood officials, for a major new festival had opened less than two hours' drive to the northwest—the Saratoga Performing Arts Center in Saratoga Springs, New York, with a handsome and sturdy open-sided theater seating 5,100 and the New York City Ballet and the Philadelphia Orchestra as its annual summer occupants.

Saratoga, however, had no adjunct comparable to the Berkshire Music Center, which in 1966 helped advance another young conductor on the

Audience even sits on the stairs during a Sunday afternoon concert by Leinsdorf. Both audience and orchestra are in shirtsleeves. (Courtesy Whitestone Photographers)

road to a major career. This was Lawrence Foster, twenty-four years old, who had worked for one year as assistant to Zubin Mehta at the Los Angeles Philharmonic. Foster, who later was to be appointed music director of the Houston Symphony Orchestra, won the Koussevitzky Prize for 1966, directing the student orchestra at its final concert of the year in Mozart's *Serenata Notturna* in D, K. 239, and Beethoven's *Leonore* Overture No. 3.

"What Tanglewood did for me," says Larry Foster, "was to open my eyes to great vistas of understanding about conducting. There was a work schedule like I'd never seen before or since. I didn't know you could prepare so many works on such short notice. You felt that you had to perform on the highest level possible. It was a great learning experience, working with the men from the Boston Symphony."

Foster returned to his job assisting Mehta in Los Angeles but came back for a second summer in 1967. With his assumption of the musical directorship in Houston in 1971 he became increasingly recognized as one of the country's brightest young musical talents. In 1973 he was invited to return as a guest conductor to Tanglewood, directing in the Shed the orchestra he had observed so admiringly as a student.

In 1966 for the first time an outside educational organization became involved in the operations of the Berkshire Music Center. The Boston University School of Fine Arts launched a summer program on the grounds, offering two-week sessions, for college credit, in various cultural areas including music, dance and playwriting. Eventually the program concentrated on music, with about 150 students enrolling either for four-week or eight-week periods at their option. They were formed into their own orchestra, and received instruction from Boston Symphony members not hitherto involved in teaching activities. The Boston University Young Artists orchestra, made up mainly of players of high school age, each year gave its own series of concerts, usually with a remarkable degree of polish. By 1975 Boston University's Tanglewood Institute, directed by the composer Norman Dello Joio, a Berkshire alumnus of 1940 and 1941, was also offering a Young Vocalists Program, a Piano Seminar and sections in Applied Music and Harp Studies, all for college credit and with a tuition range of from $250 to $500. Occasionally the B.U. program has been the start of a notable career: trumpeter Rolf Smedvig was a member of the Young Artists Orchestra from 1968 through 1970, played in the Berkshire Music Center Orchestra in 1971 and 1972 and "graduated" into the Boston Symphony where he is now third trumpet. Trombonist Norman Bolter and violinist Gerald Elias followed the same route to join the orchestra in 1975.

Tension at the Top

Despite the step-up in activities and the profusion of ideas introduced by Leinsdorf—or, possibly, because of them—relations between him and the orchestra's management worsened year by year. Tanglewood did not lie at the center of the dispute; after all, it represented only eight of the fifty-two weeks that Leinsdorf was music director. In Boston there were arguments over personnel, programming and policies. Each side has its own stories to tell. Leinsdorf says that the orchestra's trustees, especially Henry Cabot, "preferred a music director who was not an activist." By way of explanation he adds: "Cabot was like Big Bill Thompson, the Mayor of Chicago, who kept on getting reelected by fighting Great Britain. When I was in Tanglewood, Cabot was still fighting Koussevitzky." Perry, who as the orchestra's manager in those seven years was often a participant in the give and take of the struggle, says that for all his gifts as a musician, as an administrator Leinsdorf was inflexible and often impractical. One of the conductor's closest musical associates adds: "Leinsdorf was a complex man. He had to be in charge of everything and was incapable of delegating anything. Between loving them to death and tyrannizing them, he left the orchestra bitter at him."

One of Leinsdorf's recurrent conflicts with the orchestra stemmed from rehearsal problems. This is a difficulty that besets every conductor at Tanglewood, or for that matter at any summer festival. When the Boston Symphony performs during regular winter season, it customarily prepares and gives one program a week, repeating it three or four times at subscription concerts in Symphony Hall or taking it to Providence, Hartford, New York and other cities on its circuit. At Tanglewood, however, three *different* programs are played on the three concerts each weekend, and each must be individually rehearsed. Thus, from the standpoint of the preparation required of the orchestra and the conductor, the eight-week Tanglewood season is the equivalent of twenty-four weeks in Boston, and the available rehearsal time is often inadequate.

This is one reason why orchestras in summer festivals tend to repeat works from their regular season—works they know thoroughly and can perform with only a quick preliminary brushup, or not even that. Leinsdorf became adept at "stealing" time from repertory the orchestra already knew well and utilizing it for the preparing of the more unusual and unfamiliar music. Nevertheless he kept running into problems of overtime and union regulations. In a privately distributed brochure entitled "Leadership in the Arts"* put out in 1975 by the Harvard University Institute in Arts Adminis-

*Courtesy the Institute in Arts Administration.

tration he described to an interviewer a crisis that arose over his demand for adequate time to prepare a concert performance of the original 1805 version of Beethoven's opera *Fidelio*.

We did, in 1967, at Tanglewood, the performance of Beethoven's original Leonore, the first version of 1805, and this was done on a Saturday night, and on Friday morning after having rehearsed very nicely the days before, I started at ten thirty and said, "This is a general rehearsal and I do not want to stop so I warn you if something happens, don't pay any attention. At the end of each big block, the two basic halves of the work, we'll make our comments, we'll have our questions, but we will not stop. I'll run this like a dress rehearsal." So the first act went that way and went very well. During the intermission I called the personnel manager* in and said, "Bill, we will have to go overtime because I can already see by the time we have our intermission, there will not be enough time to play once through the second half. Even without stops, it will go beyond one o'clock, because the rehearsal was two and a half hours. We figured out that I would start at 12:15 or 12:20 or something like this, and that would not give us enough time to finish by one.

So he said, "Well, that is all right, Mr. Leinsdorf; the overtime is, of course, necessary, but we have it in the master contract that five minutes after you start overtime you have to give an intermission of another five minutes."

"But," I said, "not during a dress rehearsal. Have it accrue to them at the end."

"No, no. It has to be done five minutes after one o'clock."

I said, "Now, Bill, I want to tell you something. I am not going to stop. I'm going to put my foot down in this instance, and whatever the consequences, if you find that the union insists that you stop me, then you have to do it before the people present on stage because I'm going to challenge the whole affair. This kind of thing cannot go on because either we do special things or we don't do special things. If we can't do them, then we throw away the whole thing and do a few symphonies and a few concertos and give up special programs."

So he said, "Well, it's going to be a lot of trouble."

I said, "I hope not, but I am going to take the chance."

Well, nobody stopped me. I finished the opera. But, as I understand it, there were meetings for weeks. The Committee visited Mr. Perry, and it was very disagreeable. There were protests and complaints that the contract had been violated. Well, this is what I mean. These stories could go on and on and on. . . .

* William Moyer, a former trombone player with the orchestra.

Despite such backstage incidents, Tanglewood flourished in Leinsdorf's last years. The school expanded its contemporary activities, celebrating the twenty-fifth anniversary of the Koussevitzky Music Foundation with a Fromm Festival that coincided with the annual conference, held on the grounds, of the Music Critics Association. The regular Shed concerts drew capacity audiences despite the general increase in prices which were beginning to become endemic on the American scene. Attendance in 1967 dropped slightly below the previous year's record level but still was the second highest in history. The summer was abnormally rainy; as if Leinsdorf did not have enough problems, an invasion of bugs in the humid weather made life miserable for everybody. So prevalent were the mosquitos and other insects that female soloists wearing low-cut gowns were sprayed with a special insecticide before going on stage; otherwise, Leinsdorf informed a postseason interviewer, "the girls would have had to swat themselves while performing, which is not easy to do."

A major increase in Tanglewood's attendance occurred in 1968, when the Festival, largely at the instigation of Schuller, decided to add a Tuesday-night series of rock-and-roll attractions to its hitherto strictly classical programming. To maintain some aura of artistic justification, the project was dressed up with the portentous title of "Contemporary Trends," but by any other name it would have remained recognizably rock. Recalls Harry Kraut, then the Berkshire Music Center's Administrator: "We had the feeling that while our audiences might not be getting smaller, they were getting older. All agreed that we needed some good rock music at Tanglewood to get more young people in; and we also thought we could make some money on it. We hoped to develop an audience not so much from New York or Boston, but from a 150-mile radius around—Hartford, Springfield, Albany and Schenectady. We went into it with trepidation and we were a little dazed by what happened."

What happened was that huge crowds turned out, creating monumental traffic jams on the roads to the grounds and covering the lawns with what Kraut describes as "wall-to-wall people." Among the participants in various events in the series were the Modern Jazz Quartet, Judy Collins and Ravi Shankar. The climax was reached on the night of the August 12 concert when a combined attraction of B. B. King, The Who and the Jefferson Airplane was greeted by a roaring crowd of 22,000, shattering all previous Tanglewood attendance records.

Another new audience was inveigled into coming to Tanglewood by a new community outreach program entitled "Days in the Arts," in which inner-city children were brought to the Berkshires to attend performances and to visit with students and orchestra members. The program, which at first entailed brief visits, was eventually developed into an annual five-day stay at Tanglewood, funded by the Massachusetts Department of Education, for groups of sixth-grade students from Boston, Brookline and Newton. The children were housed in the dormitory of a nearby private school, and Berkshire Music Center students helped provide hospitality by giving instrument demonstrations, talking to them about music and taking them for swims at the private beach on Lake Mahkeenac that Tanglewood maintains for its community. The "Days in the Arts" have become an eagerly awaited summer respite in many a Boston inner-city household.

But even as the Festival expanded into new areas and attracted new audiences, the behind-the-scenes quarrels between Leinsdorf and the orchestra's management grew more and more intense. Nevertheless, at the end of the 1967 Tanglewood season Leinsdorf expressed his elation with the summer's performances; called the Tanglewood audiences "wonderful," and said that he and the orchestra were working well together "now that we knew each other." Public statements to the contrary, however, Leinsdorf was at loggerheads with most (though not all) of his musicians, on the outs with the manager, and quarreling with the trustees. About the only thing that seemed to be going well, somehow, were the actual concerts.

In any case, it grew clear to all concerned that both the conductor and orchestra needed a change. In December of 1967 Leinsdorf announced his intention to resign as music director of the Boston Symphony effective twenty months later, when his contract expired. He gave a "heavy work load" as the reason. There was no doubt that his step was mutually gratifying to both parties.

Thus the 1969 Tanglewood season became his valedictory and, with his administrative duties about to end, he never conducted more brilliantly. He gave two operas in the Shed, Mozart's *Abduction from the Seraglio* with Beverly Sills and George Shirley on July 12, and Verdi's *Otello* with Richard Cassilly, Maralin Niska and Sherrill Milnes on July 26. Some management officials were unhappy over such presentations, arguing that they were expensive and did not attract unusually large audiences; however, since it was Leinsdorf's last season the complaints never advanced beyond the grumbling stage.

Perhaps the most unforgettable event of the summer was another opera, given not by the Boston Symphony but by the Berkshire Music Center. Alban Berg's modern classic *Wozzeck* was produced with stunning effect by an all-student cast, headed by Richard Taylor and Alexandra Hunt, and orchestra.

Arthur Fiedler rehearses a 1969 *Peter and the Wolf* with Joan Kennedy as the narrator. (Courtesy Whitestone Photographers)

Leinsdorf conducted and Michael Tilson Thomas assisted in the musical preparation; the result was an extraordinarily moving performance of a difficult work. Leinsdorf says he regards his student *Wozzeck* as the high point of his seven summers at Tanglewood.

Even with the finale at hand the discord between the conductor and the management continued unresolved to the end. It cropped up when guest conductor Pierre Boulez ran into costly overtime while rehearsing the orchestra for a program consisting of Haydn's Sinfonia Concertante, Op. 84, Bartok's Two Rhapsodies for Violin and Orchestra with Silverstein as soloist, and Debussy's *Jeux* and *La Mer*. Boulez, absorbed in his rehearsals, unwittingly shot past the time limit set by the union contract. Leinsdorf, undoubtedly remembering his own similar experience, was quick to defend his colleague. "The man needed the time," he said. "He wanted to do it his way." He enlarged his comments to a further criticism of the administration in general by saying: "My concept that musical organizations should be run by musicians is no longer valid. . . . If the conductor here has to continue to base his programs on the repertory accumulated during the regular season, Tanglewood is in trouble."

For their part, neither the Boston Symphony trustees nor the Tanglewood administration chose to reply directly to their departing conductor. But Talcott M. Banks, who had become president of the board of trustees, did disclose that Tanglewood, with a total attendance for the summer of 236,937, had amassed a deficit of $350,000 for its 1969 operations.

Leinsdorf's last Tanglewood concert, and his final appearance as music director of the Boston Symphony, was on August 24, 1969. The program consisted of the Royal Hunt and Storm music from Berlioz' opera *Les Troyens* and Beethoven's Ninth Symphony, with a vocal quartet made up of Beverly Sills, Florence Kopleff, John Alexander and Justino Diaz, and the Berkshire Chorus—consisting largely of singers from the surrounding communities— and the Tanglewood Choir. A crowd of 14,120 was on hand and gave Leinsdorf a five-minute farewell ovation.

He has never been to Tanglewood since. Summing up his experience there he says: "Maybe I was not always successful. But there was a plan of the season, a thrust, a line—an attempt to make something beyond a sequence of concerts."

Leinsdorf acknowledges an ovation. (Photo by Eugene Cook)

Ozawa and Bernstein during the period of the "troika," which took over Tanglewood administration in the 1970s. (Courtesy Whitestone Photographers)

6. The 1970s

The Troika Takes Over

Leinsdorf's successor as the music director of the Boston Symphony was a surprising choice—William Steinberg of the Pittsburgh Symphony. The surprise had nothing to do with Steinberg's musical qualifications—he was among the world's ablest conductors, superbly grounded in classical style—but with his age. Steinberg was seventy years old when he was put in command of the Boston Symphony. He had appeared frequently both at Symphony Hall and in Tanglewood and was a great favorite with audiences. In fact, he had been a leading candidate to succeed Munch in 1961, and many had expected him to get the job. Allegedly one of the reasons he was passed over was his age. Now, nine years later, the position was suddenly his. It was almost as if the trustees were publicly admitting they had erred in 1961.

Steinberg, who was born in Cologne and driven from Germany by the Nazis in 1936, had become one of the first leaders, with Bronislaw Hubermann, of the newly founded Palestine Symphony (later Israel Philharmonic) Orchestra, and subsequently Toscanini's assistant with the NBC Symphony in New York. In 1945 he was made director of the Buffalo Philharmonic and in 1952 of the Pittsburgh Symphony. Even after coming to Boston, he retained an affiliation with the Pittsburgh orchestra.

There was one significant difference between Steinberg's regime in Boston and those of his immediate predecessors. It was made clear from the very start that while he would be in full charge at Symphony Hall, he would have no responsibilities, even nominal, at Tanglewood, except to appear there occasionally as a guest conductor. Since Steinberg had no interest either in the educational or the administrative side of the Festival, the trustees, rather than repeating the directorial vacuum of the Munch years, decided to institute an entirely new setup. Instead of concentrating the job of running Tanglewood in one person, they named a triumvirate—or troika, as it was promptly labeled—consisting of Seiji Ozawa, Gunther Schuller and Leonard Bernstein. In announcing the appointments at a press conference in New

207

York, Talcott Banks, speaking for the trustees, said that Ozawa would be in charge of the Festival programs and conduct many of them himself, Schuller would head all educational activities, and Bernstein would serve as general adviser and, in effect, provide a link between Tanglewood's past and present.

In many ways, it was an inspired decision, emphasizing Tanglewood's continued commitment to youth and change. Mrs. Olga Koussevitzky said she was gratified that the summer operation would now be in the hands of "young alumni, exactly as Dr. Koussevitzky would have wanted." Michael Steinberg, music critic of the Boston Globe, expressed pleasure in the idea that Tanglewood would "be run by three professional swingers."

Certainly the appointment of the "troika" indicated a determination to keep step with the rising musical generation. Bernstein, who had had little to do with the Festival in Leinsdorf's years and had not held an official position there since 1955, was now back in the picture. At the age of fifty he was just leaving the music directorship of the New York Philharmonic, which he had headed since 1957, and while he would not be in residence at Tanglewood, it was expected that he would make guest conducting appearances in the Shed and do some teaching at the Berkshire Music Center—as indeed he did. As for Schuller, his appointment to head the Berkshire Music Center confirmed formally the function he had been actually performing for several years, that of serving in Copland's old role as mentor, guide and father-figure to the students, especially the young composers.

The key man in the triumvirate was Ozawa, who, in the decade since leaving Tanglewood, had developed into one of the world's most spectacular and exciting young conductors. After his brilliant Berkshire student year in 1960 he had gone to Germany for further studies with Herbert von Karajan. His Tanglewood performances had also brought him to the attention of Bernstein, who went to hear him perform in Berlin and engaged him in 1961 as an assistant conductor of the New York Philharmonic. Charles Munch also took a deep interest in him; it was largely on Munch's recommendation that Ozawa was appointed music director of the Toronto Symphony, a post he held until 1969, when he was named to head the San Francisco Symphony. To this day Ozawa regards Munch as a kind of spiritual father and the conductor who had the most to do with shaping his musical career. Munch, unfortunately, did not live to see his protege succeed him as director of the Berkshire Festival. The French conductor died on November 6, 1968, at the age of seventy-seven in Richmond, Virginia, while leading the Orchestre de Paris on a tour of the United States.

In addition to conducting in Toronto and San Francisco, Ozawa had become a familiar figure on the American summer festival circuit. He made his first guest-conducting appearance in the Tanglewood Shed in 1964, only four years after his student summer there, leading the Boston Symphony in a program consisting of Bizet's Symphony in C, Hindemith's *Mathis der Maler* and Moussorgsky's *Pictures at an Exhibition*. His supple, quick-moving figure and his general choreographic approach on the podium reminded some watchers of Bernstein. With subsequent appearances he became one of the Festival's most popular guest conductors. He made a similar impression on audiences at the Ravinia Festival in Chicago; so much so that he was engaged in 1964 as permanent music director there, remaining five years and leaving only to take command at Tanglewood.

In mapping the course of the Festival during the 1970s, Ozawa and his colleagues displayed from the start an ability to put together programs that were an adroit mixture of unusual works and crowd-pleasers. Ozawa's first appearance in his new capacity, on the opening day of the 1970 season, offered a program made up of Bernstein's Chichester Psalms, a graceful gesture to one of his fellow triumvirs; Gyorgy Ligeti's *Atmospheres,* a symbol of the attention to be paid to new music, and Berlioz' *Symphonie Fantastique,* an exemplar of the big, romantic orchestral pieces in which the young conductor excelled. On July 5 Bernstein conducted, devoting his entire program to Mahler's Symphony No. 2. He received an eleven-minute ovation, and the crowd blocked his dressing room for fifteen minutes; obviously his return to the Tanglewood scene was a highly popular move. Schuller directed a Shed program that included his own *Spectra* as well as Scriabin's *Poem of Ecstasy*. William Steinberg came to Tanglewood later in the summer to direct three Beethoven concerts in memory of the 200th anniversary of the composer's birth, one of which was given over to the *Choral Fantasy* and the Ninth Symphony. Tanglewood personalities also figured among the guest conductors, with appearances by Copland and two Berkshire Music Center alumni, Michael Tilson Thomas and Kenneth Schermerhorn. At the final concert of the season Ozawa conducted the Berlioz Requiem and dedicated it to the memory of Munch. The operatic highlight was Mozart's *Così fan Tutte,* conducted by Ozawa in the Shed with a cast predominantly of Tanglewood alumni: Phyllis Curtin, Teresa Stratas, Rosalind Elias, George Shirley, Tom Krause and Ezio Flagello.

With succeeding summers Ozawa displayed a continuing predilection for large, complicated and spectacular works. In 1971 he performed Berlioz's *Damnation of Faust,* in 1972 Mahler's ''Symphony of a Thousand,'' in 1973 Berlioz' *Lélio* and the Verdi Requiem. Other conductors were encouraged to do the same; in the same season, for example, Michael Tilson Thomas conducted both Monteverdi's Vespers of 1610 and Carl Ruggles' *Sun-Treader,* works vastly different in spirit, time and content, yet both presenting a tremendous challenge to their performers, and both previously unknown to the vast majority of their listeners at the Festival.

A similar indication of a new approach was apparent in the choice of solo performers; the Tanglewood authorities had discovered that "name" artists frequently filled the Shed to overflowing and had no scruples about engaging them. But from now on, many of those invited to appear were members of the rising generation, the young stars rather than the old familiar faces—Itzhak Perlman and Pinchas Zukerman among the violinists, Vladimir Ashkenazy, Stephen Bishop, Christoph Eschenbach, Byron Janis and Garrick Ohlsson among the pianists.

The Berkshire Music Center, with Schuller firmly in charge, also underwent changes. The faculty for 1970 included such figures as George Crumb, Mel Powell and Paul Zukofsky, all associated with the avant-garde. With Schuller conducting, the student orchestra was likely to find itself playing not the Three Bs, but music by Crumb, Luigi Nono and Krzysztof Penderecki. It was at Tanglewood in the summer of 1970 that Crumb, who had been a Berkshire Music Center composition student in 1955, wrote one of his most admired pieces, *Ancient Voices of Children,* a song cycle based on poems by Federico Garcia Lorca.

Henceforth it became the policy of the Center to involve its entire student body in contemporary music performances during the Fromm festival-within-a-festival, rather than utilizing specially designated "Fromm players" or outside groups. Moves in this direction had been started under Leinsdorf, but now a policy of total immersion in new music became the rule during Fromm week every summer.

"We discarded the concept of having the contemporary music played by a special V.I.P. group, apart from everybody else," explains Schuller. "We thought it a shame to segregate and limit contemporary music to twelve chosen players. That way, the others don't get to learn about it."

Schuller believes that the integration of contemporary music performance into the Berkshire Music Center's regular routine has worked out well for both the music and the students.

"The reactions of the students fall into three categories," he says. "First there are those who have had contact with the music at their regular schools or universities, such as the New England Conservatory, Indiana, Michigan. They're interested. Then there are those who come from schools at the other end of the spectrum—I won't name them—where they're full of Tchaikovsky concertos and Brahms symphonies. They've usually had no experience in playing contemporary music and—what bothers me more—are intensely prejudiced against it.

"The third group consists of kids who have played, let's say, the Prokofiev Quintet or maybe a piece by Webern. They confuse contemporary music with Sibelius, Ravel or Rachmaninoff. You ask them, 'But what have you played?' and they say, 'Well, a Bartok quartet.' They don't really know contemporary music, but they have an open mind and know it's a necessary part of their professional equipment.

"One of the most exciting by-products of the whole program—really, its goal—is that we sometimes have kids from the first category who by their first or second summers here become so skilled and involved in it that they become the leaders of contemporary music activities in their own communities—Cincinnati, Spokane or wherever. They start a contemporary music ensemble, they go out and get funding, they develop audiences. With others, the injection doesn't work. I'd say that about sixty percent of the students get valuable experience in contemporary music, that for about forty percent it's a lost cause, and that one or two each year become leaders in the field. I don't think we should ever go back to operating with specialists in the field of new music."

Not everybody, it must be admitted, was raised to a state of ecstasy by the Festival's renewed devotion to the cause of contemporary music. In 1972 Michael Tilson Thomas led the Boston Symphony in a special concert marking the twentieth anniversary of the establishment of the Fromm Music Foundation. Included were Ruggles' *Evocations for Orchestra,* Copland's *Twelve Poems of Emily Dickinson,* Stravinsky's *Rite of Spring* ("the only old-fashioned piece on the program," one wag remarked) and the world premiere of Charles Wuorinen's Concerto for Amplified Violin and Orchestra with Paul Zukofsky as soloist.

It was the Wuorinen Concerto, an avant-garde piece fiendishly difficult to play and not especially easy to listen to, that stirred up the storm. Some members of the orchestra expressed their dislike of it by booing it at the final rehearsal, and a few catcalls were also heard at the actual performance. Afterwards the composer reportedly remarked to friends that he thought the orchestra had played his work poorly. However, resistance to the avant-garde was by no means universal in the orchestra's ranks; in fact a number of its members, including violinist Ronald Knudson, bassist Lawrence Wolfe, flutist Paul Fried, clarinetist Felix Viscuglia and percussionist Frank Epstein, participated in a group called Collage which that summer put on some contemporary chamber music performances of their own. The students of the Berkshire Music Center meanwhile staged their own twentieth-anniversary Fromm concert, the program consisting of Luciano Berio's *Circles,* Elliott Carter's Double Concerto, and premieres of Gunther Schuller's Music for Chamber Ensemble and Bruno Maderna's *Giardino Religioso,* with both composers on hand to conduct in person. There were no demonstrations.

Rock and Opera

Two problems that confronted Ozawa and his associates—not to mention the board of trustees—involved the future at Tanglewood (a) of rock concerts and (b) of operatic activities. The rock concerts, launched in 1968, had been a thriving addition to the Festival's gate receipts, with young people flocking to them from much of New England and upstate New York. Some Tanglewood officials, not to mention a substantial number of townspeople in Lenox, Stockbridge and Great Barrington, were not overly enthusiastic about the noisy outpouring of young people, many of them well supplied with their own drinking and smoking supplies, who descended upon the area for the Tuesday rock concerts. Rock never turned Tanglewood into a Woodstock, but it did not exactly draw a Symphony Hall crowd either. So with the 1972 season the management decided to order a one-year hiatus in the Contemporary Trends concerts, in order to "reassess" their place.

When they resumed, the hard-rock orientation was considerably softened, and the pseudoartistic title "Contemporary Trends" was dropped in favor of the more prosaic "Popular Artists Series." Instead of having the concerts administered by the Berkshire Music Center they were henceforth to be produced by a Boston entrepreneur, Don Law. Most important of all, the new attractions consisted of performers like Roberta Flack and John Denver, who presumably appealed to more quiescent crowds than the Jefferson Airplane and Santana. Audiences for the Popular Artists series average about 11,000 and on the whole fit comfortably into the Tanglewood scheme of things.

One department, however, would not mind seeing them disappear altogether. That is the groundskeeping crew headed by Jim Kiley. "It's improved somewhat," says Kiley. "Tuesday nights I used to put on twelve or fourteen extra men to clean up. The main problem was broken bottles. We get a lot of people on the lawn for weekends, sprawling out or leaning back. Nobody wants to get a piece of glass in a bare foot or hand, so every shard has to be picked up. In 1975 we put an absolute ban on bringing bottles or cans into the grounds for the Popular Artists Concerts."

Tending the Tanglewood grounds has always been a major task, if only because of the size of the expanse and the proclivity of crowds, whether devoted to rock or Bach, to scatter everything from candy wrappers to programs. Thanks to Tanglewood, the Boston Symphony is the only orchestra in the world that owns a fleet of trucks and tractors and a seven-gang lawnmower. Kiley works with a year-round staff of four men which he enlarges to ten during the summer months. Maintaining the verdant, parklike beauty of Tanglewood is not merely a matter of regular cleanups; it entails a year-round program of grounds care.

"We don't just lock the gates in August and say, 'That's it until next July,'" explains Kiley. "When the season ends we literally tear the lawn apart. We break up the impaction and let air, water and fertilizer in. I remember when I bought our first fertilizer-spreader—people just wouldn't believe that the Boston Symphony had use for a fertilizer-spreader. When we get through breaking up the lawn it looks awful, with plugs of grass left all around on the surface, but it works. We've established a good grassy roots system."

To keep the grass trim, Kiley has devised his seven-gang lawnmower, a tractor with two units mounted in front and five behind. "It's a Rube Goldberg thing, but it works," he says. To cart away debris he and his men employ seven-foot-high bins mounted on wheels. Eleven of these huge containers are scattered around the grounds, and visitors often toss their own debris into them over the sides. But their main function is to serve as receptacles for the cleanup crews, who hook them behind trucks and drive them for emptying to the local dump. Of his mechanical devices, Kiley says: "We've tried them all, but there's no magic contraption that can clean up as well as ten men walking around with sticks in their hands." After almost any concert, the grounds staff can be seen patrolling the grounds gathering up the debris almost as soon as it is deposited. "One thing we've never run out of here," says Jim Kiley, "is work."

Running a successful popular music series at Tanglewood has proved to be a simpler problem to overcome than resuscitating the operatic department which died with Goldovsky's departure. The first sustained effort to reestablish a substantial operatic program was made in 1971, the second year of the new regime. Singers had continued to come to Tanglewood all along, but they concentrated on recital and lieder work rather than operatic study. Phyllis Curtin, who had gone from her own summers of study at the

(Left) Not Coney Island,
but the lawn at Tanglewood just before
a rock-and-roll concert. (Courtesy
Whitestone Photographers)

(Right) Clean-up job the morning after.
(Courtesy Whitestone Photographers)

Berkshire Music Center to stardom at the Metropolitan and other opera houses, has been the mainstay of Tanglewood's vocal department since 1963, when she was asked by Berkshire Music Center Administrator Harry Kraut to establish a master class.

"There was no opera department then," she recalls, "but there was a group of ten or twelve singers being used in the various Tanglewood programs. After the season was under way some of them complained to Harry that they didn't have enough to do. So he asked me to try to give them something that would keep their interest."

Miss Curtin, who has a home in nearby Great Barrington, established her class in the East Barn, one of two ramshackle farm structures just below the main Tanglewood grounds, close to the Hawthorne Cottage. Working with an upright piano, Miss Curtin and her young singers spent the rest of the summer working on vocal repertory. So exhilarating was the experience, she says, that the class was scheduled for the following summer on a full eight-week basis. The "Phyllis Curtin Seminar" has become a seasonal perennial ever since, with as many as 600 applicants a year for the approximately thirty places that are available.

The 1971 attempt to revive opera, entitled the Music Theater Project, was headed by Ian Strasfogel, chairman of the opera department of the New England Conservatory of Music, and funded by grants from the National Opera Institute, the Martha Baird Rockefeller Fund and other outside sources.

Ideally, the project belonged in the Theater-Concert Hall, the scene of Goldovsky's triumphs, but the necessary electric lines, stage machinery and other equipment had either deteriorated through lack of use or been removed. So the Music Theater Project was carried on in the more modest and remote surroundings of the West Barn, across a lane from the East Barn, and rather like it in appearance though slightly more commodious. The singers performed on an open, curtainless platform-stage, the orchestra occupied an enclave to the side, and the audience sat on a steeply raked bank of chairs. Nobody could complain of an inability to see or hear in this mini-theater, and most of the works given were intimate or small-scaled.

The Music Theater Project lasted only three years, after which its funding was not renewed. Its productions evoked a certain amount of controversy, and it never approached the scale or importance of Goldovsky's department. But it contributed to Tanglewood's liveliness and adventurousness, and there is no telling what it might have become had it been able to move into the Theater, which probably is the only place in which opera can really take root in the Berkshires.

Part of the action in Kurt Weill's *Mahagonny* took place in a prize-fight ring.
(Courtesy Whitestone Photographers)

The opera *Chocorua* premiered in 1972 and had an Indian as its central character.
(Courtesy Whitestone Photographers)

In their first summer in the West Barn Strasfogel and his students put on five short chamber operas—the original "Singspiel" version of Kurt Weill's and Bertolt Brecht's *Mahagonny*, Erik Satie's *Socrate*, Harrison Birtwistle's *Down on the Greenwood Side*, Gyorgy Ligeti's *Aventures et Nouvelles Aventures* and Jacques Offenbach's *Croquefer*—most of which came as discoveries to their performers and auditors alike.

The next year the Music Theater Project staged a double bill consisting of another Weill-Brecht work, *Der Jasager*, given in English under the title of "The Yes Man," in which a student baritone named Lenus Carlson made a strong impression, and *Chocorua*, a new opera by Robert Selig, a thirty-three-year-old composition student at the Berkshire Music Center. *Chocorua*, an intense thirty-minute-long work about a New Hampshire Indian who falls in love with the wife of an English settler in Colonial times, made a considerable impact on many of its listeners. Michael Steinberg in the *Boston Globe* called it "impressive" and Ellen Pfeifer in the *Boston Herald Traveler and Record American* found it "very listenable" with "a sure dramatic sense." In 1972 the Project also put on Monteverdi's *The Coronation of Poppea* in a version edited and conducted by Bruno Maderna. Monteverdi's music was a revelation to many in the audience, but even more startling was the production style, for the performers were clad in futuristic costumes and the set consisted chiefly of what one observer described as "a wraparound clear plastic curtain embossed with a Warhol-like repetition of Nero's androgynous face."

In 1973 the Music Theater Project wound up its existence with a season that included the American premiere of Maderna's *Satyricon* and an entertainment, devised by Strasfogel, entitled *Wolfgangerl: A Portrait of W. A. M.*, based on Mozart's youthful letters.

Since then, there has been no formal operatic program at Tanglewood, although attempts to find the necessary funding have continued. These efforts seemed near success in 1975, and plans were actually announced for a large-scale program in the summer of 1976 under the direction of Nathaniel Merrill, a stage director of the Metropolitan Opera and a 1951 Tanglewood alumnus, with Peter Wexler as design director. Performances were projected both in the West Barn and in the Theater-Concert Hall, which was scheduled for remodeling. The opening operatic production was even announced—Verdi's *Falstaff*, with Ozawa to conduct it. However, the expected funding failed to materialize, and the Berkshire Music Center was compelled to announce a postponement. Hopefully, opera will return to the Berkshires in the summer of 1977.

Berkshire Balance Sheet

For Seiji Ozawa, it is no exaggeration to say that Tanglewood was the proving grounds that led him to the music directorship of the Boston Symphony Orchestra. As music director at Tanglewood since 1970 he had established stronger and stronger ties between himself and the orchestra's musicians and audiences alike. William Steinberg, as deeply admired as he was, was well into his seventies and his health was impaired, and it became evident that the symphony had need of a younger and more resilient leader. In 1972 Ozawa was designated "music adviser" of the Boston Symphony, and in the fall of 1973 he was named, at the age of thirty-eight, its music director. Almost simultaneously the British conductor Colin Davis, who had also proved popular with both the orchestra and its audiences, was given the title of Principal Guest Conductor.

Crowds throughout the summer of 1973 were enormous, with the largest total weekend attendance of 42,604 occurring during a series of three all-Beethoven concerts led by visiting conductors Eugene Ormandy and Stanislaw Skrowaczewski—a tribute no doubt to those two estimable maestri, but also to the coincidence of it being parental visiting weekend at the more than forty children's camps in the Berkshires. In fact, camp visiting weekend *always* produces the heaviest attendance of the year at Tanglewood, no matter who is conducting or what the program. In 1975 the Berkshire Hills Conference, the local tourism promotional organization in Pittsfield, was trying to devise a plan to have *two* visiting weekends at the camps to spread out the influx.

At the Berkshire Music Center a boom year also was in progress, with 461 students, the highest enrollment in history. One attraction was a piano seminar given by André Watts; another was a new class entitled Listening and Analysis, taught by Peter Gram Swing and Leonard Altman. These sessions, covering musical fundamentals and tied in to the Shed programs of the Boston Symphony, represented the newest reincarnation of the "secondary" student body made up of intelligent amateurs and people whose musical interests were chiefly nonprofessional. The classes, which have continued annually ever since, are usually held in the Hawthorne Cottage, which has two large studios fitted out with pianos. The pupils range from schoolteachers to amateur guitarists, and the topics from sight-reading to twelve-tone music. "My job is to expand their horizons," Altman says. "You hear so much music here that you can't help but broaden and expand as the weeks pass. Nobody comes and goes exactly the same. Your ears change."

The decor of *The Coronation of Poppea* reminded some listeners of a shower curtain.
(Courtesy Whitestone Photographers)

Total attendance for the year reached an unprecedented 313,774, a rise of 23 percent over 1972. Financial returns were up commensurately. Yet the annual state of the Boston Symphony made it clear that Tanglewood, like the orchestra's other activities, remained a deficit operation. These were the figures officially given, with separate entries for the Berkshire Festival and the Berkshire Music Center:

BERKSHIRE FESTIVAL

	Income	Expenses
Receipts from concerts	$795,505	
Other receipts	46,698	
Compensation of players, conductors and soloists		$ 646,372
Other direct concert costs		230,689
Direct administrative costs		181,997
Totals	$842,203	$1,059,058
Deficit		$216,855

BERKSHIRE MUSIC CENTER

	Income	Expenses
Tuition, dormitories	$165,358	
Receipts from concerts	19,590	
Other receipts	59,291	
Faculty salaries		$ 86,036
Fellowships and awards		53,696
Dormitory cost		110,239
Direct concert costs		5,335
Direct administrative costs		155,545
Totals	$244,239	$ 410,851
Deficit		$166,612

Thus the combined loss for the Tanglewood operation during a single summer was calculated at $383,467—despite an annual grant, instituted in 1971, of $100,000 from the National Endowment for the Arts to the Berkshire Music Center. It was not a deficit likely to diminish over the years.

From the standpoint of the Boston Symphony Orchestra players, however, the summer in the Berkshires represents a considerable plus. The annual base pay for a member of the Boston Symphony Orchestra as of 1975 is $18,720—many make more, of course—plus a recording guarantee of $1,000 from Deutsche Grammophon. Under their contract, the players also receive a per diem allowance at Tanglewood, just as they do elsewhere away from home, even though many of them own summer cottages in the Berkshires. The per diem for eight weeks comes to $2,000. On top of that they are paid $750 to teach in the orchestral or chamber music programs at the Berkshire Center, and $1,500 if they work in both. Thanks to Tanglewood, the actual annual remuneration of the average Boston Symphony member is close to $25,000. For the musicians Tanglewood has become an economic necessity as well as an artistic entity.

Much the same is true of the Festival's effect upon the Berkshire region as a whole. The area attracts tourists the year round, with foliage watchers journeying there in the autumn and skiers in the winter, but it is the Tanglewood influx every summer that provides the largest number of visitors and the highest volume of income. Sixty percent of the 300,000 who come to the Festival annually remain in the region at least two and a half days and spend about $30 a day. "It's not only the money that's important but the publicity the Festival gives," says Roy R. Kennedy, chairman of the Berkshire Hills Conference. "You can't buy that kind of coverage."

Most of the year-round residents—as distinguished from summer-home owners—who purchase tickets do so for two events, Tanglewood on Parade and the Arthur Fiedler Pops concert. But both the natives and the summer people cooperate in providing many of the volunteer services that are essential to the Festival. The parking-lot attendants, who guide the departing cars with flashlights, are paid a small sum. But the 175 ushers and 125 program girls who make themselves available for work during the weekend concerts throughout the summer receive no remuneration. In 1975 seventy-three-year-old Harry P. Stedman, a retired teacher and personnel director, marked his fifteenth successive year as head usher in the Shed. Volunteers may apply for the concerts they wish to work, and Stedman says he can predict the size of an audience by the number of requests he gets for each date. Tanglewood has one of the most elegantly clad corps of ushers to be found anywhere, with the women invariably turning up in long gowns, just as in Gertrude Robinson Smith's day.

A locally based organization that plays an important role in the Festival is the Friends of Music at Tanglewood, established in 1970 in place of the Friends of the Berkshire Music Center. The Tanglewood Friends group numbers 2,265 members, 700 of whom reside in Berkshire County with the rest coming from out of the area, mainly New York. The Friends' office, along with the music store on the grounds, offers such souvenirs as Tanglewood posters and a Seiji Ozawa jigsaw puzzle. It also maintains its own refreshment tent on the grounds and, most important of all, entitles its members to free admission to all Berkshire Music Center concerts and other events. The money it raises is used to benefit the Festival and to provide fellowships for students at the Berkshire Music Center.

Two Birthdays

The summer of 1974 marked the one-hundredth anniversary of the birth of Serge Koussevitzky on July 26, 1874. In a way the entire Festival that year constituted a memorial to him; it always seemed singularly appropriate that Koussevitzky's birthday should occur right in the middle of the Tanglewood season, which, of all his endeavors with the Boston Symphony, meant the most to him.

By any standards, 1974 would have been counted among the most exciting and distinguished of Tanglewood seasons. The guest conductors on hand included Thomas, Ormandy, Bernstein, Karl Richter and Eugen Jochum. Attendance surpassed even the previous year's record, hitting an all-time high of 319,774. The programs ranged from the traditional small-orchestra Bach-Haydn-Mozart series—this time with Stravinsky's *Pulcinella* thrown in for good measure—to a generous representation of music by Arnold Schoenberg, whose centenary was being commemorated. The climactic work was his *Gurrelieder*—the first performance of that massive composition for narrator, solo voices, chorus and orchestra ever given anywhere by the Boston Symphony. Marita Napier was scheduled to sing the role of Tove, but when she became indisposed, that Tanglewood veteran Phyllis Curtin stepped into the part. Other soloists were Lili Chookasian, James McCracken, Jerry Jennings, David Arnold and George London in a speaking role, plus the Tanglewood Festival Chorus. To make up the huge array of instrumental forces called for by the score—twenty-five woodwinds, twenty-nine brasses, and strings in proportion—members of the Berkshire Music Center Orchestra played side by side with their older colleagues in the Boston Symphony.

But the most memorable date of the 1974 season was July 26, Koussevitzky's 100th birthday, when a program was held such as even Tanglewood had never witnessed before. In the manner of Tanglewood on Parade it went on all day, but with none of the spirit of spoofing or tomfoolery that marks that annual event. Instead the nearly 12,000 who attended the marathon, paying premium admission prices of up to $15 a ticket—proceeds went to a Koussevitzky Centennial Memorial Fund—were treated to an extraordinary procession of eight and a half hours of concerts, held in the Shed, the Theater, the Chamber Music Hall and practically anyplace else there was room to squeeze in performers and listeners.

The first formal concert began at 2:30 P.M. with the Boston University Young Artists Orchestra, conducted by Lawrence Smith, playing Prokofiev's Fifth Symphony. At 4 P.M. Bernstein gave a concert consisting of William Schuman's *American Festival* Overture and Berlioz' *Symphonie Fantastique,* conducting the World Youth Orchestra, a group of gifted players aged sixteen to twenty-three assembled by the Jeunesses Musicales organization. At 6 P.M. Gunther Schuller directed the Berkshire Music Center Orchestra in Howard Hanson's *Elegy to My Friend Serge Koussevitzky,* Schoenberg's *A Survivor From Warsaw* and Stravinsky's *Symphony of Psalms,* with the Tanglewood Festival Chorus. At 7:30 Bernstein took over the Music Center Orchestra to perform his *Age of Anxiety.* The Boston Symphony itself entered the day's activities at 9:30 P.M. when Copland conducted his own *Quiet City.* Then, for a finale, Ozawa directed a brilliant performance of Beethoven's Ninth Symphony. It was a day with emphasis on youth, novelty, adventure and musical achievement, such as Koussevitzky himself might have reveled in.

The Centennial was marked not only by music but by seminars and speeches. Every one talked about Koussevitzky, often with different forms of address. At one symposium it was noted that Ozawa invariably referred to him as "Maestro Koussevitzky"; Aaron Copland and Richard Burgin as "Dr. Koussevitzky"; Lukas Foss as "Koussevitzky"; and Bernstein as "Koussy." The most formal, and perhaps most thoughtful, speech of the summer was made by Paul Fromm during the annual contemporary music week. Addressing the Friends of Music at Tanglewood on August 8, Fromm said:

> Even those of us who never knew Koussevitzky personally are so influenced by the spirit of Koussevitzky which hovers over the Berkshires that we begin to forget that we did not actually know him. . . . Each year as we return to Tanglewood, the Koussevitzky legend persists and even grows. We compare his musical miracles with our own efforts to carry on what he began, and we start to believe that while he was a magician, we live in a time when miracles seem to be no longer possible. . . .
>
> Koussevitzky's commitment to new music had a most practical base. When someone once objected to his playing of contemporary scores, he insisted, "If you do not play the new, eventually you will not have the old." In other words, an art form in which there is not continuing creation will eventually disappear. . . .

Tanglewood on Parade in 1975 found Seiji Ozawa and Arthur Fiedler riding an old railroad locomotive imported for the occasion. (Photo by Marian Gillett)

The Berkshire Music Festival and the Berkshire Music Center stand as a lasting tribute to Serge Koussevitzky, who in 1974, the 100th anniversary of his birth, is still our contemporary.

Just as 1974 constituted a homage to Koussevitzky, so was the 1975 season, at least in part, a tribute to Aaron Copland, who in the course of the year marked his seventy-fifth birthday. Copland, as in seasons past, continued to be listed in the official Berkshire Music Center brochure as Chairman of the Faculty Emeritus, but this summer he actually spent some time again at Tanglewood, performing his music and participating in student seminars and discussions. At Tanglewood on Parade he conducted his *El Salón México* with the Berkshire Music Center Orchestra in the Shed, and his *Connotations for Orchestra,* composed in 1962, was played by Schuller and the student orchestra as a feature of the Fromm contemporary festival. Copland, his spare, lanky form looking perfectly at home amid old surroundings, also was invited to participate with Schuller and Earle Brown in a Composers' Forum in the Theater-Concert Hall, listening to new music by the students and offering comments upon them. Copland's remarks were as candid and to-the-point as they had been during his active teaching days. After listening to a program of four new pieces he remarked: "I can't say there's anything in these works so striking that I'll remember them." Then, alluding to one of the compositions, he said: "It seemed to me to be awfully spurty—it didn't seem to have any reason for proceeding the way it did. There were little globs of sound that didn't seem to be adding up. I'm being a little severe, but why not?" On the program as a whole: "It's difficult to summarize my impressions. In one way, this Forum seems like what we had here ten or twenty years ago. There was a lot of diversity in the music, but the general nature of the animal seems to be about the same—young composers looking for new ways to express themselves, preferably with unconventional means." Schuller, by way of rebuttal, defended his young composers as more professional in approach than those in the past, and a lively discussion ensued. To Aaron Copland it must indeed have seemed like old times.

Guest composer for the 1975 season at Tanglewood was Olivier Messiaen, who at sixty-six was making his second visit. Twenty-five years before, when he was scarcely known in this country, he had been invited by Koussevitzky to teach composition in the Berkshires; now he returned as a kind of elder statesman, his exotic, Eastern-tinged music having found a widening public. With Messiaen came two longtime associates, his wife Yvonne Loriod, who gave seminars in piano and chamber music, and her sister

Jeanne Loriod, a specialist in the Ondes Martenot, an electronic instrument first used in France in the 1920s. A good deal of Messiaen's music was played during the summer, climaxing in a performance, directed by Ozawa, of his *Turangalila-Symphonie,* a massive, sprawling, ten-movement work commissioned in 1949 by the Koussevitzky Foundation in connection with the composer's first visit to Tanglewood.

Guest conductors during the summer included Bernstein, who conducted the opening Haydn-Mozart program, Zinman, Ormandy, Edo de Waart and Skrowaczewski—all by now familiar figures. Making their first appearances at Tanglewood were the British conductor Neville Marriner, the German Klaus Tennstedt and the Russian Mstislav Rostropovich. The latter appeared in a double capacity, for he was soloist in the Shostakovich Cello Concerto No. 2 under Ozawa's baton on August 10, a week after he had conducted a stunning performance of Verdi's Requiem in which the soprano part was sung by his wife, Galina Vishnevskaya. For the final concert of the season, Ozawa conducted a Sunday matinee performance of Mahler's Symphony No. 2 before a crowd that filled the Shed despite a heavy rain that beat down all day.

With a season that ranged from Mozart to Messiaen, that pitted Copland and Schuller in lively debate, that was distinguished alike by conductors making their first appearance in the Berkshires and conductors who had lost count of theirs, Tanglewood could make some claim to maintaining its creative role in American musical life as it moved into the last decade of its first half-century.

Aaron Copland on porch of main house with a young violinist and two cellists.
Bulletin board at rear keeps students informed of class assignments, rehearsals, and
other activities. (Courtesy the *Berkshire Eagle*)

7. At The Center

Opening Day

A hand-lettered sign atop a bulletin board near the stage of Tanglewood's Theater-Concert Hall, where most of the student performances are held, reads:

> *Remember*
> **The Orchestra**
> **That Plays Together**
> **Stays Together**

No one knows how long the sign has been there, or who put it up, but it summarizes, if a bit wryly, the concept of musical cooperativeness that is Tanglewood's philosophy. The young men and women who make up a class at the Berkshire Music Center essentially are there to learn the art of making music *together*. In 1835, commenting on Berlioz and his *Symphonie Fantastique,* Robert Schumann wrote: "It is not greater technical proficiency that he asks of the instrumentalist. He demands sympathy, study, love. The individual must subordinate himself to serve the whole, and this in turn must subject itself to the will of the leader." In a like spirit, Tanglewood has produced its share of solo performers and virtuosi, but essentially its task has been to further the craft of the ensemble musician. It is no accident that forty-one of the current members of the Boston Symphony—two-fifths of its personnel—were once Tanglewood students.*

For a time, when Erich Leinsdorf instituted a full fellowship program at the Center, some consideration was given to doing away with the term "student" altogether, but "fellow" seemed a bit awkward as an everyday term and no one could come up with a better substitute. So students they remain, though in a most advanced sense of the word.

Most of them live in the dormitory facilities which Tanglewood rents

---

*Alumni are strongly represented in other orchestras as well—for example, twenty-two in the Philadelphia and seventeen in the New York Philharmonic.

from various private preparatory schools in the area. Some students, usually in groups of three or four, prefer to rent accommodations in private houses in the Lenox-Stockbridge area. A few camp out for the summer on the shore of Lake Mahkeenac where Tanglewood maintains a pleasant campgrounds and a beautiful little beach and bathing area open to members of the Berkshire Music Center community. The Center rents a small fleet of school buses to transport the students back and forth between the dorms and the concert grounds; the lineup of yellow vehicles waiting at the gates is a regular feature of the Tanglewood landscape. So are the boys and girls thumbing their way along Route 183, carrying instrument cases or scores. Tanglewood is one of the few institutions that, far from discouraging hitchhiking, urge motorists in the area to pick up students heading for classes or concerts. One way or another, everybody gets there.

For a visitor, the ideal introduction to Tanglewood and its ways is by attending the opening exercises of the Berkshire Music Center, held in the Theater-Concert Hall generally on the last Sunday in June. The entire program and the beautiful grounds themselves are open without charge, and the theater is usually well filled with students, parents, friends, neighbors and summer visitors.*

Andrew Raeburn, a British-born musician who spent nine years at Tanglewood as musical assistant first to Leinsdorf and then to William Steinberg, says he could guess what instrument each of the students played just by their appearance and demeanor the first day. "Viola players never smiled," he says. "Brass players were hippie types, and with a solid, bulky build. Flutists tended to look delicate. And the student conductors you could always spot. They were in a great hurry, looked very important, and carried great sheafs of music about."

Most onlookers at a typical convocation of the Berkshire Music Center would be less quick at identifications but would be struck by the seriousness and enthusiasm of the young musicians. At the opening exercises they invariably sit through a barrage of speakers, all introduced by Tod Perry.

Mrs. Olga Koussevitzky, who still spends her summers at Seranak, the spacious house high on a hill a mile from the grounds, is present, as she always is at a Tanglewood festivity, and is introduced for a bow, a personification of the legacy of the past. Boston University's Norman Dello Joio, talks about the Young Artists' summer program, which he directs. But the two

---

*During the day time, Tanglewood's grounds are open to the public free throughout the year; only at concert time are tickets required.

Every summer Tanglewood's faculty and students gather for a group picture. This is a photograph of part of the 1948 "class": 1. Sarah Caldwell 2. Hugh Ross 3. Felix Wolfus 4. Boris Goldovsky 5. Rosario Mazzeo 6. Richard Burgin 7. Gregor Piatigorsky 8. Darius Milhaud 9. Ralph Berkowitz 10. Aaron Copland 11. Leonard Bernstein 12. Serge Koussevitzky 13. Eleazar de Carvalho 14. Irving Fine 15. Lukas Foss 16. Roger Voisin 17. Margaret Grant 18. Frederick Fennel 19. Irwin Hoffman 20. Seymour Lipkin 21. Howard Shanet (Courtesy Howard Shanet; photo by Howard S. Babbitt, Jr.)

principal speakers are the co-directors of the Center, Gunther Schuller and Seiji Ozawa—the day-in, day-out leader of education affairs; and the conductor who started his own American career in this same rough-hewn, rustic hall.

Schuller's annual speech is full of the practicalities of everyday Tanglewood life. "Tanglewood is a polishing school, a finishing school," he says. "Except that we know as musicians that the job is never finished, so let's call it a beginning school, where you can refine the raw material of your talent. Concentration is the key word; leisure moments are a struggling minority.

"Only four days from now, those of you who are in the orchestra will play a concert under Seiji Ozawa. You'll play as if you've been together for months. Or let's hope you will—don't let me down. Don't think of Tanglewood as another 'gig,' a place to play a few weeks and then split. The pace is hectic and the work exhaustive. But eight weeks here will be the musical experience of your young lives. I predict that not until next winter, or even a few years from now, will you fully appreciate the Tanglewood experience."

Ozawa's speech, delivered in his understandable though accented and slightly awkward English, takes on an even more personal aspect. He is well aware that he is a living example of what Tanglewood is all about. "Every year I sit in this ceremony," he says, "and I think it was fifteen years ago—fourteen years ago—thirteen years ago—that I was here, like you, a student. When I came here, I thought I had enough training and enough of music school. But I found completely new things that I had missed for myself. It is good to find your weak points, and to strengthen them. You are here for hard work, and we in the Boston Symphony are not here to get relaxed, either. When you have music in your mind, and see beautiful nature all around, as you do here, the two things together, then suddenly you see why God gave us music, and if you see that, you know why you are here."

The climactic moment of every season's opening of the Berkshire Music Center is the singing of Randall Thompson's *Alleluia*. The students have been seated in a bloc in the middle of the audience and each has been given a copy of the music. They rise in their places, boys and girls in shorts, blue jeans, T-shirts, sandals and even bare feet, and sing Thompson's lovely music with the same feeling and fervor as generations of their predecessors did in their saddle shoes, sweaters and even ties and jackets. Thompson's five-minute work has become a favorite of choirs and glee clubs the world over and turns up everywhere from concerts at Carnegie Hall to small-town high school graduations. It never sounds more beautiful than at its annual performance by the young voices of Tanglewood.

The Tanglewood beach on Lake Mahkeenac, which is used by students, faculty, and other members of the Berkshire Festival community. (Courtesy the Boston Symphony Orchestra)

In a studio in the Hawthorne Cottage a student composer
tries out some ideas at the keyboard. (Photo by Marian Gillett)

Says Dan Gustin, the Berkshire Music Center's young and resourceful administrator: "A lot of work and preparation goes into each Tanglewood season, not just during the summer but throughout the year. It's a big effort to get it opened. I never hear that *Alleluia* every summer without tears coming to my eyes—not just because it's so beautiful, but because I know that another season is here and we're really under way."

As the session ends, everyone streams out for afternoon tea, which is served in what Serge Koussevitzky, in his ineluctable accent, used to call "the fummil garden"—a pleasant area of flagstone walks and carefully cropped high hedges. The tea is poured in paper cups and the cookies come in packages, but somehow there is a touch of elegance that also is characteristically Tanglewood.

Ordeal by Audition

A typical Tanglewood class will be made up of around 440 students, split approximately evenly between men and women. Of these 133, or nearly one-third, are on full fellowships—ninety-five orchestral instrumentalists, nine pianists, thirteen vocalists, eight composers, five conductors, two vocal coaches and one administrative intern. Virtually all have been accepted on the basis of auditions, most of them held during the previous winter. In most cases it is the head of the appropriate Boston Symphony section who makes the selection.

Auditions are held at stated dates at Symphony Hall in Boston, Carnegie Hall in New York and similar centers. But the first-desk men of the Boston Symphony make it their business to hear applicants all over the country throughout the year. Whenever the orchestra arrives in a town while touring, Tanglewood auditions are announced in schools and conservatories or wherever else young musicians gather. The news is spread on bulletin boards, in various publications or by that most ancient and effective method of communication, word of mouth. Many more are heard than can possibly fit into the available places. "This year 200 flutists auditioned for the five open places," says Richard Ortner, assistant administrator. "For some reason there always are a lot of flute applicants." Sometimes unsuccessful candidates are put on a standby basis, in case someone fails to appear, or are asked to reapply the following season. Acceptance into this school which offers no degrees, diplomas or academic credit has been an honor cherished by young musicians ever since Koussevitzky and Copland first extended invitations to the likely youngsters they had heard.

No one especially likes the competitive audition as a method of evaluating a performer's skill and musicianship; it produces unnatural pressures and tension, and sometimes does not bring out the best in a player. Many young musicians, like many academic students, do not "test" especially well. But no other satisfactory method has yet been devised, and musicians are faced with auditions all their lives. So here, too, Tanglewood quickly places its students on the path to professionalism—a rocky one at times.

In the past, all the fellowship students were invited to spend the summer working at Tanglewood at no cost to themselves. But starting in 1975 they were asked to make a small contribution toward the expense of their room and board. The others, including those enrolled in the B.U. program, the Listening-Analysis seminar, and the remaining instrumentalists, pay varying amounts for their summer's immersion in music.

The orchestral fellows, who make up the largest bloc of the Tanglewood student body, will work on various levels—as members of their instrumental sections, as members of the full orchestra and as participants in various chamber ensembles. The schedule of their daily activities, the road map and guide to all of Tanglewood's musical doings, is mimeographed and distributed weekly.

"We would degenerate into just as big a bureaucracy as anywhere else, but we don't have time," jokes Dan Gustin. "We're here only eight weeks. We try to maintain a professional situation. For the student orchestra, Joe Silverstein, the Boston Symphony concertmaster, makes out the string seatings. Gunther Schuller makes the brass and wind assignments. These change as we go through the summer."

"Seatings," of course, are the locations of each player in the student orchestra—who sits among the first violins and who among the seconds; who is concertmaster; who plays first horn and who fourth; who gets the solo trumpet part. These are questions of highest importance to professional symphony players, and they also are a matter of moment to these young musicians who—sometimes for the first time in their lives—are measuring themselves against instrumentalists of equal caliber.

To determine their placement in the orchestra, the young players are once again put through auditions soon after their arrival. The auditors include Ozawa and Schuller, as well as the appropriate faculty members. The stakes are not so high as they were in the original auditions for admission, of course, yet even now there is an inevitable feeling of tension and pressure. The string auditions are held in one of the oddest of the many jerry-built structures that have been erected among the trees and groves of Tanglewood. Called the

"Rehearsal-Stage," it is just that—a full-sized enclosed theater-stage, well stocked with chairs and music stands, but with no auditorium attached. Into this curious shed students are called one by one while their fellows wait on the grass outside and cover up their nervousness with small talk. "Who knows, they may be auditioning us for jobs in a few years," quips a tall, bespectacled young cellist from Massachusetts who is spending his summer on a Tanglewood fellowship prior to entering Yale. At seventeen he is one of the youngest fellowship students, and he also appears to be one of the most confident. A stocky, curly haired violinist who attends the New York State University system during the winter emerges rather crestfallen from his session. "I played some of the Mozart Fifth Concerto, and part of a Christian Sinding Suite, and then they asked me for some of Brahms' Third Symphony and Copland's *El Salón México*," he says. "One of them told me he hadn't heard the Sinding in years, but at the end all they said was, 'You can go now.' Oh yes, they also told me to work some more on the Copland."

Two girl viola players, one from Ann Arbor, Michigan, the other from Manhasset, Long Island, both seem reasonably satisfied with their performances. The girl from Ann Arbor has spent several summers at the National Music Camps at Interlochen, but says she feels Tanglewood will give her more performing opportunities and on a higher level. The Manhasset player, whose viola is a bit undersized, explains: "My hands are small, so my viola is made an inch smaller than usual. They're making them that way now for women—it's become an equal opportunity instrument." As far as Tanglewood is concerned, she says that its superiority over other summer programs lies in the opportunity of working with conductors like Ozawa, Schuller and Bernstein. "The real weak point of other places is that the conductors aren't very strong," she says. "Playing in an orchestra can be heaven or hell, depending on the conductor. I'm looking for heaven."

When the seatings for the first orchestral rehearsals are posted the following day, the Yale-bound cellist is at the first-desk position, both the violists are well up front, and the worried fiddler has made it to the first violins, but just barely, at the last stand. Later on during the season the positions will be rotated for the various concerts given by the student orchestra; nevertheless, a certain initial precedence has been established, and the students have begun to appraise their own capacities.

The orchestra is not the only Tanglewood department in which there is jockeying for position. Placement also is important in the chamber music program in which all the instrumental fellows participate. The students are split up into various trios, quartets, quintets and so on, up to octets and nonets, in which they will explore different aspects of the chamber music repertory, not to mention the niceties of ensemble playing itself. These combinations will also shift and vary during the season; generally the same players spend no more than one week working on a piece, then move on to a new grouping and a new composition.

The assignment of students to the various chamber groups is influenced by the Boston Symphony Orchestra faculty members, but much of it devolves upon James Whitaker, a former trumpet player and Tanglewood alumnus of the famous class of '42, who now is in charge of student scheduling. It is to Whitaker that the administrators turn when it develops that a string quartet lacks a second fiddler or a wind group has one horn too many. Whitaker, accordingly, is admired by those students who are pleased by their assignments and is resented by those who are not. "I've done all right in the orchestra," mourns one violinist, "but in chamber music I've done nothing but play second violin in a lot of quartets I've already played. It's disappointing."

Whitaker says complaints used to be made in his day, too. "The students haven't changed much," he says. "In the fellowship program they always were highly intent and serious. I think perhaps they're a little better qualified today than they used to be. That's because public school instruction in music is much better. When the Berkshire Music Center first started there was nothing else like it in the country. We had the complete pick of young talent, the cream. When I was here in '42 there was no other place to go. Now there's Blossom, Aspen, all the other festivals and schools. There's competition. But we still do all right."

Even some of the students themselves seem deeply impressed by the caliber of their fellows. Remarks one high-school-age trumpet player, a member of the B.U. Young Artists Orchestra: "There are two kinds of players up here. The good ones and the great ones."

Students at Work

Learning at Tanglewood is an unending process. It goes on while students are attending Boston Symphony rehearsals and concerts; when they are exchanging musical small talk at mealtime; during the informal practice sessions they sometimes arrange among themselves. But its most intense manifestation is at the daily classes and performance sessions that each attends—concentrated get-togethers with a faculty member and a group of fellow students that can range in number anywhere from two or three to twenty or thirty.

Hugh Ross working with student choristers in one of the Berkshire Music Center's typically rough-hewn buildings. (Photo by Gus Manos, courtesy the Boston Symphony Orchestra)

It is no exaggeration to say that at Tanglewood classes are held wherever there are four walls and a roof—and sometimes not even that. Many a Tanglewood group, as in Paul Hindemith's day, has convened in a grove of pines or under an arching elm. But nearly every structure on the rolling 260-acre estate is pressed into educational service. The gabled Main House is partially occupied by the Center's office force and library, but most of its more than twenty rooms, opening off narrow, labyrinthine corridors, have been turned into studios. The Theater-Concert Hall is regularly used for class sessions. The Shed would be, too, if it were not so large. The East and West Barns, which actually *were* once barns, have been converted to musical uses, as has the rebuilt replica of Hawthorne's house. A chamber music hall designed by Saarinen, a miniature theater whose side wall can be slid back to open upon the countryside, offers a comfortable recital stage and chairs for an audience of several hundred. Scattered about are a variety of little sheds in which the daily musical work also goes on. These plain, unfinished wooden structures, some designated by numbers, others by letters of the alphabet, are minimal in space and sparse in furnishings, being equipped only with an upright piano and a few chairs and music stands.

To make the rounds of these unpretentious learning centers on a typical Tanglewood day can be a revealing experience.

In a third floor room of the Main House a quartet of three boys and a girl are putting together the parts of Mendelssohn's String Quartet in D, Op. 44, No. 1 under the guidance of violinist William Kroll. The room is beneath the eaves of the roof, and two of its windows command a view of the lake and the blue-shrouded Monument Mountain beyond—the Berkshire vista that Nathaniel Hawthorne so admired. But the four players have resolutely turned their backs to the view and under the sloping ceiling sit facing their instructor who, like themselves, has his instrument in his hand.

"Fritz" Kroll, as he is universally known in the music world, was born in 1901 and has been playing chamber music for half a century. In the 1930s he was first violinist of the Coolidge Quartet, which played on South Mountain in Mrs. Elizabeth Sprague Coolidge's Temple of Music. In 1944 he organized his own Kroll Quartet, which ended its existence in 1971. A courtly, soft-spoken gray-haired man with a dry sense of humor, he is wearing a jacket and slacks and a checked bow tie, an outfit that contrasts strikingly with his T-shirted, blue-jeaned, sneaker-shod players. Kroll has been teaching summers at Tanglewood since 1949 and is immensely proud of being the only string man on the faculty who is not a member of the Boston Symphony.

The old Tappan house, built in 1849, has served as headquarters of the Berkshire Music Center and focal point of student activities since 1940. Practice sessions go on all day in its rooms. (Photo by Gus Manos, courtesy the Boston Symphony Orchestra)

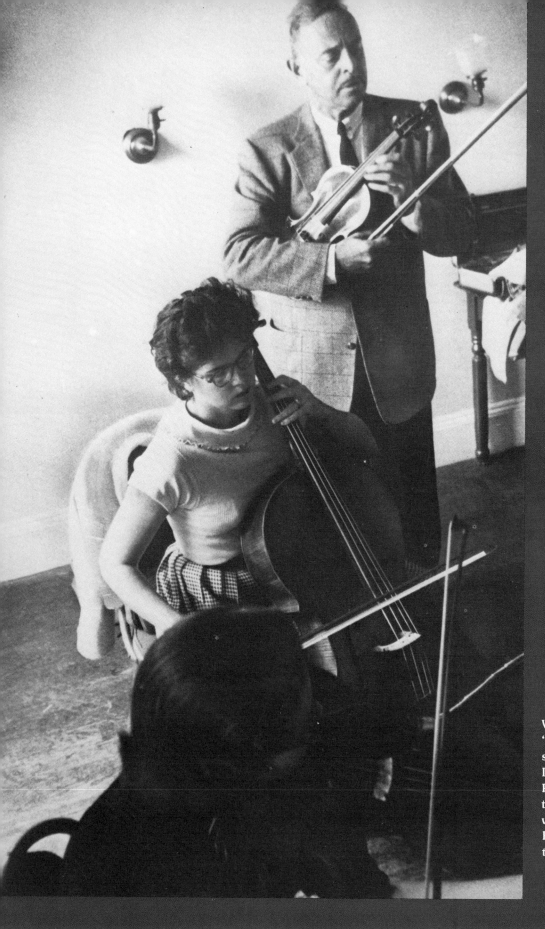

Violin under arm, William "Fritz" Kroll works with a student string quartet. Invited to join the faculty by Koussevitzky in 1949, he is the only string instructor who is not a member of the Boston Symphony. (Courtesy the *Berkshire Eagle*)

"Koussevitzky asked me," he recalls. "I played a concert in Boston in 1941 and he was there. I had injured my back and I had to wear a stiff corset, so I stood very rigid through the whole recital. Koussevitzky was tremendously impressed by my carriage. When he came backstage he said, 'You will be at Tanglewood.' Eight years went by. Then he called me and said, 'You remember I said "You'll be at Tanglewood?" Well, now you're at Tanglewood. You'll be here for life.' I thought he meant his life, but I'm still here, so I guess he meant my life."

Kroll begins his session in the most direct way possible by telling the players: "All right, let's go." Without actually playing he moves his bow in small arcs over his violin—then finally he joins in with the first violin part. "Excellent!" he calls out, then, a few moments later: "No, no, you're two measures behind." A fresh start is made, and this time things go better, with the blonde girl and the three boys—two beards and a moustache—moving smoothly through the intricacies of the music. "You're becoming accustomed to it," Kroll tells them as they continue playing, "it's really very easy—when you were late before, well, you have to realize the things that take place between the mind and the execution."

An hour and a half later, the quartets—both Mendelssohn's and the young players'—are taking shape. "When do we meet again?" asks Kroll. Everyone has some sort of a schedule conflict to overcome—except Kroll. Finally, a time for the next day is agreed upon. "I'm entirely a slave of the administration," says Kroll cheerfully.

When his pupils have packed up their instruments and departed Kroll is asked how one goes about teaching ensemble playing.

"Well," he says, "you have to find out their abilities, especially their abilities in rhythms. They have to become aware of one another, intensely aware of what the other is doing. You give them fingerings and bowings, just as you do in an orchestra. When the violins are independent, it's O.K. to play as they wish. But when they're in conjunction they must use the same bowings. Also, I must take care of the dynamics—in a room like this there's hell to pay over dynamics. They will play this piece at a concert within a week. And to form a quartet, you really must practice at least a year."

In the Theater-Concert Hall Roger Voisin is working with three instrumentalists—trumpet, bassoon and clarinet. They are going over passages from Jacques Ibert's *Capriccio*, a piece for ten instruments. It is fairly complicated to play, so Voisin is preparing the musicians in small groupings. But even with only three instruments in action there is plentiful evidence of the young musicians' bounce and vitality. Ibert's perky measures seem to brighten up the empty theater as the performers sit on the stage tooting away.

Afterwards Voisin, seated on a bench beneath a pine tree outside the theater, remarks that one of the toughest parts of his job is finding music with which to challenge his young performers.

"Students now are more inquisitive than they used to be, which is healthy," he says. "They're much more aware, and they're better and better informed repertoire-wise. It's more and more taxing to find them repertoire they haven't played before. With the Ibert, they told me they didn't know it. But then, I didn't know it too well, either."

Voisin, slender and thin-faced, retired as an active player in 1973 after thirty-nine years in the orchestra during which he rose to first desk of the trumpet section. His father, Réné Voisin, also a trumpeter, preceded him to the orchestra. "Koussevitzky heard him play in Paris and imported him 'like a piece of cheese,' he always used to say," says Voisin *fils*. "I was nine years old when we came here from France. At that time, you didn't get hired by the Boston Symphony; you were 'invited to join' it. At sixteen, I was invited to join, too. I was the youngest member of the orchestra. I had two bosses, Koussevitzky and my father. My father and I were playing side by side the night of that famous thunderstorm in the tent in 1937. My son Peter is now third trumpet in Syracuse, and he has played as an extra in the Boston Symphony. So this orchestra has had three generations of Voisins in it."

Voisin has continued to teach at Tanglewood since his retirement, working both with fellowship students in the Berkshire Music Center and with the brass ensemble in the B.U. program.

"We are not teachers of the instrument *per se*," he explains. "We teach ensemble. The problem is to make people listen to each other. All your life you have been in a room playing to yourself. Now, to play ensemble, you almost have to divorce yourself from your instrument. You must listen very carefully, you must be *sympathique* to the others. The main thing to teach these kids is to try to listen all around them. If they don't blend, they're not going to make music. Koussevitzky tried to develop this sense of chamber music even in the Boston Symphony itself."

Voisin believes there are benefits students gain in addition to musicianship from their summer-long contact·with the Boston Symphony players. "We let them absorb from us *le métier*, the profession," he says. "They see us swim, they see us play. They see us eat too much one night, and yet show up for a concert the next day. They see us in a bad temper. They see the profession as it is. We have to play as we preach; you can't teach them one way and play another at the concert that night. We teach by example.

"They also learn to realize that when last night's concert is over, it's finished. Today's another one. In a college or a conservatory they talk about a concert two weeks before it takes place and five weeks after. Here it's given, it's gone. On to the next."

At the Windsor Mountain School Phyllis Curtin is conducting a vocal seminar. The Windsor Mountain School is about a mile from the Tanglewood grounds, just outside the town of Lenox. It is one of the several private schools from which the Berkshire Music Center rents dormitory space during the summer. It also has a small, auditoriumlike room, glass walled and in a rustic setting, which is well-suited to class sessions. So Tanglewood rents that, too, and the students either hike up from the main grounds or arrive by cars which they park on a nearby grassy strip.

Miss Curtin, an unusually intelligent and thoughtful singer, puts her technical knowledge and personal experience to good use in working with her pupils. In fact, so many of them keep returning to Tanglewood that she has instituted a limit of three successive summers for attendance at her seminar.

She runs her class in a traditional manner: each student is called upon in turn, announces his or her song's title, and proceeds to sing it with the class accompanist at the piano. Everyone else listens closely both to the performers and to Miss Curtin's running critique. The idea is to learn not only from your own mistakes—and successes—but from everybody else's as well.

Some of the students at the session are working on songs by Berlioz, and Miss Curtin comments on everything from their methods of producing sounds to their French diction. "It's not easy," she tells them. "You know you're doing six months' work in about three minutes."

To one girl who has a lovely voice but too much vibrato Miss Curtin says: "Now, you must sort out a vibrato from a wobble. They're two different things. Talk yourself into a mental image. Try to *see* the note as it goes away from you. See the sound on a long black road with a yellow line down the center, all the way across the state of Kansas. That center line is endlessly long to infinity, and none of it can spill onto the black."

The young soprano nods, starts again, thinks of a long yellow line stretching to infinity. When she comes to the last words, "*le rossignol chantera,*" the notes flow out free and secure. A smile suffuses the singer's face, and the class bursts into applause.

A young tenor named Fred is having some difficulties with his pro-

Double-bass students get an outdoor workout under the Boston Symphony's Henry Portnoi. (Photo by Marian Gillett)

nunciation. He announces he will sing the aria from Mendelssohn's *Elijah* "It is ee-nough," but he immediately launches into the words "It is eh-nough." Miss Curtin stops him quickly. "We have this beautiful sound from you, Fred, but we start thinking: 'Well, how *do* you pronounce the word? How will he do it next time?' I remember when I sang in *Peter Grimes* in England how my American pronunciations stood out from the rest of the English cast's. We cannot hamper ourselves with inconsistencies, affectations, regionalisms."

Singer after singer comes forth with his or her song, goes through it and is given practical advice on voice placement or production, pronunciation or phrasing. There is a tall black youth with a truly remarkable bass voice, obviously at the point of full professionalism; a plump, pleasant-looking Rhode Island girl who brings her slumbering five-week-old baby to class in a little basket; a church mezzo from the Midwest who wants to broaden her range and repertory; singers of varied backgrounds and interests, but all eager to work and to learn.

Says Miss Curtin afterwards: "I'm not so concerned over the singers as I am over who wants to engage them. We have a funny cultural setup in this country—we put up these huge centers, but we don't know what to put in them. I sit around and listen to all these first-rate talents but I don't know who will use them. These singers are far more sophisticated as musicians than we ever were in my day as a student here—far more attuned to musical values, and to contemporary music. What I learned here as a young singer was a standard of personal excellence. The standard was so high, there was always such a looking for more and more and more, that it gave an enormous impetus to your own thinking about your own work. I found that here, and I try to give it to others."

In the Rehearsal-Stage Gilbert Kalish is holding a preparatory session for Schumann's *Andante and Variations*. The piece exists in two versions, one for two pianos, two cellos and French horn, the other, made later, for two pianos alone. The Tanglewood performance will be of the original version for the full complement of chamber players, but at the moment Kalish is working only with the two pianists, a girl in a pink blouse and white shorts, and a boy in a green sports shirt and blue jeans. The Rehearsal-Stage, that curious foreshortened structure, is cluttered with empty music stands, timpani, a xylophone and other percussion instruments shoved against the back wall. The two grand pianos are placed back to back and curve to curve, so that the pianists are seated facing each other under the upraised lids, while Kalish perches himself on a metal folding chair near by.

Phyllis Curtin's seminar for singers encompasses all branches of the vocal art from voice production (above) to projection (below). The Metropolitan Opera soprano once was a Tanglewood student herself. (Both photos by Eugene Cook)

"There's a little too much accent," Kalish tells the girl. "It has a legato sound, like this—" and he sings it for her, then, stepping to the keyboard, plays it. "I'm exaggerating, but if you could do the same in the playing, to bring out the loveliness. . . ." Then, after a time, to them both: "You must learn to work together as a team. We're being led by a staccato. It's got to be a staccato, but not a weighty staccato. It's got to have some inflection."

At the end of a passage the boy says: "Can I ask a question?" Kalish replies quickly: "You never have to ask if you can ask a question." The boy smiles: "All right, I have a question." Kalish, with mock brusqueness: "Sorry, no questions." The question, as it turns out, has to do with fingering, but the ensuing discussion is inconclusive. Kalish finally says: "It's for you guys to work out—you have to get that lower part so it sounds right. You both sound a little sluggish today. . . . Now, *that's* it. That's excellent, much better right there."

"When the others are here it'll be better," puts in the boy. "Very true, but it sounded confusing," says Kalish. "It's a very elusive little section."

Gil Kalish, born in 1935, is a pianist of broad musical sympathies and prodigious technique, who specializes in performing new music. He first came to Tanglewood as a sixteen-year-old student; nowadays he is in charge of its piano department. "You find yourself standing in the place where you were sitting," he says. "It's an odd kind of *déjà vu*." He does his own auditioning and heard a hundred pianists before selecting the nine who make up the summer's crop. "Mostly they were in Boston and New York," he says, "but there were some in Los Angeles and other cities. I make a point of auditioning when I tour. I find out their backgrounds, their teachers, and that's a factor, too. This year about twenty of the hundred I heard were on tape. That girl you just heard in the Schumann, she was picked off a tape. I took a chance. She sounded like a really interesting player. I checked with her school, Eastman, and also with some pianists I knew in Rochester. Mostly I'd rather not hear them on tapes—it's unfair. But a live audition can be unfair, too. I once heard twenty-eight people in seven hours in Boston. You get tired listening. I believe pianists are more carefully selected now than in the past. In my time I'd say that only two of the ten pianists we had were on a really high level. We also keep them busier. In the past some pianists sat around without assignments for two weeks."

Kalish, voluble and intense, is an enthusiast for the idea of student involvement in contemporary music performance. "The secret of playing new music," he says, "is the same as the secret of playing ensemble music of any kind—you have to listen to each other and yourself. An instructor has to insist that the students keep on doing that—it's a continuous discipline. In the contemporary field they used to hire ringers up here. Paul Jacobs used to do all the piano playing; they brought in the Lenox Quartet and the Dorian Quintet. Then Schuller decided not to use outsiders but to bring everybody into it, and why not? It makes for an iffy situation, but educationally there's no question that it's of greater value.

"Tanglewood is a professional proving ground. The young musicians see if they can do it, if they can take it, if they like it. These are things they have to know."

In Studio No. 2 the instructor is the Boston Symphony's first bassoonist Sherman Walt, and the subject is the Thuille Sextet. And what, even a knowledgeable music-lover may ask, is the Thuille Sextet? It is a work for flute, oboe, clarinet, bassoon, horn and piano by Ludwig Wilhelm Andreas Maria Thuille, a composer and pedagogue who was born in the Tyrol in 1861 and died in Munich in 1907. His music, well-tailored to the instruments and discreetly romantic, is nowadays played mostly in conservatories. "A very nice piece, but if you get too involved in it it gets boring," comments Sherman Walt diplomatically. "I wouldn't want to work on it for a month."

The six Tanglewood students will work on it for only a week. They can hardly squeeze into the tiny hut of a studio illuminated by two small windows and an unshaded light bulb. The bassoon player, particularly, has developed a case of claustrophobia, not because he hasn't got room to maneuver his unwieldy instrument, but because of the sound. "There are too many echoes," he complains. "It's hard to hear."

Walt, a moustached, sporty-looking man who rides a motorcycle to and from work, is trying to get the young wind players to play softly—not because of the chamber's acoustics, but because excessive loudness is ruinous to chamber playing. "It's hard not to crescendo," he tells the students. "Think diminuendo, then you'll get the piano." Later he interrupts them: "On those last notes, *every* one of you was just a little late, which means you're counting and not listening." Trying to get more legato out of the bassoonist in the gavotte movement Walt says: "You're making it too cutesy. I want a lift there, but you're putting a hiccup in it. That's one way of doing it, of course. I did it that way when I was at Curtis. But when I came out, I changed. I find that in playing a piece I might be hung up on, the best way to overcome it is to sing it. If you sing it, you can't play it wrong."

Then, summing up the art of instrumentalism in a word, he says: "The difference between first-class playing and great playing is phrasing. What else is there?"

Walt, like most of the Boston first-deck men, does his own auditioning, listening to fifty or sixty bassoon applicants a year. When the Boston Symphony is on tour he visits conservatories and schools to hear prospects, and in New York he holds open auditions. He also listens to tapes. "A girl stopped me in Philharmonic Hall in New York while I was playing in the Mostly Mozart there," he says. "She wants to come up here next year. We'll listen, and maybe she will."

Like Roger Voisin, Walt sometimes has trouble finding repertory for his players. "We play eight pieces in eight weeks," he says. "It's not like with the string players, where there's so much repertory. But the chamber music program is essential. Wind players tend to play too strongly—they're all tuned to playing like in an orchestra. In chamber music you have to listen to one another more than in an orchestra—there's no conductor. Have the students changed over the years? Yes, they have. They've improved. When I first came here they were looking for the basics of orchestral performance. Now they're ready for jobs."

On the open lawn near the back entrance to the Tanglewood grounds that is known as the "Lion Gate" sits a seventy-five-year-old retired member of the Boston Symphony named Albert Bernard. Around him are gathered six young men, all members of the conducting class at Tanglewood. The subject is solfège, a somewhat vague and mysterious musical term which one popular dictionary defines as "a course in ear-training and general musicianship." Essentially it is a system of sight-reading in which the notes are sung with a certain syllable attached to each note. Solfège—the name comes from the notes *sol* and *fa*—is used widely in France and is taught at a number of American musical institutions, the Berkshire Music Center among them.

"It is not the grammar of music, but it is the reader," explains Albert Bernard in the pleasant French accent he has never lost in his fifty years in America. "Koussevitzky started the teaching of solfège at Tanglewood and we have always continued it. But I have only the conductors and the vocalists in my classes—not the instrumentalists, though they need it, too."

Bernard was another of the Parisian musicians imported like a piece of cheese by the Boston Symphony; he came here in 1925, and played the viola until his retirement. For the last twenty years he has been teaching solfège at Tanglewood, and during the winter he teaches it at the New England Conservatory. At his classes he distributes sheets of exercises involving intervals, time spans and transpositions; and he and his students sit on the grass in a semicircle, almost like monks in a medieval monastery, singing notes and beating time.

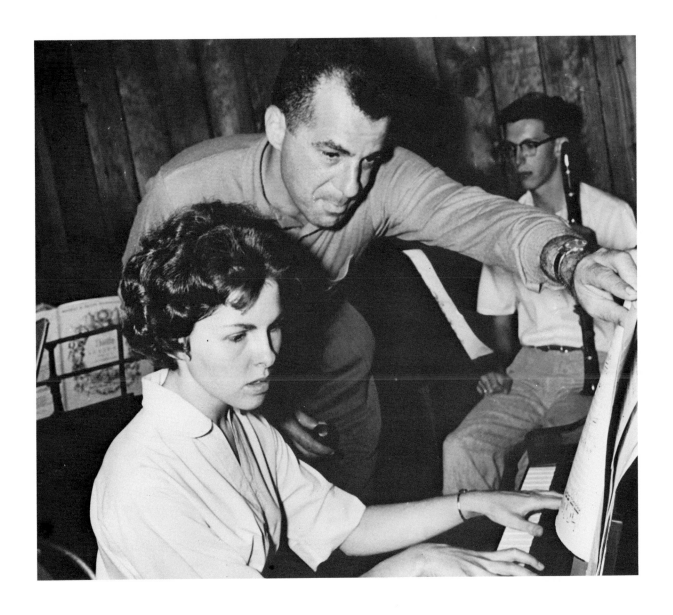

Instructor Sherman Walt, in his moustacheless days, guides his students through the Thuille Sextet, a favorite practice piece. (Courtesy Whitestone Photographers)

But he also interjects into his conductors' class little aphorisms culled from his half-century's orchestral experience: "If one player makes a mistake it's his fault—if a whole section makes a mistake it's your fault." "It's just as bad to anticipate a beat as to come in too late." "There is no such thing as being a little out of tune. You're either in tune or not. It's like being a little bit pregnant."

Later he tells a visitor: "They get the technique of conducting from their conducting classes. I want to give them a musician's slant. So I tell them things like 'Don't beat with your foot' or 'Don't turn your back on a section.' I try to show them how to bow, how to act on the stage—things not taught in technical courses. I want them to know that to gain the respect of the orchestra it's important to catch the little mistakes. Everyone notices the big ones. There is a constant battle between the musicians and the conductor—it's in the nature of things—and the conductor must impose his will on the players. So when the conductor points out a mistake, and the musician will say 'Show me,' the conductor must be able to show him." Albert Bernard's solfège, like Tanglewood itself, covers a lot of ground.

Putting It All Together

Of all of Tanglewood's institutions, probably the most remarkable is the orchestra assembled every summer from the students at the Berkshire Music Center. Each year it is made up of different people, yet each year it achieves within an incredibly short time an extraordinarily high standard of performance, with a blend of skill and enthusiasm that give it a distinctively vibrant quality.

Foremost among its accomplishments is its capacity to prepare and put together a program in a brief period of time. At the end of its first week of existence it is being conducted by Ozawa in a public concert consisting of Berlioz' *Roman Carnival* Overture, Beethoven's Symphony No. 2 in D and Copland's *El Salón México*. The rehearsal time would be short even for an established orchestra working with a new conductor; for an orchestra whose members have never met each other previously the task requires extreme diligence and application. Ozawa, wearing a rumpled white tunic and trousers, makes every minute of each session count. In Beethoven's Second he demands more tension in the strings. "It's too easy, the way you do," he says. He gets off his stool to crouch over the orchestra from a standing position, stamping and shouting, his long black hair flying as he conducts. By the fourth movement he has the young orchestra whipped up to a peak of

(Above) The student orchestra is the core of the Berkshire Music Center's activities, with faculty members closely supervising work of instrumentalists and conductors. In this 1975 picture student Thomas Fulton conducts while Bernstein looks on.

(Below) Jose Contreras is on podium with Ozawa standing in the middle of the orchestra. (Courtesy Whitestone Photographers)

excitement. By the day of the concert he is leading them—without the shouting and stamping—in a performance whose precision and vigor bring an ovation from the audience.

In its second week of existence the orchestra begins work with Leonard Bernstein on another program consisting of Ravel's *Alborado del Gracioso* and G Major Piano Concerto (with the conductor as soloist) and Sibelius' Fifth Symphony.

"People will tell you I'm crazy to make such a difficult program in one week," Bernstein tells the students gathered on the stage of the Theater-Concert Hall for his first nighttime rehearsal. "But I'm sure we can do it. I've been looking forward to this."

He is wearing a tan gabardine suit and a blue shirt with an open collar. He starts by hanging his coat over the back of a chair, shaking hands with the leaders of the string sections in front of him and seating himself on a stool.

"Now you all know what this means," he says. "'Alborado' is a morning song or dance. 'Gracioso' is a clown. So it's a clown's morning song. It's fun, dewy, morning bright. Try to be aware that it's a French piece although it's also a Spanish piece. It has very sharp accents—brilliant, light dry. Even in the fortissimo it has to be light, the exact opposite of the Sibelius, when we get to that."

Bernstein uses a quiet, conversational tone in talking to the students in the orchestra, and some lean forward to listen. Other students—in fact, the entire Tanglewood corps—are in the audience, but it is more difficult to hear him there. Seiji Ozawa, still in rumpled white, is on hand, too, and he interrupts to suggest that the conducting students in the audience move up to the stage and sit at the sides and rear of the orchestra so they can hear and observe better. Ozawa himself begins to carry folding chairs for them onto the stage.

Alborado del Gracioso is a short, brilliant piece full of tricky instrumental solos. Bernstein begins to conduct it, calling out approving comments as he goes along. "Excellent!" he says as the plucked strings open the work incisively. Then, "That's *terrific,* charming, nice" to various instruments as they make their entrances. To a girl bassoonist he says: "Keep on without taking a breath as though you were this big gypsy contralto. . . . Try and make up some words for yourself, something that sounds vaguely Spanish." Then, when she finishes the plaintive passage: "That was wonderful. You just broke my heart."

Sometimes, though, the comments, humorously couched as they are, are exhortations to do better. To the tuba player: "How old are you? Gee,

I could play a tuba louder than that when I was twenty-three. And I never had tuba lessons. . . . That's better. . . . That's *terrific!*" To the harpist: "You want to sound like a guitar there, but a Spanish guitar. That was a Nashville guitar." To the trumpet players after a difficult passage: "That's *practically* it. Don't be scared that you're all alone. You've always got each other."

All through the piece Bernstein is in motion, signaling to players and sections, getting caught up in the music, doing a little Spanish dance at a flamencolike episode, talking, encouraging, cajoling. At a tricky rhythmic passage he says, "You have to understand the ambiguity of this Hispanic music—six-eights and three-fourths simultaneously. You're not sure whether it's in three-fourths although it's not written that way. Rehearse at first as if we're all playing the same." After a little while the passage is being done to his satisfaction. He apologizes: "I'm sorry we're taking so long with this piece, but what the hell is the point unless we learn it? Everything you learn with this piece you can apply to all music of this sort." All through, the comments are frank and direct, but never given impatiently or with a sharp edge to them.

Finally the piece is played to the end and a ten-minute break is announced. Bernstein, who is covered with perspiration on this warm summer's evening, goes out to change his drenched shirt. The students don't leave the stage but buzz excitedly among themselves, with some trying out some of the *Alborado* passages they have just played. Ozawa talks quietly to one or two of them, and the conducting students go into a little huddle of their own at the side of the stage.

Bernstein reemerges in a fresh shirt. "Now the Sibelius," he says, resuming his place on the podium, "is the exact opposite. There's nothing in the first movement with the attack or the sharpness of that French music. Most of the time you don't know where the notes are coming from. Mysterious, like a sleeping giant—there's an awful lot of force inside that has to be awakened. You see, it's marked piano, but it must be as though you're playing forte."

The Sibelius goes much more arduously than the Ravel, but Bernstein continues to work with the young musicians patiently. Finally, when time is running out he leads them in what is little more than a sight-reading of the score. When it is finished, he remarks: "Nobody ever said music was easy—especially this music. When do we meet again?" At the next rehearsal—the following day—there will be time to work out the problems.

Talking about the session afterwards—after one more change of shirt—he says: "I really do come here to learn. All those things I teach the kids, I'm learning. Nothing is so exciting to a young person as a chance of getting better. And having been that myself, having gone all through that in this very place, I relate very strongly to them. I feel very strongly for these kids. I feel when they're bored and when they think 'Oh, this is all too heavy, why are you talking so much, why don't we just play it?' and then when they realize *why* I'm going into it in such detail, then I feel very rewarded.

"It is very, very hard for young people to absorb what I was trying to tell them about the Sibelius tonight. I did talk too much because I was trying to get the point across. This is basically a philosophical kind of music, born of years of brooding and trying to cope with history. But it will be fine, you'll see. I have every confidence that by the time we get finished next week it will be beautifully done."

And so it was.

Koussevitzky's Children

As befits an educational institution that gives no diplomas to its graduates, the Berkshire Music Center offers very little in the way of ceremonial flourishes as its season draws to an end. Tanglewood on Parade might be considered a kind of Class Day, for it belongs largely to the students, who usually begin the festivities by welcoming the first visitors through the gates with a fanfare, and close it by joining the Boston Symphony in a suitably noisy and large-scale work, like Tchaikovsky's "1812" Overture.

The closest the Center comes to holding a commencement is its final concert, held the last Saturday afternoon of the season in the Theater-Concert Hall. As at all its concerts throughout the summer, the orchestra is attired in concert dress—white jackets and dark trousers for the men, white dresses for the women. Each student conductor directs one of the works on the program. In 1975 they were Rossini's *Semiramide* Overture, Mendelssohn's "Italian" Symphony, Haydn's "Clock" Symphony and Stravinsky's *Petrouchka*. Inevitably, there is a feeling of competition in the air, for the awards to outstanding students, including conductors, will be announced by Seiji Ozawa and Gunther Schuller at the end of the concert. However, the prizes are for the entire season's work, not merely for these final performances.

As the awards for each category are called out, the students in the orchestra and the audience alike greet the names with cheers. The winner of the Koussevitzky Prize is most eagerly awaited; nobody has to be told that the award has served as a springboard for some notable conducting careers. As occasionally happens, 1975 is a year in which no single individual is adjudged outstanding enough to receive the award, so it is withheld. The four young competitors are disappointed, but each has a job lined up for the season ahead, ranging from an assistant conductorship with the San Francisco Symphony to the musical directorship of a chamber orchestra in Brooklyn Heights, New York. Everyone of them leaves Tanglewood a more accomplished and confident conductor than he came. And although the formal sessions of the Berkshire Center are over for the summer, no one is thinking of departing until after the next day's final Sunday afternoon concert by the Boston Symphony.

Of all the ceremonies that are held at Tanglewood during the summer the one that best conveys the unique spirit of the place occurs not at the end of the season but in the middle, and not on the Festival grounds but two miles away in the Church on the Hill, a dignified white edifice built in 1805 that stands on a rise just beyond Lenox on the Pittsfield road.

There every year on the Sunday closest to July 26, the birth date of Serge Koussevitzky, a memorial service is held in his honor. Unlike most memorial services, it is not a funereal affair. Rather it is what Mrs. Olga Koussevitzky calls by the Russian word *pominki*—a festive gathering that is a celebration of a life rather than a commemoration of a death. It is fitting that the mood be one of a family coming together, for Koussevitzky, who had none of his own, regarded and referred to the Tanglewood students as his "children," and for many of them, from Leonard Bernstein and Lukas Foss on, he has remained a father figure.

At the church, the regular Sunday-morning Congregational service is performed and a brief meditation is read by the Reverend H. B. Hinchcliff. Then a musical service, in the form of a brief solemn concert, is performed by a group of students from the Berkshire Music Center. The program varies from year to year: it can encompass a Gabrieli fanfare, Copland's Threnody or Haydn's *The Seven Last Words*.

When the music has ended, the entire congregation files into the hilltop cemetery behind the church and gathers around Koussevitzky's grave. There the students from Tanglewood sing Randall Thompson's *Alleluia*. Then a huge white cake inscribed "Berkshire Music Center" with the appropriate year is brought out, and Mrs. Koussevitzky slices it and distributes the pieces to the throng. "His students shared his birthday cake every year in life," she says, "and now they continue to do the same."

Koussevitzky himself chose this grave site. A few years before his death he told his wife that he wished to be buried in the hilltop churchyard "because it overlooks Tanglewood." Though there was little room left in the cemetery, which has headstones dating back to Colonial days, the church elders readily consented, and a site beneath a huge, centuries-old maple tree was selected. In 1974, the year of the centenary of the conductor's birth, one day after the annual graveside ceremony was held, for no apparent reason the great tree fell. Only the fact that it landed on two heavy branches prevented it from cracking or possibly shattering the Jerusalem marble headstone. "When it happened," says Mrs. Koussevitzky, "I thought to myself, 'This tree was for the first hundred years, and now something new has to start.' So I asked Mr. Woodger, who takes care of the church grounds, to get me a fir tree. He got a Canadian evergreen, and it is here now." Afterwards, watching the students and the other celebrants walk down the path that will take them back to their cars and their work at the Berkshire Center, Olga Koussevitzky says: "I think Tanglewood will be alive as long as there are young people."

Among those who share her belief is Seiji Ozawa, the man who will have more to do than any other individual with shaping the future course of Tanglewood. Ozawa is almost exactly the same age as the Berkshire Festival: he was born in 1935, one year after Hadley started it and one year before Koussevitzky took it over. He has himself undergone significant changes since he first came there in 1960 as a student, a total stranger in this country, speaking no English, and with little money in his pockets. His hair was cut short, he dressed conservatively, and he impressed everybody by his great earnestness. "When I came here as a student," he says, "there were many things I didn't know besides the language. I didn't know about Mahler, I didn't know about opera—at least I was way behind in opera. Also, I didn't have an aggressive way of expressing things. In Japan, conductors conduct with less energy, in a neater way. So I learned the positive approach of young people in America. As a young kid here I learned the energy of the young. I developed a more positive, forceful approach."

Ozawa's conducting technique and his personality both have flowered at Tanglewood. The very first performances he gave with the student orchestra stirred great interest among the faculty and among the other students as well; clearly he was headed for an important career. Later on he was able to transfer the same incisiveness and authoritative technique to more formal concert halls. His musical range, limited when he first came here, has expanded enormously, so that he is now at home in a wide variety of styles and epochs. But as a superb organizer of tonal forces he retains a particular affinity for large-scale splashy works—works that sometimes seem almost

Beads flying and score closed, Ozawa is in command of a Boston Symphony performance in the Shed. (Courtesy the *Berkshire Eagle*)

In Loving Memory
of
Serge Koussevitzky
by the Members of
The Israel Symphony Orchestra
To Whom He Was A Great and Inspired Leader
and A Loved and Honored Friend

Each summer on the Sunday closest to Koussevitzky's birthday, Berkshire Music Center students gather at his grave to sing Randall Thompson's *Alleluia*. Mrs. Koussevitzky stands at right. The cake that will be served afterward rests on a bench behind the gravestones. Marble slab in foreground is Jerusalem marble sent from Israel. (Courtesy Whitestone Photographers)

too vast and sprawling for the confines of the normal concert hall. That is one reason, perhaps, why he is such a successful summer festival conductor, scheduling compositions written for huge choruses and expanded orchestras, deploying his forces across the great stage of the Shed, sending audiences home in a frenzy of excitement and delight. Tanglewood can expect to see and hear many more such works in the future.

In dress and demeanor Ozawa also is altered from the rather timid young man who arrived from Europe with the Besançon prize and Munch's recommendation as credentials. During class hours, as a matter of fact, he is one of the most easily recognizable sights on the Tanglewood "campus," as he moves quickly about clad in a sloppy white tunic, trousers and sandals, his long black hair flying behind him, beads jiggling around his neck. The beads often also are part of his evening concert costume, for at Tanglewood, at least, Ozawa has discarded customary formal garb in favor of his own neatly tailored tunic, trousers and turtleneck style, sometimes black, sometimes white. Says Sherman Walt: "It took a while, but the real Seiji finally came out."

In his personal style, as well as in his musical outlook, Ozawa exhibits a continuing close kinship with the Tanglewood students. Asked what he feels he can best give them as Boston Symphony director, he says: "These young people, they can do almost anything. But there are two things working against each other, two things they must get. One is the discipline, the style, of ensemble playing—that I feel I must give. But sometimes I also wish I could give a feeling of how beautiful a particular line is in a musical work, of how wonderful music is.

"I want to give them a sense of excitement and emotional involvement. They have this, of course, but they need even more. They hold back. Between the music on the stand in front of them and the conductor on the podium they become timid. They should feel they are expressing their musical experience and feeling through their place in the orchestra."

Future seasons will see Ozawa spending more, rather than less time at Tanglewood, both in directing the Festival itself and in working with Schuller in the educational activities of the Berkshire Music Center. "I should be involved on both sides," he says. "I have no trouble crossing the lawn." Having cut his remaining ties to the San Francisco Symphony and curtailed his guest-conducting activities elsewhere, Ozawa is likely henceforth to be as much a summer fixture in the Berkshires as any other member of the Boston Symphony.

For Leonard Bernstein, however, the picture is less clear. Bernstein

Students with instrument cases are an integral feature of Tanglewood's scenery.
(Courtesy the *Berkshire Eagle*)

Ozawa acknowledges applause after a 1975 performance of Tchaikovsky's *1812 Overture*. On this occasion students of the Berkshire Music Center played side by side with members of the Boston Symphony Orchestra. (Photo by Marian Gillett)

has Tanglewood in his blood; there is no reason to doubt his repeated asseverations that he never feels happier or more useful than when he is there. But Bernstein is not a conductor, he's a conglomerate. His musical activities are so numerous, intricate and far-flung that they leave no room for a permanent, specific commitment to Tanglewood. His advent as "adviser" was invaluable in bridging the gap between Leinsdorf's departure and Ozawa's full take-over; but in actuality, after the first few summers he became gradually less and less active in the necessary policy-making and decision-taking. Nevertheless he very likely will continue to conduct and teach at Tanglewood for limited periods, and judging by past experience, no visitor will be welcomed more eagerly both by audiences and students.

Koussevitzky—Bernstein—Ozawa: the three represent a continuity, a renewal, a passing of an old tradition to youthful hands. Ozawa—who enjoys flavoring his speech with Japanese-accented Americanisms—is as aware of this as anyone. Walking across the lawn on his way from a conducting class in the Theater to a rehearsal session in the Shed he says happily: "Koussevitzky was big poppa to Lenny and Lenny was big poppa to me."

Now as a big poppa himself, it is Ozawa's task in the years ahead to make Tanglewood increasingly unified, cohesive, purposeful and productive. Certainly there is every reason to believe that he will be able to do so. Securely grounded in the past, deeply committed to the future; as beautiful as ever to those who know it and as exciting as ever to those just discovering it, Tanglewood seems well equipped to maintain its position of leadership among this country's, and the world's, music festivals. Koussevitzky's children are flourishing.

A Tanglewood Chronology

1934: First Berkshire Symphonic Festival held August 23, 25 and 26 at horse ring on the Dan Hanna Farm near Stockbridge, with Henry K. Hadley conducting sixty-five members of the New York Philharmonic-Symphony Orchestra. Opening attendance: 3,000.

1935: Hadley conducts a second summer of concerts, this time with eighty-five in orchestra drawn largely from Metropolitan Opera personnel. First talk heard of "an American Salzburg."

1936: Serge Koussevitzky and Boston Symphony Orchestra invited to be resident performers of the Festival, held under a tent at a new site, "Holmwood." Total attendance for three concerts is 15,000.

1937: Site moved again, this time to estate at "Tanglewood" donated by Mrs. Gorham Brooks. On August 12 a rainstorm disrupts a Wagner concert, and a campaign for a permanent structure is begun on spot by Miss Gertrude Robinson Smith.

1938: The Tanglewood Shed is inaugurated on August 5 with Koussevitzky conducting Beethoven's Ninth Symphony.

1939: A record attendance of 7,000 is established for a single concert, with a seasonal total of 38,000, up 2,000 over the previous year. Koussevitzky introduces his newest discovery, young soprano Dorothy Maynor.

1940: The Berkshire Music Center, a school for young professionals, opens on grounds, running concurrently with the concerts. Koussevitzky's first conducting class includes young hopefuls Leonard Bernstein, Lukas Foss, Thor Johnson and Richard Bales.

1941: New 1,200-seat Theater-Concert Hall is added to facilities at a cost of $40,000. U.S. Army bandsmen from Camp Edwards pay visit as European war shadows close in. Koussevitzky leads Beethoven's *Missa Solemnis*.

1942: With entry of United States into war and ensuing transportation shortages, Boston Symphony Orchestra concerts are canceled. However the Berkshire Music Center carries on with Koussevitzky conducting performances by student orchestra and audiences getting there as best they can.

1943: Koussevitzky announces entire Festival must suspend temporarily owing to war conditions.

1944: An abbreviated Festival is given: four Mozart concerts in the Theater-Concert Hall by an orchestra of thirty.

1945: Reduced activities continue, with a three-week Bach-Mozart Festival and a slightly larger orchestra.

1946: Full-scale Berkshire Music Festival and Music Center both resume. Nine concerts given on three weekends. First Tanglewood on Parade is held. Benjamin Britten's opera *Peter Grimes* receives American premiere with composer on hand.

1947: Leonard Bernstein and Eleazar de Carvalho assist Koussevitzky in Berkshire Music Center instruction. All nine Beethoven symphonies played. Season attendance is 100,000.

1948: Replica of Hawthorne Cottage given to Festival by National Federation of Music Clubs. New attendance record for single concert of 14,700 is established.

1949: Koussevitzky, seventy-five, conducts his farewell season as musical director of Boston Symphony. Two Benjamin Britten United States premieres: *Spring Symphony* and opera *Albert Herring*.

1950: Koussevitzky continues as active as ever as Tanglewood director and conducts Bach's B Minor Mass. Sarah Caldwell stages Mozart's *La Finta Giardiniera*. Mrs. Eleanor Roosevelt is narrator in *Peter and the Wolf*.

1951: Koussevitzky dies on June 4; a *Missa Solemnis* he was to have led on August 9 is conducted by Bernstein and dedicated to his memory. Charles Munch, Koussevitzky's successor as Boston Symphony musical director, makes his first Tanglewood appearances. Boris Goldovsky directs Tchaikovsky's opera *Pique Dame*.

1952: Pierre Monteux and Artur Rubinstein make Tanglewood debuts. Goldovsky and Sarah Caldwell give Mozart's last opera *La Clemenza di Tito* its first complete American performance. Munch closes Festival with Berlioz Requiem.

1953: Arthur Fiedler and the Boston Pops make the Tanglewood scene. Leontyne Price and William Warfield sing Act II of *Porgy and Bess* under Bernstein. Munch moves Thursday-night concerts to Friday nights, thus achieving a concentrated weekend.

1954: Twentieth-anniversary season brings new attendance record of 155,325, with twelve concerts in the Shed instead of the previous nine. Munch conducts concert version of Berlioz' *Damnation of Faust.* Aaron Copland's opera *The Tender Land* is performed.

1955: Hurricane Connie almost disrupts final weekend, but 9,750 sit through Beethoven's Ninth in a rain-lashed Shed. Wet summer fails to prevent still another attendance record.

1956: Fromm Foundation of Chicago inaugurates series of contemporary music concerts. Boston Symphony plays five new works commissioned for its seventy-fifth anniversary. Munch leads two Wagner programs; Benny Goodman plays Mozart's Clarinet Concerto and Clarinet Quintet.

1957: Opening of Massachusetts Turnpike halves travel time from Boston to Tanglewood. Berlioz' *L'Enfance du Christ* and Beethoven's Ninth among works led by Munch.

1958: Bach's B Minor Mass is conducted by C. Wallace Woodworth, retiring as director of Harvard Glee Club and Radcliffe Choral Society. Bumper crop of young conductors includes Claudio Abbado, Zubin Mehta, David Zinman.

1959: Twenty-fifth-anniversary season achieves total of 181,715 visitors with total ticket sales of $327,055.50. A new stage canopy for the orchestra is dedicated.

1960: Festival opens a few days after Boston Symphony returns from an eight-week tour of Far East and Pacific. Munch leads all Shed concerts except four by Monteux. Luciano Berio is composer in residence. Seiji Ozawa wins Koussevitzky Prize for conducting.

1961: Festival increases duration from six weeks to seven. Danny Kaye and Eugene Ormandy make Tanglewood debuts. Critic's complaint of conservative Shed programs brings rebuttal from orchestra manager.

1962: Thirteenth and last year of Munch's tenure as Boston musical director; season lengthened to eight weeks. Evening concerts now begin at 8 instead of 8:30. Increase in modern works: Lukas Foss and Leon Kirchner conduct own compositions.

1963: Erich Leinsdorf's regime begins with announcement of new emphasis on contemporary music; a Prokofiev cycle is given. Britten's *War Requiem* has American premiere July 27. Mozart's Requiem is given in memory of Pope John XXIII.

1964: Thirteen works by Richard Strauss played in honor of 100th anniversary of his birth. Three-day musicological conference is held on the grounds in mid-July. Ozawa back as a guest conductor, four years after leaving the Berkshire Music Center.

1965: Twenty-fifth anniversary of Berkshire Music Center is celebrated at a concert at which Bernstein, de Carvalho and Leinsdorf conduct. Leinsdorf directs a complete *Lohengrin,* one act per evening.

1966: "The Romantic Concerto" is selected by Leinsdorf as the summer's theme. He also inaugurates 9 P.M. starting time Fridays, with main concert preceded by a "Weekend Prelude" of chamber music or solo recital in the Shed.

1967: William Steinberg is guest conductor in all-Beethoven program. Leinsdorf directs a concert version of Beethoven's opera *Fidelio* in its original version. Music critics' conference coincides with mini-festival of seven modern-music concerts.

1968: Conductor Josef Krips and soprano Beverly Sills make first Tanglewood appearances. Leinsdorf leads all-Beethoven, all-Mendelssohn, all-Wagner and all-Brahms programs. All attendance records shattered by turnout of 22,000 for rock concert on August 12.

1969: Leinsdorf's last season highlighted by concert versions in the Shed of two operas, Mozart's *Abduction from the Seraglio* and Verdi's *Otello,* and by Berkshire Music Center's fully-staged performance of Alban Berg's *Wozzeck.* His finale is Beethoven's Ninth.

1970: Ozawa and Gunther Schuller share artistic direction of Tanglewood, with Bernstein as adviser. New seats are installed in Shed. Berkshire Music Center alumnus Michael Tilson Thomas makes Tanglewood debut guest-conducting Boston Symphony. Friends of Music at Tanglewood organized.

1971: Bernstein leads *Missa Solemnis* in Koussevitzky Memorial Concert; Ozawa directs *Damnation of Faust.* Music Theater Project under Ian Strasfogel revives student operatic activities for three seasons.

1972: Ozawa directs Haydn's *The Seasons* and Mahler's "Symphony of a Thousand." Thomas leads Boston Symphony in all-modern program of music by Ruggles, Copland, Stravinsky and Wuorinen. Rock concerts suspended for a year.

1973: Verdi's Requiem and Haydn's *Creation* are conducted by Ozawa, and Handel's *Messiah* is led by Colin Davis. André Watts gives a piano seminar; Listening and Analysis course is instituted at Berkshire Music Center.

1974: Koussevitzky Centennial is marked by a day-long marathon of orchestral concerts, culminating in Beethoven's Ninth led by Ozawa. Final concert of season is devoted to Schoenberg's *Gurrelieder.*

1975: Aaron Copland's seventy-fifth birthday is observed. Composer-in-residence Olivier Messiaen's *Turangalila-Symphonie* is played by Ozawa. Neville Marriner, Klaus Tennstedt and Mstislav Rostropovich make Berkshire conducting debuts.

1976: Schedule includes *St. Matthew Passion* conducted by Ozawa and *Missa Solemnis* by Davis. Twentieth anniversary of beginning of Fromm concerts at Tanglewood. Plans to revive student operatic activities are deferred to 1977.

Bibliography

Briggs, John: *Leonard Bernstein.* New York, 1961.

Canfield, John Clair, Jr.: *Henry Kimball Hadley: His Life and Works.* Florida State University, 1960 (unpublished dissertation).

Dickson, Harry Ellis: *Gentlemen, More Dolce Please!* Boston, 1969.

Holland, James R.: *Tanglewood.* Barre, Mass., 1973.

*Howe, M. A. DeWolfe: *The Tale of Tanglewood.* New York, 1947.

Johnson, H. Earle: *Symphony Hall,* Boston. Boston, 1950.

Leichtentritt, Hugo: *Serge Koussevitzky, the Boston Symphony Orchestra, and the New American Music.* Cambridge, Mass., 1946.

Lourie, Arthur: *Serge Koussevitzky and His Epoch.* New York, 1931.

*Mahanna, John G. W.: *Music Under the Stars: A History of the Berkshire Symphonic Festival, Inc.* Pittsfield, Mass. (no date).

Meyer, Robert, Jr.: *Festivals, U.S.A. and Canada.* New York, 1970.

Selznick, Daniel, ed.: *A Tanglewood Dream* (Koussevitzky Music Foundation), New York, 1965.

Shanet, Howard: *Philharmonic: A History of New York's Orchestra.* New York, 1974.
Smith, Cecil: *Worlds of Music.* New York, 1953.
Smith, Moses: *Koussevitzky.* New York, 1947.
Wood, David H.: *Lenox: Massachusetts Shire Town.* Lenox, Mass., 1969.

Of the books above, only the two that have been starred deal with Tanglewood's history. Howe's is a brief survey of the first twelve years, from the standpoint of the official historian of the Boston Symphony Orchestra. Mahanna's is an account of the founding based on the records of the Berkshire Symphonic Festival, Inc.

Acknowledgements

As indicated throughout the text, I have made copious use of the New York and Boston newspapers, as well as of various magazines both musical and general, from 1934 to the present. Most of these articles and reviews were consulted in the Library of the Performing Arts of the New York Public Library of Lincoln Center and at the Boston Public Library, and I wish to thank the staffs of both institutions for their helpfullness.

My gratitude also goes to the Lenox Public Library, which is the repository of the official records of the Berkshire Symphonic Festival, and to the Stockbridge Public Library, whose material includes an oral history collection relating to Tanglewood. *The Berkshire Eagle* in Pittsfield generously opened both its clipping and its photographic files to me.

In addition to the individuals named previously in the Introduction, I would like to express my deepest gratitude to the many people who aided my researches either by granting me the time for interviews or by supplying me with important data and information. If some have been inadvertently omitted from the list which follows, I ask their pardon, and there are many, I full know, who deserve far more than a brief alphabetical mention.

My thanks, then, to Leonard Altman, Milton Bass, Harry Beall, Ralph Berkowitz, Albert Bernard, Martin Bookspan, Engelbert Brenner, Leonard Burkat, Shirley Burke, Sarah Caldwell, Margaret Carson, Aaron Copland, Phyllis Curtin, Dinah Daniels, Margaret Downs, Alice Edman, Lukas Foss, Lawrence Foster, Paul Fromm, Boris Goldovsky, Dr. Joseph L. Gottesman, Larry and Ted Gross, Daniel R. Gustin, Edith Hall, Dennis Helmrich, Robert Holton, Harriet Johnson, William Judd, Gilbert Kalish, Margaret Kennard, Roy Kennedy, James F. Kiley, Penelope Knuth, Harry Kraut, William Kroll, Pierre LaGrange, Ken Lieberson, Erich Leinsdorf, Patricia McCarty, Haden McKay, Zubin Mehta, Audrey Michaels, Sam Morgenstern, Carlos Moseley, Richard Ortner, Seiji Ozawa, Thomas D. Perry, Jr., Polly Pierce, Joel Pitchon, Andrew Raeburn, Francis Robinson, Beth Rosenfeld, Muriel Rukeyser, Marvin Schofer, Gunther Schuller, Howard Shanet, Joseph Silverstein, Louis Snyder, Sheldon Soffer, Steven Solomon, Jane Taylor, Walter Trampler, Roger Voisin, Sherman Walt, Heinz Weissenstein, and James Whitaker.

Index

279

280